# RENZO PIANO

# RENZO PIANO

*Logbook*

THE MONACELLI PRESS

# Contents

7    **Placeform and Produktform**
Kenneth Frampton

10    **The Profession of the Architect**

22    **1966: Early Works**

32    **1970: Cusago (Milan)**
Free-Plan Houses

34    **1970: ARAM Module**

36    **1971: Novedrate (Como)**
B & B Italia Offices

38    **1971: Paris**
Centre Georges Pompidou

50    **1978: Otranto**
UNESCO Urban Reconstruction Workshop

54    **1978: Corciano (Perugia)**
Il Rigo Evolutive Housing

56    **1978: Fiat VSS/Flying Carpet**

58    **1978: Dakar**
Mobile Construction Unit

60    **1979: Habitat Television Program**

62    **1981: Montrouge (Paris)**
Schlumberger Facilities Restructuring

68    **1982: Turin**
Alexander Calder Retrospective Exhibition

70    **1982: Houston, Texas**
Menil Collection

82    **1983: IBM Traveling Pavilion**

86    **1983: Venice and Milan**
*Prometeo* Musical Space Design

88    **1983: Genoa**
Subway Stations

90    **1983: Turin**
Lingotto Factory Conversion

98    **1984: Montecchio Maggiore (Vicenza)**
Lowara Company Offices

99    **1985: Novara**
Institute for Research into Light Metals

100    **1985: Cagliari**
Credito Industriale Sardo

102    **1985: Genoa**
Columbus International Exposition

112    **1986: Rhodes**
Ancient Moat Rehabilitation

113    **1986: Valletta**
City Gate

114    **1986: Lyons**
Cité Internationale

122    **1987: Bari**
San Nicola Stadium

130    **1987: Pompeii (Naples)**
Intervention in the Excavated City

132    **1987: Matera**
Restoration of the Sassi

134    **1987: Charenton le Pont (Paris)**
Bercy 2 Shopping Center

138 **1987: Paris**
Rue de Meaux Housing

146 **1988: Saint Quentin-en-Yvelines (Paris)**
Thomson Optronics Factory

148 **1988: Paris**
IRCAM Extension

150 **1988: Osaka**
Kansai Air Terminal

164 **1989: Kumamoto**
Ushibuka Bridge

166 **1989: Scoglio Nave (Genoa)**
UNESCO Laboratory and Workshop

174 **1991: Nouméa**
Tjibaou Cultural Center

184 **1991: San Giovanni Rotondo (Foggia)**
Padre Pio Pilgrimage Church

188 **1991: Lodi (Milan)**
Banca Popolare di Lodi

192 **1992: Berlin**
Potsdamer Platz Reconstruction

208 **1992: Houston, Texas**
Cy Twombly Gallery

212 **1992: Amsterdam**
National Center
for Science and Technology

218 **1992: Paris**
Reconstruction of the Atelier Brancusi

220 **1992: Riehen (Basel)**
Beyeler Foundation Museum

224 **1993: Sindelfingen (Stuttgart)**
Mercedes Benz Design Center

228 **1994: Rome**
Auditorium

234 **1995: Saitama (Tokyo)**
Multifunctional Arena

236 **1995: Nola (Naples)**
Service Complex

238 **1995: Paris**
Renovation of Centre
Georges Pompidou

240 **1996: Maranello (Modena)**
Ferrari Wind Tunnel

242 **1996: Sydney**
Mixed-Use Tower Complex

246 **From Builder's Son to Architect**

260 **The "Workshop" of Architecture**
Giulio Macchi

264 **Biography**

266 **Register of Works**

278 **Renzo Piano Building Workshop**

280 **Collaborators**

282 **Bibliography**

288 **Photography Credits**

I dedicate this book to the three people, sadly no longer with us, who have had the greatest influence on my development as an architect: my father, who in the eyes of a child was the greatest builder in the world; my brother, the best of all; and Peter Rice, engineer and humanist, irreplaceable traveling companion for twenty years.

By Renzo Piano with the assistance of Roberto Brignolo

Conceived and realized by Renzo Piano with Giorgio G. Bianchi, Roberto Brignolo, Alberto Giordano, Giulio Macchi, and Franco Origoni

Graphic design and layout by Renzo Piano Building Workshop, Giorgio G. Bianchi, François Bertolero, Stefania Canta, Toma Damisch, Giovanna Giusto, Paola Rossato, Franc Somner

Franco Origoni & Anna Steiner with the collaboration of Giovanna Erba

Translated from the Italian by Huw Evans

The original edition of this book was published to coincide with the traveling exhibition "Renzo Piano: Out of the Blue," prepared in collaboration with the Kunst und Ausstellungshalle der Bundesrepublik Deutschland, Bonn.

First published in the United States of America in 1997 by
The Monacelli Press, Inc.
10 East 92nd Street, New York, New York 10128.

Library of Congress Cataloging-in-Publication Data
Renzo Piano. English.
Renzo Piano : logbook.
p.  cm.
Includes bibliographical references.
ISBN 1-885254-65-2
1. Piano, Renzo—Criticism and interpretation. 2. Architectural practice, International. 3. Architecture—Environmental aspects. 4. Architecture, Modern—20th century.
NA1123.P47R4513   1997                    97-5774
720'.92—dc21

Printed and bound in Italy

# Placeform and Produktform

Kenneth Frampton

Perhaps the single most exceptional aspect of Renzo Piano's production is the remarkable scope of the work, with buildings extending across a wide typological spectrum, constituting a great variety in terms of form, material, and structure. Thus one passes, in the space of seven years, from the vast megastructure of the Kansai Air Terminal (1990–94) to a housing complex on the Rue de Meaux, Paris (1987–91), or from the San Nicola Stadium, Bari (1987–90), with its capacity for sixty thousand, to the unique Tjibaou Cultural Center in New Caledonia, on which work first began in 1991. Thus over the last decade the Renzo Piano Building Workshop has worked across the world from Northern France and Southern Italy to Southern Japan and a remote island in the Pacific.

Simultaneously Piano's expression has alternated in terms of membranes and images, involving an equally diverse range of components and finishes. It has passed, in the aforementioned works, from an elongated stainless-steel shell to a tessellated terra-cotta facade and from a heavy cantilevered concrete stadium, capped by a light parasol, to a series of monumental mahogany screens or "kivas." These last were conceived as double-layered, three-dimensional basketlike shells erected to represent ethnographic origins for the cultural center now nearing completion in Nouméa, New Caledonia.

The works of varying size designed and realized over the last fifteen years seem to have done more to establish the current reputation of the Building Workshop than any other commission since the completion of the Centre Georges Pompidou. In all this, the Menil Collection in Houston, Texas (1982–86), seems to have played a decisive role in raising the level of the practice, largely because of a concious differentiation between the topographic character of site and the mode of production.

This implicit opposition between *placeform* and *produktform* ought, ideally, to be capable of resolution, and this is indeed what happens in the Menil Collection.

Throughout his career, Piano has sought an architecture free of myths, save for the myth of primordial making; that is to say, the inborn, world-creating drive of the *homo faber,* which in Piano's case has a peculiar significance, due to the maritime craft culture of the Mediterranean from which his family stems. The anti-academicism that is such a profound aspect in his character is pre-Renaissance in its fundamental spirit, which surely accounts for certain conflicting aspects of his professional career: on the one hand, his debt to Baconian empirical science, that is, to the Anglo-Saxon pragmatic tradition; on the other, his respect for Italian craft production, for *il mestiere,* the mastery that may be acquired only through apprenticeship.

In terms of professional politics Piano has steered an independent course, while remaining faithful to the critical ethic of teamwork (perhaps no one practicing today has acknowledged his collaborators more fully) and to the inescapable truth that in the field of *Baukunst* there is no single author. In contrast to the late-modern world, in which architecture constantly overreaches itself in a grotesque attempt to prove its claim as a new formula species of fine art writ large, Piano insists on the need for architects to maintain their command over the building process in all of its aspects. For Piano and his Building Workshop, the future of the profession, as it enters the next millennium, must turn on its ability to resolve the ever-increasing complexity of the building task at the highest possible level. Whether this will result in an architecture that will be recognizably part of the humanist tradition or not is a question that, as far as Piano is concerned, is to be left discreetly open.

# The Profession of the Architect

## An Ancient Profession

The architect's profession is an adventurous one, a job on the frontier. The architect walks a knife-edge between art and science, between originality and memory, between the daring of modernity and the caution of tradition. Architects have no choice but to live dangerously. They work with all sorts of raw materials, and I don't just mean concrete, wood, metal. I'm talking about history and geography, mathematics and the natural sciences, anthropology and ecology, aesthetics and technology, climate and society—all things that architects have to deal with every day.

The architect has the finest job in the world because, on a small planet where everything has already been discovered, designing is still one of the greatest adventures possible. As far as exploring the physical world, our ancestors have beaten us to it. People like Columbus, Magellan, Cook, and Amundsen have already discovered everything. We are left with the adventure of the mind, which can bring as much anxiety, bewilderment, and fear as an expedition to a land of ice and snow.

Designing is a journey, in a way. You set off to find out, to learn. You accept the unexpected. If you get scared and immediately seek refuge in the warm and welcoming lair of the already seen, the already done, it is no journey. But if you have a taste for adventure, you don't hide, you go on. Each project is a new start, and you are in unexplored territory. You are a Robinson Crusoe of modern times.

Architecture is an ancient profession—as old as hunting, fishing, tilling the fields, exploring. These are the original activities of human beings, from which all others are descended. Immediately after the search for food comes the search for shelter. At a certain point the human being was no longer content with the refuges offered by nature, and became an architect.

Those who build houses provide shelter: for themselves, for their families, for their people. In the tribe, the architect performs a role of service to the community. But the house is not just protection: this basic function has always gone hand in hand with an aesthetic, expressive, symbolic yearning. The house, from the very beginning, has been the setting for a quest for beauty, dignity, and status. The house is used to give expression to a desire to belong, or to a desire to be different.

The act of building is not and cannot be just a question of technique, for it is charged with symbolic meaning. This ambiguity is only the first of many that mark the profession of architecture. Any attempt to resolve the ambiguity is not the beginning of a solution— it is the first sign that you are giving up.

## A Profession in Crisis

I have always talked about the fear that the profession of architecture is coming to an end. I have said that the architect's job is in danger of disappearing, like that of the lamplighter or the dowser. This is a provocation, of course: architecture is still necessary, more than ever before. Incompetence, irresponsibility, arrogance, a lack of love for the craft: these are the things that diminish and frustrate our work. I believe that this profession needs to be given new dignity; and for that, we have to go back to its origins.

First, who is the architect? Architecture is a service: this is a sober lesson that we need to keep in mind every time our discipline gets lost in the maze of fashions, styles, tendencies. This is not moralism; perhaps it is just a kind of modesty—a way of putting things in perspective.

Second, architects are people who know how to make houses for people. They know which materials and structures to use; they study the direction of the wind and the level of the tide. They control the process of production and the tools with which they must work—in other words, they know why and how houses, bridges, and cities are built.

In every crisis there is an element of self-indulgence. Some architects relish their social uselessness, whether real or presumed. It is a classic case of prejudice against oneself. And so it becomes an excuse for taking refuge in pure form, sometimes in pure technology. Such individuals reject their role as craftspeople to promote themselves as artists—and then rapidly slide into academicism. I do not believe I am generalizing. I said earlier that this profession walks a knife-edge between technique and art; and it is right on that edge that I think it should stay. As soon as you accept that division you are bound to fall—on one side or the other.

When building is reduced to mere technique—a matter of machinery, organization, money—it loses all its expressiveness, all its social significance, all contact with life. Our coastlines and cities are filled with examples of this. However, as a wise Russian once said, facts are the most stubborn thing in nature. Building is necessary. And building is a technical activity, as well. Many people believe that technique should be placed in the service of art, that it has to be an instrument of art: this is almost a religious point of view. As happens with every faith, it gives rise to a heresy—the position that, on the contrary, art is technique. I don't agree with either of these positions, but I find the second more congenial.

I like to think of the architect as a person who uses technique to create an emotion, an artistic emotion, to be precise. When you listen to the performance of a great musician (I am thinking of the pianist Maurizio Pollini, or the violinist Salvatore Accardo, just to mention a couple of friends) you realize that their technique has sunk in so deeply that it has been metabolized, that it has turned into art.

"Learn all about music and your instrument, then forget it and play how you like"—I think it was Charlie Parker who said that. I believe you have to do the same with architecture.

## The Adventure of the Architect

Creating means peering into the dark—with tenacity, obstinacy, even insolence. There are moments of suspense and waiting that cause anxiety—but if you don't accept the challenge, you are left with no alternative but to work with what already exists. That is where academicism starts. When you place your certainty in something, that thing does not become the root of your thinking, but the crutch that allows you not to think: it becomes a refuge from your fear. Adventure also means going the wrong way. The risk has to be taken. If you want to be sure, take the highroad; but that is not exploration.

When you enter a dark room, your eyes adapt after a while—this is an observation of a physical character. The mind adapts too. And that is the beginning of a moment of creation. Creation. Perhaps we ought to find another word. The whole adventure of design is studded with moments of excitement, but the real moment of creation, if it ever existed, can only be reconstructed in your memory. Looking back, six months, a year later, you say to yourself: that day was the turning point. And you wonder, but why didn't I hear trumpets blaring, or at least bells ringing? In reality, the idea is not a solitary stroke of genius, nor a word whispered in your ear by the muse. It is a synthesis of all the efforts that have gone into research, into experimentation; it is that "trying over and over again" that Galileo used to talk about. The idea derives in such a natural way from the process that it is really hard to recognize the moment when it arises.

These thoughts form part of my personal struggle to free myself from the mythology of "creation." Artists are not people who have a "gift"; rather they are people who master a *tekné* and use it to attain their objective, which is art.

## The Obligation of the Architect

Architecture is a socially dangerous art, because it is an imposed art. You don't have to read a bad book. You don't have to listen to a terrible piece of music. But the ugly block of apartments in front of your house leaves you with no alternative: you have to look at it. Architecture inflicts a total immersion in its ugliness; it leaves the user with no choice. This is a heavy responsibility, and one that involves future generations as well. This is not an idea of my own, but it helps us to broaden the scope of our reflection.

So what is the obligation of the architect? Neruda declared that when someone is a poet, whatever he or she has to say will be said in poetry. There is no other way to express it. As an architect, I don't preach morality—I design it and build it, trying to maintain the profound nature of our profession, that of architecture as a service, as a project for the community.

Even in this, architects can become dangerous. Their utopias, unlike the utopias imagined by other people, are destined to come true. The architect's vision of the world becomes the world. And then they can start to see themselves as demiurges, come to believe that they have been entrusted with the task of inventing the future. Or more modestly, they can accept the fact that they have set a process in motion.

I believe that our work is always an unfinished project, for it is in the nature of human relationships (and therefore of cities, too) to be a process in constant evolution. The architect sets something off; but its future, of course, is unknown. This is all the more reason why the starting point has to be on firm ground—because it is here that the architect asserts his or her values and morality.

## The Culture of Doing

I was born into a family of builders. They were all contractors: my grandfather, father, brother. I should have become one too, but instead, I decided to be an architect. My father accepted the news as a glitch in evolution: for him, a builder who never attended university, evolution implied that his sons should be builders with degrees—engineers, in other words. This choice was to be a sort of paradigm for my many subsequent heresies.

Someone once said that everything we know we learned in our childhood, and that inventing means spending your life digging through your childhood memories. I was very conscious of the family trade, just as anyone growing up in the circus knows that he or she is a born acrobat. My childhood as the son of a builder left me an important legacy: the passion for construction or, to put it more boldly, the culture of doing, which has left a deep mark on my approach to my work.

There is always a temptation for a young architect to start out with style. But I started with "doing": with the building site, with research into materials, with the knowledge of construction techniques, conventional and otherwise. My journey through architecture started out from technique—and has gradually led me to an awareness of its complexity as space, expression, and form. The first few years after my graduation, from 1964 to 1968 (what I call my prehistory), were years of play, that is, of experimentation. It was a very important time, even though I constructed no buildings that were destined to last. Perhaps it was just that period spent trying over and over again that protected me from academicism.

I remember my first experiences on the construction site, when I went there with my father. For a boy of eight or ten the site was a miracle: one day I saw a pile of sand and bricks, the next I saw a wall that stood all by itself, and eventually turned into a tall, solid building, in which people could live.

I hold another image of my father in my memory. My relationship with this taciturn man was always very strong. Once, when he was already over eighty years old, I took him to one of my own construction sites. We were building a tensile structure and carrying out tests. He smoked his pipe quietly and watched us. On the way home, I asked him, "What do you think of it?" "Hmm," he replied. Perhaps he added, "Who knows if it will stay up." It was clear that he was thinking about it.

## The Magic of the Building Site

I still love building sites. They are wonderful places, where everything is in movement, where the landscape changes every day. They are a great human adventure, and one that fills me with pride at being able to play a part. The building site is always a place of extraordinary discoveries. It is not true that everything is in the plans. It is on site that you understand the hierarchies, that you decide to give importance to something that appeared irrelevant on paper.

In a sense, the process of construction is never complete. I believe that buildings, like cities, are factories of the infinite and the unfinished. We must be careful not to fall into the absurd trap of perfection: a work of architecture is a living creature that changes over time and with use. We live with these creatures of ours, linked to them by the umbilical cord of an adventure that has no end.

The concept of endless construction, of the imperfect work, lends substance to the idea that architecture is a tainted art, tainted by everything that is ugly in life: money, power, haste, complications. But it is also tinged by everything that is beautiful, healthy, authentic: the roots of things, innovation, nature, people's needs.

These taints, for better or worse, are the limits that our profession imposes on us. I say "imposes," but I ought to have said "offers," because the contaminations, constraints, and obligations are not obstacles. On the contrary, they enrich architecture. Contamination is not a restraint, but a guide that leads us by the hand. It allows us to perceive the stimuli and influences that come from the tradition of places, from technology, from the history of peoples, from human tastes and expectations.

## Curiosity and Disobedience

The sea: the other face of the Earth, the face that we do not know.

Perhaps my curiosity was born out of walks along the seaside. I was an inquisitive and disobedient child. I don't know why, but these two things always go together. In fact, at school I was considered a very bad example.

I think it is right to connect disobedience with independence of thought. In my case, however, it was the latter that stemmed from the former. It started as a character trait, a wholly involuntary one, and only later turned into an intellectual attitude, one that is naturally reflected in my work.

The Centre Pompidou, for instance, was to some extent a form of civil disobedience. It represented the refusal to inflict an institutional kind of building on a city already overburdened with memories. But dumping this out-of-scale object, disturbing in its dimensions and appearance, in the center of Paris (creating an effect a bit like that of an ocean liner passing through the Giudecca Canal in Venice) was obviously a deliberate taunt aimed at the most conservative sort of academicism—all this, after winning an international competition with almost seven hundred participants.

Perhaps it is also the fault (or the merit) of the Centre Pompidou that my career as an architect has been a long series of heresies. For decades I was a sort of outcast, blacklisted from the clubs, the schools, the academies. As a true ne'er-do-well, this excommunication has always been a source of satisfaction. To a degree, I have now been admitted to the "temple." Maybe I liked it better before.

I often remember a story about Jean Prouvé. He—undoubtedly the last heir of Le Corbusier and the great French masters—was completely outside the academic world: he didn't even have a degree. One day some common friends and I decided that it was time to get him an honorary degree. When this was proposed to him, Jean hesitated a long time, and then one evening said to me: "Renzo, I'm grateful to you, I'm grateful to all of you, you've been very kind—but I don't want the degree. Let me die ignorant." He wanted to end his days as an outsider, just as he had always been.

## Genoa

There are certain moments, certain images that are always coming to mind: I call them "postcards from the past." Some of them bind me very strongly to Genoa, my hometown. For Paolo Conte, from Asti, Genoa is "a gleam of sunlight on the windshield" and "that sea that moves even at night, that never stays still." The light and the sea: for me, these two things together mean the port.

The port is a powerful landscape made up of elements that are both grand and ephemeral, that are continually changing—reflections on the water, suspended loads, swiveling cranes, and of course ships coming and going. Who knows where that ship is coming from, in what direction it is headed? Many years ago the art critic Giovanni Carandente pointed out to me that the Centre Pompidou is in some way a tribute to the port. I had never thought about it that way, but it's probably true.

Another postcard is the historic center of Genoa. I was born and grew up in Pegli, just outside the city. In my memory, everything is magnified by the imagination of a child. Every so often my mother took me to Genoa, and this was a great occasion: it meant going to this ancient and rather gloomy center, which smelled of chickpea flour. So maternal and protective, it was the exact opposite of the port. In my imagination, the port is as ephemeral as the heart of the city is fixed, permanent, eternal.

I have always had a love/hate relationship with Genoa, one that implied not just flight but return as well. "It is curious to realize what deep traces this land leaves," said Montale. Perhaps it would be more logical for me to live in Paris or London, but I prefer to come back here, whenever I can.

## The Conditions for Creating

As an architect, I believe that place influences every human perception, emotion, activity. So at a certain point in my life I asked myself the question of what the place where I work ought to be, what characteristics it should have. Creating something is difficult, but putting yourself in the right state to create is even more difficult. You need peace and quiet, but also tension; calm, but energy too; time, but speed as well. The creator walks a tightrope "suspended between memory and oblivion," as Jorge Luis Borges put it. I wanted a place like that.

And so the UNESCO Laboratory and Workshop was born on the coast west of Genoa, between Voltri and Vesima. Perched on the rocks and surrounded by the sea, it is half rock, half ship. And in fact the place is called Punta Nave: Ship Rock. Here I find calm, silence, and concentration—all things that are essential to my personal way of working.

I don't want to give the wrong impression. This office is no hermitage, first of all because a lot of people from many different countries work here, and also because it communicates in real time with the rest of the world. The workshop is here, but it is also in Osaka, Nouméa, Sydney. I believe that human beings have always wanted to be in several places at once, and to some extent we have achieved this today. Only this ubiquity is not physical, but technological—or as people like to call it now, virtual.

Our links with the world are provided by technology: it is an opportunity that was not available to our forebearers, and for me it is a great luxury. The telephone, fax, modem, and internet allow me to live by the sea, which is like the cosmic soup in which we all live, a true network of the collective psyche. I have built this place, and decided to locate it here, because living in a word of telecommunications has made it possible.

The choice of working on the Punta Nave certainly has something to do with the postcards from the past, but there is another reason too. I love this workshop because it provides a meeting place for craftsmanship and high technology, daring and patience, persistence and reflection, teamwork and privacy.

At the same time, I love Paris, and I love my studio in the Marais. I like to stroll through the quarter on a Sunday morning: it is a place where you go around on foot, where you meet people, where you greet the *boulanger* and the *bouquiniste*. Social life, meetings, and exchanges: these are necessary, just as at other moments a refuge is what you need. Thus Paris is information, sociability in the highest degree—sometimes to the point of excess. The Punta Nave is reflection, solitude. I need both, in my life and in my work.

It is a bit like composing a large mosaic: you have to work up close, because each tessera has to go in exactly the right place, but then every so often you have to take a step back, so as to get the whole picture. The Marais is confusion, but it is also the richness of the close-up view. The Punta Nave is a hot-air balloon that allows me to look at things from above.

## Architecture is a Patient Game

There is a light way to use intelligence, and a heavy one. What I am trying to do is to use intelligence lightly. It is not a program; it is not an ideology or a manifesto. It's simply what works for me.

Architecture is a game that requires patience. Our work never gets off to a flying start. It isn't done urgently. No one says: "That's how it is, it'll do." The ideas have to be allowed to settle for a while, like wine: only if you do things this way can you tell what is really good. Allowing ideas to settle means working as a team, so that the best proposal comes out on top, whomever it comes from.

There is a lot of talk about teamwork, when what is actually going on is a step-by-step process: one person does something and then passes it on to somebody else, who then does something else but with a smaller degree of freedom. The process continues, but with greater and greater restrictions at each step. That is not what I mean.

Teamwork is when you throw out an idea, and it comes back at you, like a game of Ping-Pong—four can play it, or six, or eight, with the balls moving back and forth at such a speed that they are flying in both directions at once. Everything gets mixed up. When the project finally takes shape, you can no longer tell who put what into it.

## "Trying Over and Over Again"

Designing is not a linear experience, in which you have an idea, put it down on paper, then carry it out and that's that. Rather it is a circular process: your idea is drawn up, tried out, reconsidered, and reworked, coming back again and again to the same point.

As a method it seems very empirical, but if you look around, you realize that it's typical of many other disciplines: music, physics, astrophysics too. I once discussed this with Tullio Regge and Luciano Berio, and the analogy was clear—one was talking as a mathematician, the other as a musician, but the essence was the same.

In scientific research you have to deal with equations with too many variables. In nature, the variables are virtually infinite. So you fix some on the basis of an intuition that stems from your experience. At that point it becomes possible to solve the equation. Then you test what you have found. If it doesn't work, you start again. You formulate another hypothesis, you go back over what you've done, and so on. In the process, you narrow the circle, like a hawk closing in on its prey. Note that circularity, in this sense, is not just methodology, and still less procedure. It is, to use high-sounding words, a theory of knowledge. Trying over and over again is not just a means of correcting mistakes. It is a way to understand the quality of a project, or of material, light, sound.

## Experimentation

In ancient times, designing also entailed inventing the machines that were needed to carry out the work. Antonio Manetti recounts that Brunelleschi studied the mechanism of the clock so that he could apply it to a system of great counterweights; this system was then used to raise the beams for the dome of the Florence Cathedral. The means and the end were the fruit of a single experience, of one and the same process.

The moment of testing is not the execution of a work that someone else has written down and directed—it is interpretation, performance; it is part of the creative process. When you work in a circular way the technical aspect returns to its place at the center. It is given back its dignity. Experimenting serves to link together the idea and its material consequences. While working on the Menil Collection, in Texas, we made a little machine—which we called, a bit pompously, "the solar machine"—that would allow us in Genoa to find out the position of the sun in Houston. We also built one-to-ten scale models, which we put in the garden to study the diffusion of light. All the projects that come out of the Building Workshop have stories of similar experiments.

Knowing how to do things not just with the head, but with the hands as well: this might seem a rather programmatic and ideological goal. It is not. It is a way of safeguarding creative freedom. If you intend to use a material, a construction technique, or an architectural element in an unusual way, there is always a time when you hear yourself saying, "It can't be done," simply because no one has ever tried before. But if you have actually tried, then you can keep going—and so you gain a degree of independence in design that you would not have otherwise.

While we were building the Centre Pompidou, we had to make a structure out of pieces of cast metal. The entire French steel industry rose up in arms: it refused point-blank, saying that a structure like that wouldn't stay up. But we were sure of our facts, Peter Rice above all, and passed the order on to the German company Krupp. And so it was that the main structure of the Centre Pompidou was made in Germany, even if the girders had to be delivered at night, almost in secret. This was one case in which technique protected art. Our understanding of structures set free our capacity for expression.

In a rather bizarre way, what with old postcards and building sites, Robinson Crusoe and jazz, I have tried to introduce the works described in the following pages—introduce them in the way that you would introduce friends.

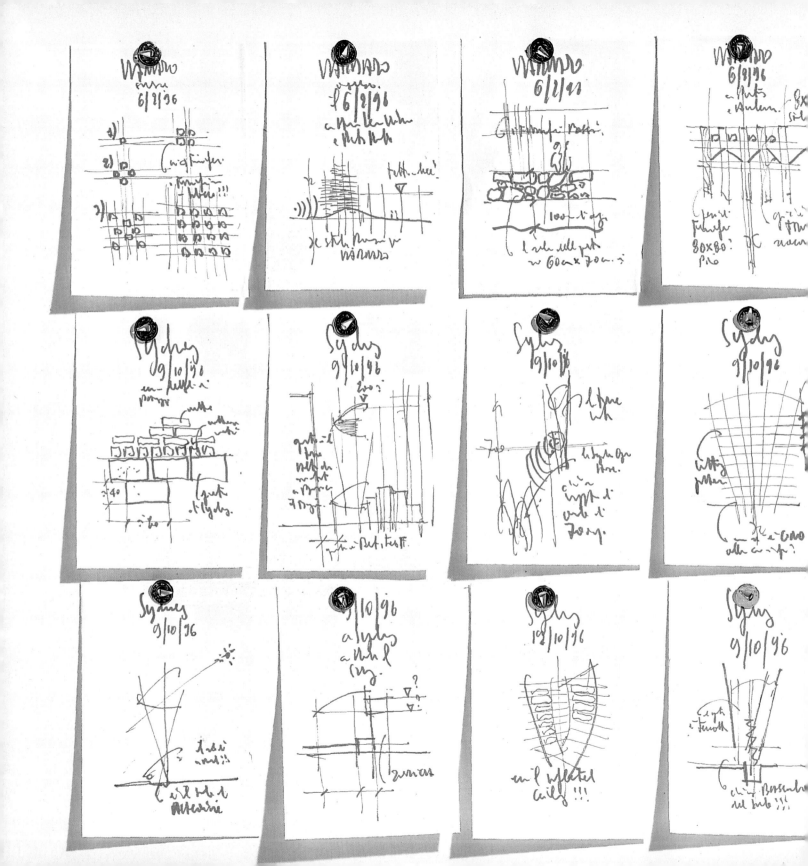

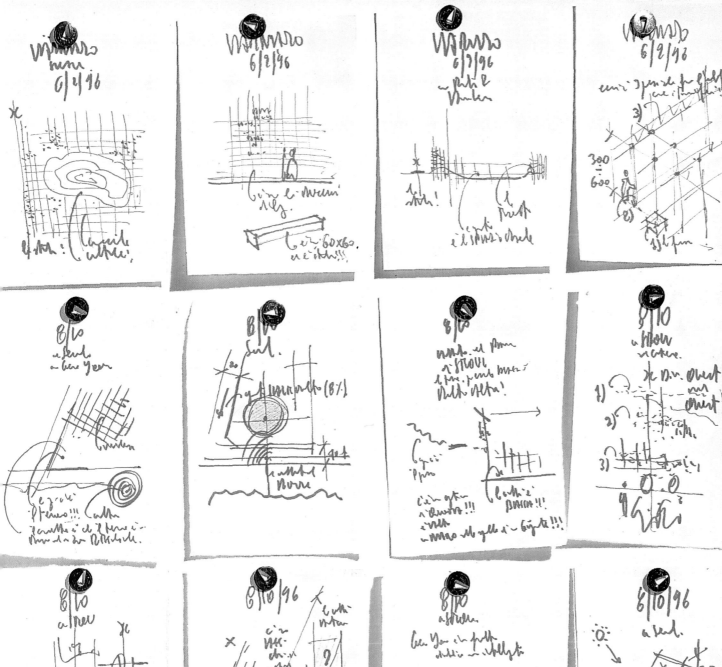

# 1966  Early Works

Construction: 1966–70

**Mobile Sulfur Extraction Factory, Pomezia (Rome), Italy, 1966; Pavilion for the 14th Triennale, Milan, Italy, 1967; Studio Piano, Genoa, Italy, 1969; Italian Pavilion, Osaka Expo, Japan, 1969. The early years were years of research rather than of real projects; lightness, flexibility, and ease of construction were the main subjects of study.**

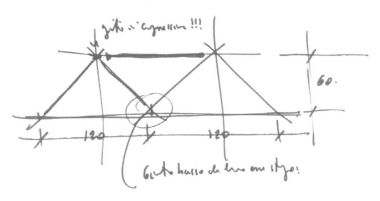

In retrospect, there was a utopian element in my early works: I was looking for an absolute kind of space without form, of structure without weight. Perhaps I was seeking an elegance without architecture. At the time, the theme of lightness was a game in the best sense of the word, a line of research that was very much based on instinct. I felt that I was part of the great circus of construction. For me, these slender, "impossible" structures were acrobatic exercises, carried out without the safety net of the already seen, the already done.

Like everyone, I had teachers. Whom I will list in haphazard order: Pierluigi Nervi, for he taught how to build things, rather than just design them; Jean Prouvé, for the way he eluded any attempt at categorization (was he an engineer, a constructor, a designer?); Buckminster Fuller, because he raised questions about the great themes of architecture in a very free and nonconformist way (where are we going? what does it mean to build? and so on).

Franco Albini was my teacher in a more literal sense, since I worked in his studio in Milan. I spent more time working with Albini than at university, in fact. I learned a lot about the relationship between form and material from Marco Zanuso (I was his assistant at the Milan Polytechnic for two years). The man who taught me most about spatial structures was Z. S. Makowski in London.

Later, toward the end of the sixties, I had the opportunity to work with Louis Kahn on the Olivetti-Underwood factory at Harrisburg, Pennsylvania. Although our conceptions of architecture have nothing in common, Kahn taught me a lot about life and character. He had a quality that I respect very much and find essential in our profession: a patient determination.

When someone talks about lightness, about the effort to take things away, there is a tendency to see this as an attempt to create a wholly aesthetic effect. In reality it was not like that. There was, even then, a careful study of the relationship between structure and function.

When we designed a factory at Pomezia for the extraction of sulfur, I came to the extremely banal conclusion that the cost of mining was all in the transport of the material, since it obviously had to be taken to the place where the work was

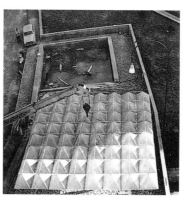

Spatial structure of reinforced-polyester pyramids.

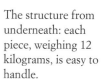

The structure from underneath: each piece, weighing 12 kilograms, is easy to handle.

The same structure, here in an arch.

Opposite: Detail of the translucent structure. The piece was taken to the extreme limit of detail, as in an industrial product. Thus the quest for lightness resulted in an essential language made up of openings and transparencies.

done. So I decided to turn the problem on its head: instead of moving the material, I moved the building. The plant was a tunnel-shaped structure; as the sulfur was dug out, the rear part of the tunnel was moved to the front. This was made possible not just by the modular construction but also by the lightness and limited size of the individual elements, which allowed the structure to be dismantled and reassembled by hand.

This example serves to show two things: that we were paying attention not only to the elegance of the design, but also to industrial costs; and that we did it with that rather wayward approach that still leads us to overturn established solutions today, to change the rules of the game.

I have literally started with the subject of mining. In fact, this whole section, devoted to my first works, is a sort of mine. During our childhood, adolescence, and the early part of our careers, we all develop a great potential for dreaming, which our technical, cultural, and economic means are not capable of fulfilling. When, as we grow up, we have more means at our disposal, it may prove necessary to start digging to find the dream again.

The research into shell-shaped structures was partly motivated by the curiosity that led us to investigate the properties of shells, which allowed great rigidity to be achieved with very thin materials. There was, however, a desire to imagine new worlds as well. One of these projects, the most interesting, was produced for the 14th Milan Triennale in 1967.

Already working with me, Flavio Marano was the engineer who helped to design these structures. From the viewpoint of structural calculation, the project's interest lay in the great versatility of forms that could be obtained by the same process of design, calculation, and construction.

Once the conceptual problems of optimization of the shell had been solved, production of the casting itself was relatively simple. This led us to devise a strange instrument: a sort of pantograph that drove a set of pistons over a rubber membrane. When the shape looked satisfactory to us, the membrane was used as a mold to produce the final casting.

An understanding of techniques means extending your research to cover the design of the machines required for the production of architectural elements: the architect has to work with the master builder, just as in the construction of the Gothic cathedrals. This remains one of my firmest principles. The shell structures did not involve just a quest for a vaguely organic elegance, but the adoption of a model of space in continuum, developed through compression, expansion, and lightening of the surface, i.e., transparency.

These forms reappeared in later works with a greater level of technical difficulty. But I like to think that in this early work it is possible to make out the germ of something that was going to reach its maturity years later in the Bercy 2 Shopping Center in France and the Kansai Air Terminal in Japan.

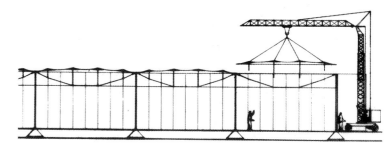

Pretensioned structure of steel and reinforced polyester.

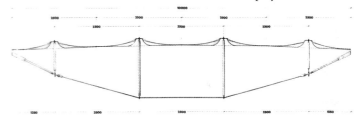

Drawing of the membrane held in tension by vertical metal struts.

Membrane viewed from above (left); detail (below left).

Opposite: Sealing the membranes of the roof.

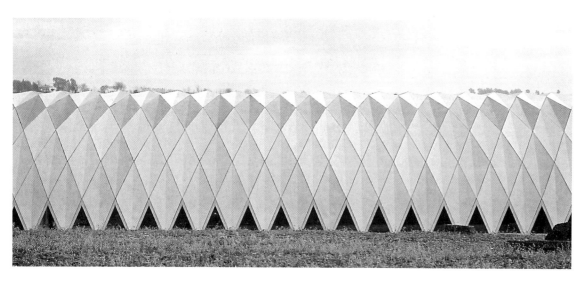

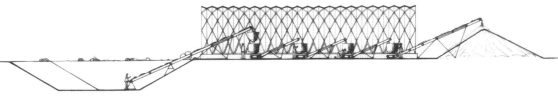

Mobile Sulfur Extraction Factory: External view (left); longitudinal section illustrating the mode of functioning (below left).

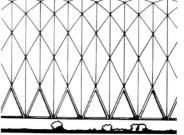

The wood workshop in Genoa (far left); a vaulted structure (left); expandable structure, which meets production needs (below left).

System of shell structures presented at the 14th Milan Triennale.
1–6. Study models of membranes.
7. System for transferring membrane obtained from model to adjustable mold for production.
8. "Reader" for the transfer.
9. Piano and Marano studying a model.
10. Trial installation of a membrane.

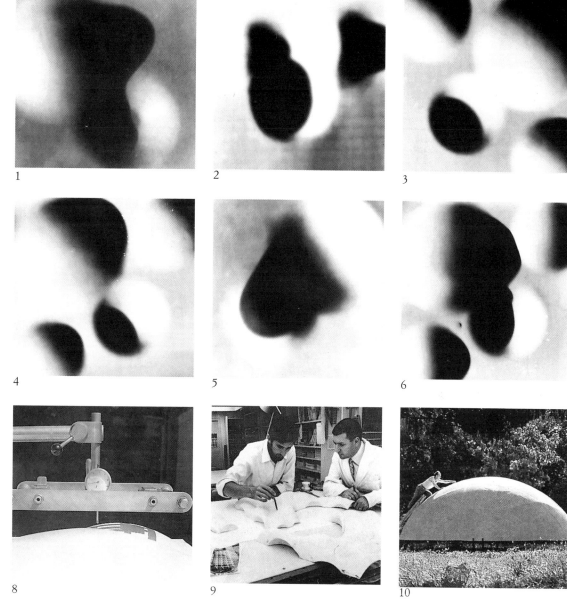

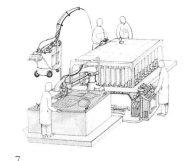

Study model.

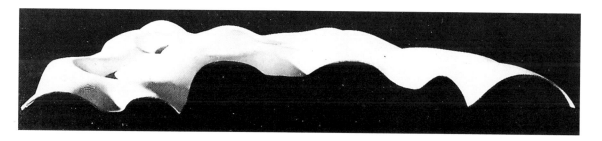

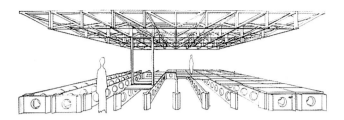

Free-plan housing at Garonne: axonometric showing assemblage of construction elements (above); model of structural casting in wood (right); mounted structure (below).

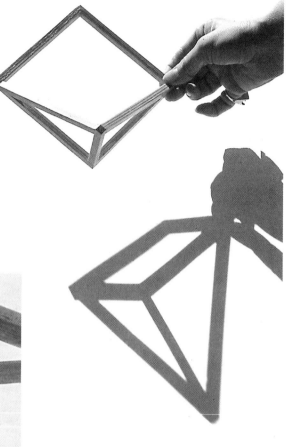

Opposite: Renzo Piano's first office in Genoa. Installation of a roofing element (top); structural elements of the roof in storage (center); detail of the frames on the facade (bottom).

The large space of the office, measuring twenty by twenty meters, with constant and diffuse light from above.

The following year we built my first studio in Genoa. Two of the themes tackled on that occasion crop up continually in later works: that of space in a free plan and that of light from above.

The studio consisted of a single space of twenty by twenty meters, with no openings at the sides. The only light available was from above. So we created a structure of very lightweight, pyramid-shaped frameworks of steel framing panels of transparent polyester (we even patented these panels, calling them microsheds).

The panels had an undulating profile with successive transparent corrugations to the north and opaque ones to the south; as a consequence only light from the north could enter and the excessive heat that would have been produced by exposure to direct sunlight from the south was filtered out. In a way we were learning even then how to work with the magic of light from above.

At the same time another important concept began to emerge: the free plan. The building is an organism subject to evolution. It is unfinished and imperfect. It must have the capacity to adapt to different uses and functions. Indeterminacy is not a shortcoming, but an openness to change. Space is volume, but it should also be opportunity.

The concept of modular space, of function that is not frozen, was taken further with the Italian Pavilion at the Osaka Expo. The pavilion had to be fabricated in Italy, dismantled, and shipped to Japan. This posed three interesting problems: lightness, portability, and resistance to atmospheric agents.

The resulting building was a very simple one in spatial terms: essentially it was a cube, constructed out of a double membrane of polyester and a system of very sturdy steel rods to keep the structure under tension and ensure its solidity. This bizarre balance between tension and lightness proved capable of withstanding gusts of wind of up to 150 kilometers an hour in Osaka during the summer of 1970.

The building was demolished in 1971, along with the majority of the other pavilions.

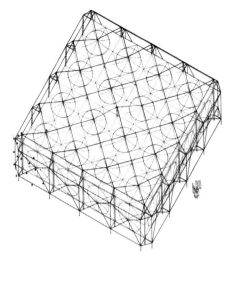

Axonometric showing structure (left); typical panel section (below left). Each panel is composed of two layers of reinforced polyester with an air space in between.

Detail of the meeting point between the metal reinforcing structure and the polyester membranes.

Opposite: The Italian Pavilion was fabricated in Italy and transported to Osaka. It was the outcome of technical research into lightness, flexibility, and the relationship between construction and cost.

# 1970 Cusago (Milan) Italy

## Free-Plan Houses

Construction: 1972–74

**Four single-family houses, identical on the outside, but with a flexible interior whose completion was left to the user. An open and flexible model of architecture.**

Not long after the Italian Pavilion at the Osaka Expo, we tackled the theme of architectural function that is not frozen (and therefore space that is not subdivided) in the context of housing as well. There were some interesting technical aspects to this, but above all, a cultural implication. The aim was to restore to housing the purity of its primary function, leaving the resident (the individual) with the responsibility for the functional and aesthetic definition of the space inside.

This is the element that characterizes four single-family houses built at Cusago, near Milan. We wanted to create a space open to any interpretation, and we achieved this by reinforcing the roofing with a steel lattice girder, making it possible to create an interior space, as broad as the front of the building (fifteen meters), with no structural constraints.

Underneath the outer layer of roofing we erected a second ceiling, that of the housing unit proper. A space between the two echoed the theme of the attic (or of the loft used to store grain in old farmhouses, if you prefer) and operated as a thermal equilibration chamber, permitting a natural improvement of the internal climate.

The oldest method of insulation relies on the mass of materials, and functions by means of the physical principle of thermal inertia. I have used this principle several times over the course of my career. For instance, I have built houses with a layer of earth in their roofs; this means that the surface exposed to the sunlight takes more time both to heat up and to release the heat stored. In the houses at Cusago, on the other hand, I used the opposite approach, based on the lightness of the materials and relying on natural ventilation of the space between roof and ceiling.

Today we would describe this method of resisting heat and cold through the use of ancient architectural solutions as "environmentally friendly," not because it "respects" nature and the temperatures that it imposes, but because it tackles the problem in a way that reduces the consumption of energy: the air space between the two layers of the roof drastically reduces the need for heating and cooling systems. Once again, the model is not "natural" architecture, but sustainable architecture.
We shall find thermal insulation systems based on the use of air spaces in many more recent projects: from Bercy 2 to the IRCAM Extension.

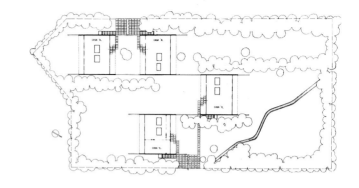

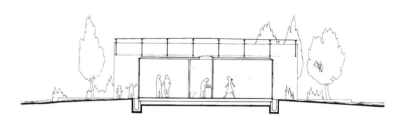

Plan showing the four houses (top); section through one house (above); house seen from the garden (left).

The four houses are
identical on the
exterior, but the free
plan allows the
occupants to organize
the interior space as
they wish.

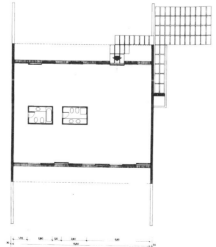

# 1970 ARAM Module

**This is a medical module, containing the most sophisticated hospital equipment, designed for mass production. The unit provides two hundred beds and was intended principally for developing countries, in both urban and rural areas.**

The theme of this project was the creation of mobile hospital units that could be transported easily and rapidly to wherever they were required (ARAM stands for Association for Rural Aids in Medicine). It fit very well into the line of research on free-plan spaces, since it shared their objective of making the functions and organization of space flexible. It also reflected a very interesting conception of medicine, which attempted to bring the health institution closer to the patient through a new relationship with local communities. This approach regarded the hospital as a medical instrument, capable of adapting to the specific needs of the place and situation.

The design was tackled on two distinct planes. On one hand is, a hard core, containing the more sophisticated equipment for diagnosis and treatment, which constituted the module proper; on the other is the accommodation of patients, already provided with the structures necessary for their care but capable of location in different places. The ARAM Module was simplified to the maximum: the whole structure was based on a compact nucleus, easy to transport and incorporating the crane required for the erection of the complex. The highly standardized components and elementary coupling systems made it possible for even a group of non-specialized volunteers to assemble the module, under the guidance of a few technicians.

The experimental module we created provided two hundred beds—a figure that we had identified as the maximum that would still permit a useful relationship with the community concerned. Anything larger than this would have brought with it the rigidity of the megastructure, conflicting with the flexibility of operation that was the central requirement of the project.

The ARAM Module could be mass produced. With a medical and paramedical staff covering all areas of expertise (with the exception of specific emergencies), a single module could meet the health needs of an area with a population of about one hundred thousand. The project was funded by the World Bank and intended for use in developing countries, with particular reference to Latin America.

Photomontages showing the module in different environmental conditions.

The module and its system of anchorage.

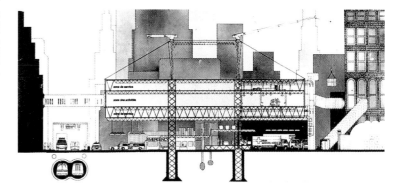

The module has a square plan, which is divided into square submodules. At the center is the so-called compact core with the vertical structure of ground support at the corners. The whole thing can be erected by non-specialized volunteers under the guidance of a few technicians.

The section shows how it is possible to obtain a totally free plan with this system. All the equipment is located in the gaps of the primary structure.

The drawings also show the positions of the cranes built into the module, used for its assembly.

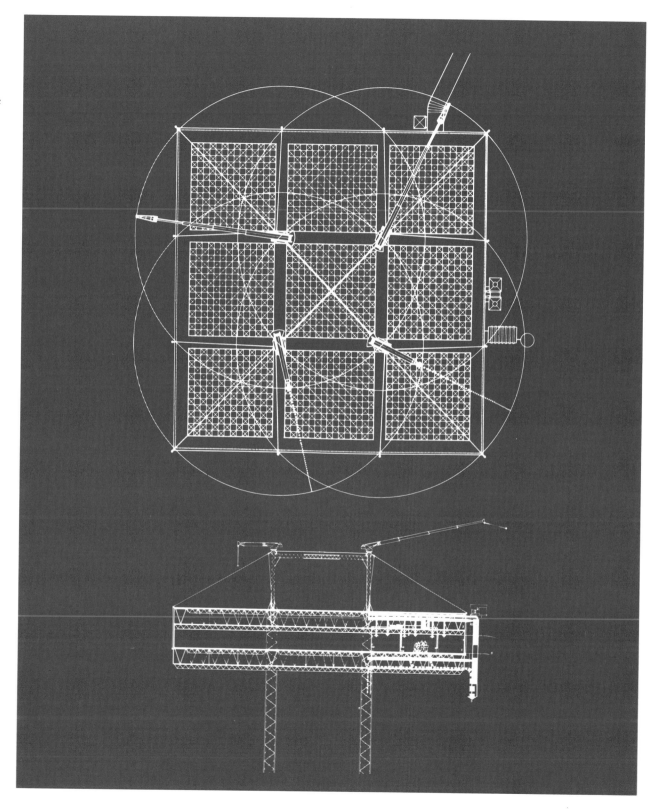

# 1971 Novedrate (Como) Italy

## B & B Italia Offices

Construction: 1971–73

**The building houses the offices of an important furniture manufacturer. It has a completely free plan, with a modular structure that permits easy expansion. The relationship with nature was primary.**

B & B is a work that overlapped with the Centre Pompidou. Obviously the larger projects cover a longer time span, and to some extent run right through this book. I point this out to excuse myself once and for all for a number of leaps forward and backward in time. In this case the chronology is important, because Piero Busnelli (the proprietor of B & B) saw the plans for Centre Pompidou, thought that we must be a bit crazy, and since he is a little crazy too, decided that he wanted to work with us.

The offices of B & B are at Novedrate, in Brianza, a place with a hot and rather stifling climate in the summer. It thereby provided an opportunity to extend the idea of the double roof (or the loft, if you prefer) to a much larger structure than the housing units at Cusago. In this case the structure between the two layers of the roof also houses the service and ventilation ducts.

We worked on this project between Paris and Genoa, and it was influenced by the Centre Pompidou. It had an influence of its own on the Paris project as well, being a small-scale dress rehearsal for it in many ways: extensive use of color, large open and flexible areas, broad spans. What was specific to this project, however, was the attempt to achieve the final result of a structure with large spans using very small elements, i.e., by fragmenting the scale.

B & B is smaller than Centre Pompidou, of course, yet it is still fairly large. I remember that we said, as a sort of challenge: "There shouldn't be any element with a diameter larger than eight centimeters." The idea was to reduce everything to a very slender structure, to a sort of filigree: at bottom, a formal and rather sophisticated exercise, an effort of stylistic and plastic research carried out with the components of metal supporting structures. This challenge provides the key to the building: a span of forty meters made with extremely light self-supporting elements. It was a work that required a great deal of patience, and some demanding acrobatics. When you fill in this lattice with totally transparent glass, set back a little, under the shade of the roof, you get a building that is so transparent to the surrounding nature that it establishes a dialogue of opposites with it. Furthermore, it has a modular structure that can be extended ad infinitum, just by continuing to add elements. The B & B is now a quarter of a century old, and I have to say that the relationship it proposes between the built and the natural remains current.

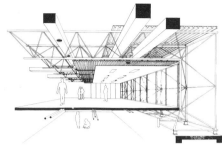

Axonometric and details of assembly.

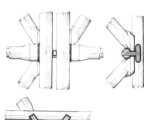 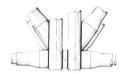

Joints of the structure of the open galleries.

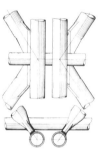 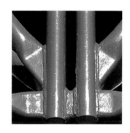

Below: East facade with elements in different colors according to their functions.

Passage from the
offices to the
production
departments (above);
entrance (below).

# 1971 **Paris** France

## Centre Georges Pompidou
Construction: 1971–78

**A hundred thousand square meters in the heart of Paris dedicated to the figurative arts, music, industrial design, and literature. The building reflects the program laid down in the competition, which indicated that culture be given a less institutional and traditional setting. With its parody of technology, but above all with its great expanse of public spaces that find their main expression in the plaza, it has become an active urban and cultural entity. Each day Centre Pompidou hosts more than twenty-five thousand people.**

Beaubourg was intended to be a joyful urban machine. You arrive in the Marais, in the center of Paris, and you find a creature that might have come from a Jules Verne book—or an unlikely-looking ship in dry dock. Over the last twenty years this idea has been described as amusing or unseemly, crude or fascinating. Over the same twenty years, a hundred and fifty million people have visited the Centre Pompidou.

Beaubourg is a provocation, as I have said more than once. This is an apt description of my feelings, but has no negative connotations as far as the quality of the design and the reasons behind it are concerned. So perhaps we need to take a step back.

In the last few years museums have undergone a genuine renaissance. Young and old, residents and tourists, everybody stands in line to see Picasso and look for poetry in the polished stones of Brancusi. But when Beaubourg was conceived, at the beginning of the seventies, no one went to museums. They were dreary, dusty, and esoteric institutions, and were perceived as politically incorrect, or rather as something for the elite. Museums did not suffer from a lack of sacred mystique, quite the contrary.

The irreverent tone of Beaubourg arose from this situation. The program itself, if I think about it, as laid down in the terms of the competition, suggested getting away from the confines, the boundaries typical of the library and museum. It spoke of culture, but also of functional versatility; of art, but also of information; of music, but also of industrial design. There was already something unconventional in this approach. All that was needed was to bring this out, push it to the limit, give it an extreme interpretation—and the most extreme interpretation, among the 681 projects submitted, was the informal and rather unruly cultural machine dreamed up by a couple of somewhat unmannerly young guys, not much over thirty years old.

Aerial view of Paris with Les Halles at right and Plateau Beaubourg at left.

Robert Bordaz, with Richard Rogers and Renzo Piano.

The team of architects on the construction site.

Pontus Hulten.

Competition drawing of the east facade.

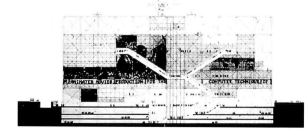

At that time I had a studio in London with Richard Rogers. It was Ove Arup, the engineering firm, that suggested we take part in the competition. One day Ted Happold came to see us on Aybrook Street, with Peter Rice (who remained my engineer until his sad death in 1992). They even promised us a little something to cover our expenses. This too came in handy. It was an open contest, and we knew that the competition would be stiff, so we decided to hold nothing back. We put our impatience with the established models together with the rationality and organization that was needed, and out popped Beaubourg.

The program was very open, highly innovative, but I don't think they expected such a radical response. Beaubourg is a double provocation: a challenge to academicism, but also a parody of the technological imagery of our time. To see it as high-tech is a misunderstanding. The Centre Pompidou is a "celibate machine," in which the flaunting of brightly colored metal and transparent tubing serves an urban, symbolic, and expressive function, not a technical one.

Beaubourg is the exact opposite of the technological model of the industrial city. It is a medieval village of twenty-five thousand people, the average population of daily visitors. The difference is that it extends upward: the layout is vertical, rather than horizontal, so the squares are set one on top of the other, and the streets run up and down.

Like a medieval village, it is essentially a place of meeting and contact: a place for wandering, for unexpected meetings, for the surprising and the curious, culturally speaking of course. This is why it has four and a half hectares of pedestrian areas at street level: a choice we have defended fiercely. This is why it has a large square in front.

It only makes sense to build a transatlantic liner of this kind if it places art at the service of social life in the city, and vice versa. So it is also right for it to be in the city center. At the time there were objections, like "It is okay to build it, but outside Paris." This is wrong: a Beaubourg in the suburbs would have made no sense.

A building of a hundred thousand square meters, as called for in the program, could never have been disguised, or made to "blend in"—as it is usually put—with the houses of the Marais quarter. But we were well aware of the need to create a relationship with the context, and chose to do it on the urbanistic plane as well as that of expression and form.

The transparency of the escalators, for instance, has been seen as a citation of high-tech—but in reality it is not technology. It is a game played with technology. When riding the escalator you are in the building, but you are outside it as well. As you rise slowly upward, you get a view of the square, then the quarter, and then the city. This is undoubtedly one of the revelations of Beaubourg.

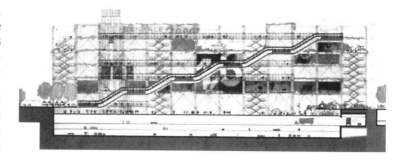

Final version of the west facade.

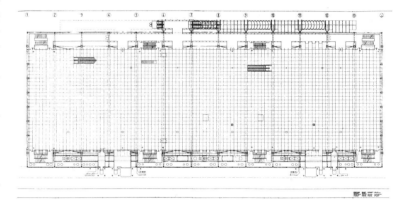

Typical floor plan.

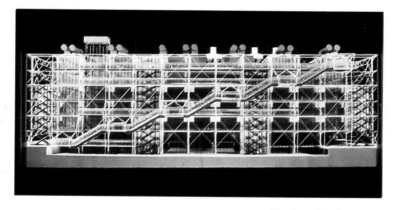

Final model of west facade.

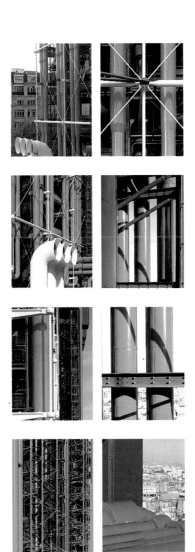

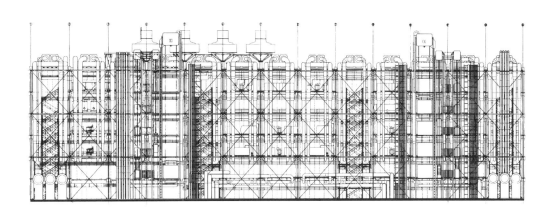

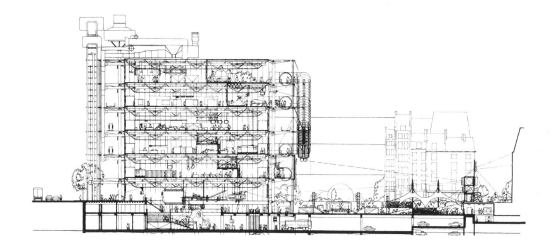

The Centre Pompidou as "celibate machine": the flaunting of colored metal and transparent tubing responds to its urban, symbolic, and expressive functions, not just the technical one.

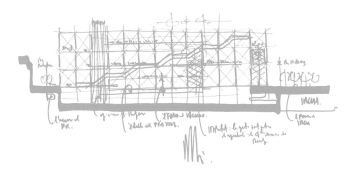

The square represents a twofold mediation: on the one hand, between Beaubourg and the quarter; on the other, between official culture and street culture. Those who perform in the square have interpreted its meaning correctly: the square is the location for art that is not formal, not institutional. Beaubourg, when all is said and done, was created not just to present culture, but to produce it. This utopian dimension may be unattainable, but is worth striving for.

Until this point, it was an adventure of the mind. But architecture is more than this: it also means navigating through storms. Real storms.

As could easily be foreseen, there were many attacks on Beaubourg: six lawsuits were brought in an attempt to halt construction, on the most bizarre grounds—including the fact that the chairman of the jury, Jean Prouvé, did not have an architecture degree. Luckily there was a sense of humor too. A newspaper published a manifesto of intellectuals against Beaubourg: it was not a fake; it was simply the text that had been drawn up by Parisian intellectuals to protest against the Eiffel Tower, copied out word for word, but with the signatures changed and "Beaubourg" inserted instead of "Eiffel Tower." What made the joke perfectly plausible was that a pressure group really had been set up to oppose us—it had given itself the pompous name of Comité pour le Geste Architectural.

Some aspects of the design were particularly unpopular: this was the case with what I call the "ears," the intakes for the ventilation system that can be seen in the square. At the time Paris did not have a mayor. There was still a prefect—just like Berlin has a burgomaster. When work started on the air intakes, the prefect of Paris told us, "It's too much, this is going too far," and prohibited their installation. So we went to Robert Bordaz, the director of the center, who said: "Let's put them in storage." Three months later we tried again—and straightaway the message came from the prefect, "What's this, are you pulling my leg?" Things went on like this for almost a year—until we received sad news: the prefect had died. The intakes were installed the next day. Umberto Eco has suggested that those ears are the means by which the population of the underworld communicates with the outside. Perhaps he's right.

The attacks on the "stagecoach" were continuous. But we learned that in architecture, too, the cavalry arrives (sometimes). Our "cavalry" was always led by Robert Bordaz.

Once, at a press conference—we were talking about the tubular structures that had been left visible, and the audience was on the point of pelting us with tomatoes—Bordaz said in all seriousness that the pipes were an explicit reference to the vertical members of the structure of Saint-Merri, a beautiful Gothic church in the quarter. How he came up with this idea I still don't know. We were red with embarrassment, but he had managed to silence the journalists.

Installation of the end of a Gerber beam, which came to be known as a "gerberette" (left); construction drawings (below left); gerberettes after casting (bottom).

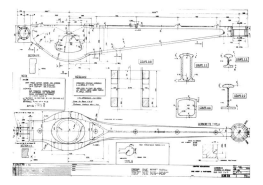

Opposite: Transport and installation of a prefabricated girder; assembly of the structure, without the use of scaffolding; placing a main girder on the end of the building.

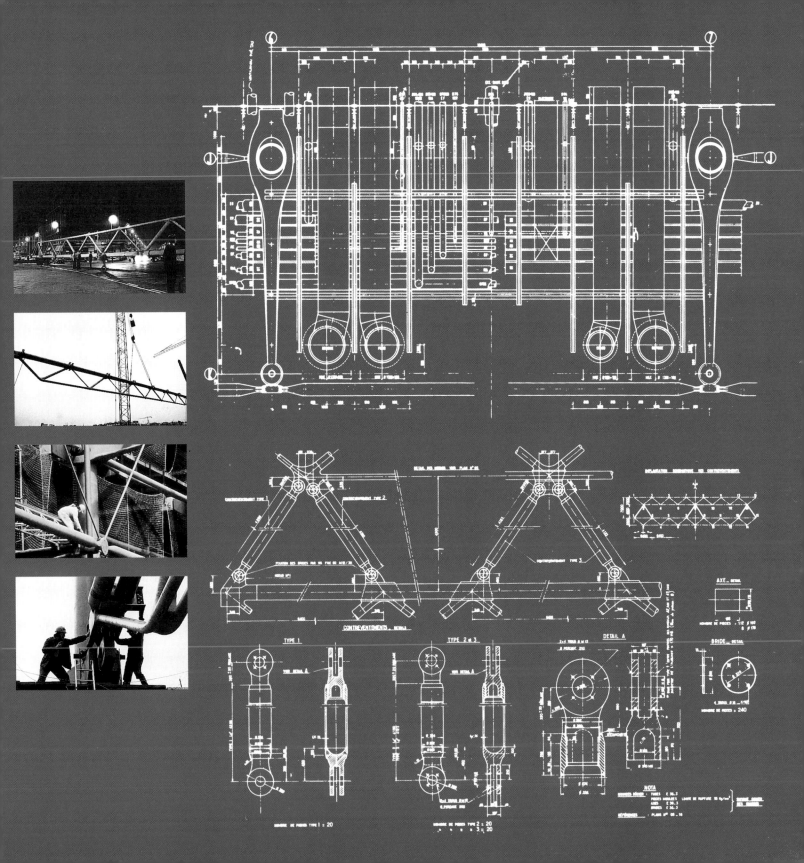

The decision to work with Krupp for the cast-metal structure instead of the French steel industry was one we could not avoid: the latter had turned us down flat. But this didn't make things any easier on the political plane. Bordaz shouldered the responsibility: very simply, he went straight to the president of the French republic—and came back with the authorization (later we discovered that we had an important ally in the Pompidou home: Mme. Claude Pompidou, who remains a great friend). Obviously there was still the problem of public opinion. We had to be careful that not too many people found out about Krupp, otherwise there would have been a lynching.

Have you ever tried to hide 50-meter-long steel girders weighing 120 tons? This is how: You bring them in on a special train. You transport them across Paris between three and five o'clock in the morning, when traffic is at a minimum. Of course, you need a huge truck, or rather two (one at the front of the girder and another at the back). Before the convoy passes, you send another truck to protect all the manhole covers along the route with four-centimeter-thick sheets of steel, which first have to be laid and then lifted with a giant magnet. When the girder reaches its destination you erect it at once, otherwise it will bring the whole construction site to a standstill. Simple, in a way.

For me Beaubourg was a school of life, not because of its scale—I could say that the rules of the construction site, whether it is small, large, or enormous, are basically the same, and I have known them since I was a child—but chiefly because up until that moment I had always worked in a rather intimate way. I had carried out my experiments more or less at home, in a manner of speaking. With the Centre Pompidou I discovered adventure—and met many of the people who are still my companions on that adventure.

Willy Sandberg, for instance, had been the great inventor of the Stedelijk Museum and then director of the museum in Jerusalem. It was he who introduced the artistic director Pontus Hulten to Bordaz. Pontus and I became great friends, and still are today. He is a man of refined and sensitive culture, but looks like a brown bear that has strayed out of the northern wastelands. Philip Johnson, a prodigy, also became a good friend.

We were a sort of foreign legion—we were building the biggest monument in France, and almost all of us were foreigners: Italians, Britons, Swedes, Americans, Japanese. It was during Beaubourg, too, that I started to work with Bernard Plattner and Shunji Ishida. The latter passed through Genoa by chance in 1971; he is still with me there. Of course the balance of the team was fully restored with Bordaz's excellent administrators and with the main contractor, G.T.M., who were all French.

Perhaps the most important partnership that was formed during those years in Paris was with Peter Rice. The Ove Arup

View from a tower of Notre Dame.

South facade, which maintains a dialogue with the IRCAM extension, built subsequently.

The escalators on the west facade viewed from the inside and from the outside. The escalators provide access to the various departments. The visitor, rising at a slow pace, is gradually presented with a view of the quarter and, finally, the city.

studio, to which Peter belonged, had supported us right from the start: when we won the competition, Peter was placed in charge of the structural engineers. The immense structure of Beaubourg is the result of the assembly of thousands of small pieces made almost by hand, and it is modular, expandable—once again infinite and unfinished—it is what is called a prototype. Structural calculation was not enough to obtain a result like this: what was needed was creativity applied to structures. And that is just what Peter Rice could do. He did it in all my most important works right up until his death. My relationship with Tom Barker, Arup's plant engineer, was the last of these great partnerships, and one that still exists.

Two other friendships that date from those years are with Pierre Boulez and Luciano Berio, which developed out of the IRCAM project. IRCAM is the Institute for Research and Coordination on Acoustics and Music, and is an offshoot of Beaubourg—also in the sense that it is located in the adjacent Place Saint-Merri. From the urban point of view, it is a nonplace, for it is entirely underground—except for the tower of course, of which we shall speak later on.

Given that it was intended for research in the field of acoustics, the first problem posed by IRCAM was one of soundproofing. Originally it was to have been located aboveground, taking the place of a rather ugly school fated for demolition. When the site had been cleared, however, we realized that the square we had involuntarily created, with the Gothic church of Saint-Merri in the background, was necessary to the proportion of the place. Building something there had become unthinkable. The underground solution amounted to a squaring of the circle: on the one hand it helped us to design an acoustically neutral structure; on the other it restored full dignity to the church, which had been suffocated before. Out of all this came Place Stravinsky at ground level, a pedestrian square dotted with the skylights of IRCAM.

My meeting with Boulez and Berio introduced me to the world of music. Previously my relationship with music had been one of well-disposed ignorance. It is significant that, yet again, my relationship with an art came out of technique—it was born not at La Scala, but at the IRCAM, which means at the music factory. This taught me a great lesson in interdisciplinary sensitivity. It was here that I began to understand just how arbitrary the borders between the various disciplines are. Certainly music is the most immaterial of the arts, and architecture the most material; but both of them operate on the basis of a similar logic, of structural discipline, of severity (mitigated by the possibility of breaking the rules), of detail, vibration, and color. Luciano Berio and I looked at our work the same way: both of us broke the rules, but methodically. We were both disobedient but precise. This marked the beginning of a deep personal friendship. Luciano is a true explorer, who leads music on incursions into the world of science and math-

Life inside and outside the Centre Pompidou. Here art is placed at the service of urban sociability and vice versa. Official culture and street culture meet in the vast public internal and external spaces.

ematics, but who also has a profound understanding of the music of the past and feels deeply grateful to it: to its history, folklore, popular traditions. It is an attitude that, in my own field, I share.

The fourth person who worked with us on IRCAM was Victor Peutz, a Dutchman who was responsible for acoustic experimentation. From Peutz I learned just how important it is, in certain cases, to take a scientific approach to architecture. We worked with analogical models, with acoustic models, for we were not building a concert hall like so many others, but an actual musical instrument. Among other things, we created a room for experimentation in which the acoustic response varied from 0.6 to 6 seconds. It was practically a machine: an underground cube of twenty meters on a side, with variable acoustics and movable ceilings and walls. The room is a banal object from the viewpoint of geometry, but still very rich, for the sound becomes part of the space: it turns into an immaterial but indispensable component.

The excavation of the IRCAM site (left); perspective of the experimental chamber (below).

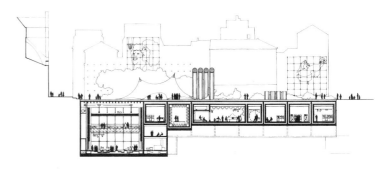

Longitudinal sections of the zone of specialized research (above) and the public zone (below).

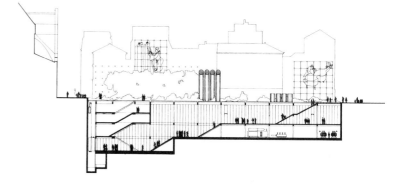

Above: The experimental chamber, with panels that can be adjusted to vary acoustic response.

Detail of the experimental chamber (below left); the anechoic chamber for testing sound (below center); a recording studio (below right).

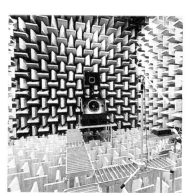

# 1978 **Otranto** Italy

## Urban Reconstruction
## Workshop

**This is a program for the rehabilitation of historic centers, supported by UNESCO. It is a unit that can be transported on a truck and set up in the middle of a city's historic area. It is organized into four sections that correspond to the four sides of a cube: analysis and diagnosis, information and education, open project, work and construction. The project was based on participation.**

In a way, Centre Pompidou was the work that every architect dreams of at the age of thirty-five: big, prestigious, visible. But Beaubourg was followed by a period of real fatigue.

The experience had lasted six years: six years of full immersion in a project and in a city. Despite the huge success of the building, it left a deep mark on us: partly in the sense that it had given Richard Rogers and me the powerful experience of working in a team. I am pointing this out to show that there was a sort of reaction, immediately afterward.

My relations with Pontus Hulten, Pierre Boulez, and Luciano Berio had allowed me to discover dimensions and disciplines I had never encountered during my university training, or during my previous career. It had been a great lesson, which stimulated me and aroused my curiosity. I had discovered the enormous possibilities opened up by learning about the experiences of other people.

Again: Beaubourg had been the construction of a cathedral—in direct contact with Culture and Politics, with capital letters. Afterward, I wanted to go back to a more direct relationship with the facts of ordinary life. I wanted to immerse myself once again in the reality of a less gigantic undertaking. I don't know if it was a strong sense of nostalgia for my Genoese past, but—paradoxically—one thing I had missed during the six years I spent in Paris was the relationship with the old city. So, when Wolf Tochtermann of UNESCO raised the possibility of working on a project in Otranto, it seemed just the right thing to do. It would take me back to working on one of my favorite themes: the current state of historic centers.

If you look around and ask yourself, "What are the great themes for an architect today?," in Europe at least there can be no doubts: the reclamation of historic buildings, the rehabilitation of decayed areas, the quality of the domestic environment. These were the problems we faced in the Otranto project.

It was a modest undertaking in terms of scale and duration, but an extremely interesting one. What we developed in

1

2

3

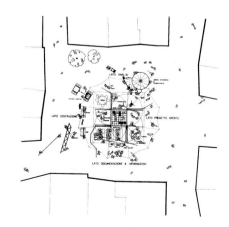

4

1. Erecting of the structure for the Urban Reconstruction Workshop.
2–4. The arrival of the workshop cube in the central square of Otranto and the various phases of assembly.

The workshop with its tent/awning of white canvas was the point of attraction for residents, whose involvement was one of the principal aims of the project.

Otranto was a district workshop based on the total collaboration of the inhabitants. We drew up the project together, made the choices together, adjusted the plans together, sometimes experimented with the means of intervention together. We even got the work underway together. The idea was to operate on the territory in the way that a good doctor works on a patient: taking a comprehensive approach, based on an understanding of the case history and not just the symptoms. In a way we have created the figure of the "local architect," performing the same kind of role as the general practitioner.

Our method was designed to keep disturbance to a minimum and to allow us to work in the area without the inhabitants having to move out. Using nondestructive techniques of diagnosis (borrowed from medicine in some cases), we started to work in a way that, instead of breaking everything down, tried to determine whether an intervention was really necessary. The reasoning was: if the wall is not unsafe, why knock it down? This may seem obvious, but it went completely against previous practice in the reclamation of historic centers. Support for this comes from an observation made by the philosopher Gianni Vattimo, who in an article described our work in Otranto as a "weak construction site," i.e., one with a "light" touch.

This experiment stirred up an interest that went beyond its material significance, which was partly due to the involvement of some top-flight people. The contractor responsible for the work was Gianfranco Dioguardi; the journalist Mario Fazio helped us to devise the methodology of the participatory process; the director Giulio Macchi was in charge of the collection of oral histories; the photographer Gianni Berengo Gardin recorded the various phases of the project; and Magda Arduino, my first wife, wrote the scripts for the films.

The intervention was divided into four phases, each covering a different sector: diagnosis, planning, operational workshop, recording. Local inhabitants were involved in all activities. In the workshop every aspect of participation and communication was brought forcefully into play. For us, it was an immersion in what I call the "art of listening."

Recently Mayor Bassolino of Naples made a very shrewd observation to me: in such cases the process of participation serves above all to reawaken people's pride in living in the old city. I have some very fine memories of this in Otranto. Some of our experiments had become an attraction—such as the camera for taking aerial surveys, which we suspended from a helium-filled balloon. Every time we launched this miniature aerostat and then brought it back down into the square, it turned into a festival. And then, of course, there were the meetings with the local people—hundreds of interested and attentive individuals, gathering around our tent in the evenings to talk about history, materials, and architecture.

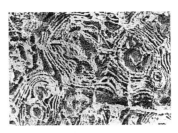
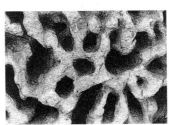

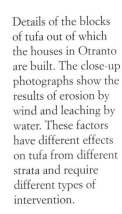

Details of the blocks of tufa out of which the houses in Otranto are built. The close-up photographs show the results of erosion by wind and leaching by water. These factors have different effects on tufa from different strata and require different types of intervention.

A camera attached to a helium balloon was used to take aerial photographs of the streets of Otranto.

It proved possible to replace structural beams inside the houses without requiring the occupants to leave.

A meeting at which videos made during the workshop's activity were shown to the residents.

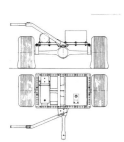

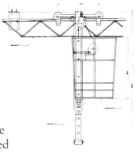

An electric vehicle was specially designed to be able to move through the narrow streets and over the flights of steps in the historic center.

Lightweight mobile scaffolding was used for interventions on facades where it was impossible to install fixed scaffolding. The basket could easily be moved sideways and vertically.

# 1978 Corciano (Perugia) Italy

## EH, Evolutive Housing

Construction: 1978–82

**Standard housing units with a width of six meters and a height of six meters, providing a floor space ranging from 50 square meters to 120. The combination of the primary space of an industrially produced external container and a secondary, internal space left up to its users.**

EH, Evolutive Housing, is a name that I don't like any more for a project that I still like a lot. It would be better to call it Corciano, after the small town near Perugia where we built the prototype.

The concept of evolutive space has fascinated me since the beginning of my career. In this project, developed in collaboration with Vibrocemento Perugia, it was applied to a low-cost product, highly flexible and easy to assemble. We wanted to take our experimentation with the concept of the "unfinished living space" to a level where it could be tried out on an industrial scale. The idea was this: industry produces the shell and the inhabitant finishes the interior according to personal taste. The house is a living organism, which should be incomplete and modifiable.

The work was carried out on two levels: the modularity of the components that make up the external structure and the modularity of the interior from the viewpoint of its user. The quakeproof shell consisted of C-shaped concrete elements: two Cs put together formed a piece with a repeatable section, which was at once floor, ceiling, and two walls. The construction was completed at the front and rear with two glass walls. The resulting space was a cube, six meters on a side. This meant it could be split in half vertically; taking the thickness of the floor into consideration, the result was two levels each with a height of 2.7 meters.

The panels that formed the intermediate floor and the inside walls were made of wood on a steel framework, and therefore very light. We did a lot of work with Peter Rice on this project, mixing and overlapping aspects of structure with those of production, aspects of typology with those of space. The standardization of the modules and of the connections to the structure allowed the inhabitants of the houses a great deal of freedom in the design of their own interiors. Different arrangements of these interiors meant that the floor space could be anything from 50 to 120 square meters. Whatever the solution chosen, two windows of six by six meters ensured excellent illumination.

You know those houses that are untouchable works of art, where the ashtray always has to be put back on the table in the same place, or else the composition of the interior decoration is ruined? Well, this was the exact opposite.

Construction under way.

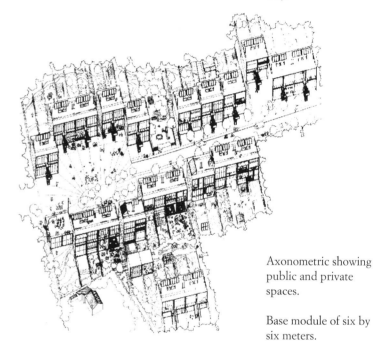

Axonometric showing public and private spaces.

Base module of six by six meters.

The house as a living and therefore adaptable organism: two large windows ensure plentiful light, and inside, residents are free to organize their apartments as they wish (right); the assembly of two structural elements (bottom left); it is possible to create a second level with light slabs supported by small beams (below center and right).

# 1978   Fiat VSS/Flying Carpet

Realization: 1978–80

**VSS: Design for an experimental automobile based on separation of the supporting structure, impact resistance, and the changes to the exterior shell.**
**Flying Carpet: A base of reinforced concrete fitted with an engine and transmission, designed for supply to developing countries.**

The application of different body components to the same chassis permits the creation of different models. The results of this research still dominate current production.

VSS was a project for an experimental vehicle commissioned by Fiat at the end of the 1970s. The company's managing director at the time, Tufarelli, asked me to carry out a study on the automobile of the future, approaching it with the same open-mindedness that I applied to the theme of the house. The basic principle of the project was to conserve energy, and to achieve this we had been given the objective of reducing the vehicle's weight by 20 percent. To develop this project we set up the IDEA institute in Turin with Peter Rice and Franco Mantegazza.

A line of research emerged right away: if we wanted to make the car lighter, its supporting function had to be shifted back from the body to the chassis. In this way the chassis would provide resistance to torsion and absorption of energy during an accident, while the body could be made lightweight, interchangeable, and flexible. Once again the approach mixed up the more technical roles with the more functional and expressive ones. This brought us into contact with one of the greatest practitioners of automobile design of all time: Dante Giacosa, the man who had introduced the idea of the supporting body into Fiat.

VSS was fundamentally a structural study and produced formal results that were highly unsatisfactory, since it had to meet the dictates of too shortsighted a view of the market. But the results of that research, which lasted for three years, still have an influence today.

Over the same period we also worked on the Flying Carpet project. We were asked to devise solution to the problem of selling the main components of the car in North Africa. When we drew these parts on a sheet of paper, they formed a complete automobile without body or chassis. So we had the idea of constructing a bed of reinforced concrete and mounting all these components on it.

The idea was an elegant one, and had a powerful commercial logic all its own—in North Africa, apparently, protection from the elements was less important than the cost, versatility, and reliability of a vehicle. And yet it didn't work, because we hadn't taken into consideration the weight of psychological and cultural expectations. The product had everything that it should have, but it did not satisfy the need for modernity of which the automobile is an expression.

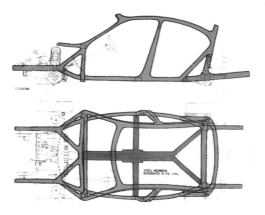

Scheme of the steel framework.

Opposite (above): Computer simulation of a collision affecting the front part of the vehicle; scheme and exploded isometric of the plastic materials of the body.

Crash test.

Model of framework.

Opposite (below): In the Flying Carpet project, the basic components of the automobile—engine, transmission, clutch, brakes, steering gear, gearbox, electrical system—made up a car with no body. So we mounted the components on a supporting bed of reinforced concrete, which led to the name "Flying Carpet."

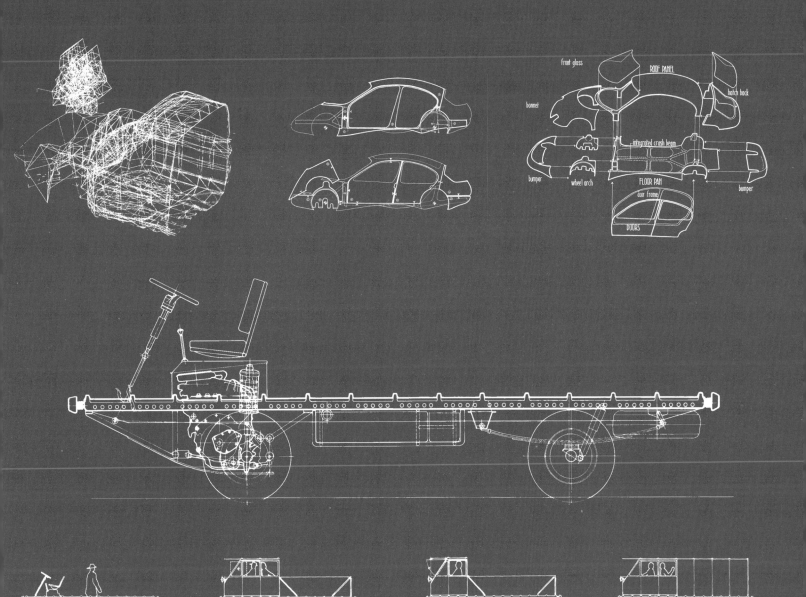

front glass

bonnet

ROOF PANEL

hatch back

integrated crush beam

bumper

wheel arch

FLOOR PAN

door frame

bumper

DOORS

# 1978 Dakar Senegal

## Mobile Construction Unit

**A project for a small mobile factory, created to make roofing elements for dwellings in situ from new plant fibers introduced to replace the traditional ones that had disappeared because of altered soil conditions. The clash between tradition and aspiration to the "modern."**

The Flying Carpet was a good lesson. We have our own cultural models, our own scale of values; and sometimes we forget that there are a lot of us on this planet, and we don't all think the same way. The problem of aspirations, and of the needs induced by our perception of modernity, was posed in just these terms by the Senegal project. We had an intelligent solution, one that responded perfectly to the program and that would have reduced the country's trade deficit drastically—but it didn't have the required symbolic value.

The project in Senegal was another one developed in collaboration with UNESCO, through its regional office in Dakar. The president of Senegal at the time was Léopold S. Senghor, a poet, writer, and man of great quality and culture, with whom we got on immediately. The aim was to devise a way that would allow people to keep their own habitat and their own homes intact, in a region where the traditional construction material was no longer available.

Fifteen years earlier, the city of Dakar had built an aqueduct. The whole of the region around Dakar is very low-lying—when the tide turns, the Senegal River even reverses its flow for dozens of kilometers. The aqueduct had lowered the water table by half a meter, with the result that the conditions for the life and growth of all plants had been altered. Even the baobabs were falling over (the baobab's roots extend horizontally, and when the wind blew they ended up on the ground like toppled pachyderms). The same thing happened to all the trees with long-grained wood. As a result the source of the material that had always been used to build huts had dried up. This meant developing techniques of rebuilding and maintenance that could substitute for these plant fibers. At least that was what Senghor thought, and so did we.

Our project provided for the creation of mobile units, capable of moving from village to village and making roofing elements out of new plant fibers made available in situ. Buying the simple machinery needed would have cost less than importing the components, and this was very important to the country's fragile economy. In some areas it would have been possible to identify new crops capable of growing under the new environmental conditions and bring them into cultivation. At the outset, the mobile units would have received advice from us on the choice of materials and use of the machinery. Later they would have become self-sufficient.

Aerial view of Dakar (above); typical hut (left).

Bricks of plant fiber laid out to dry.

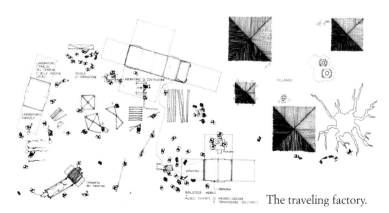

The traveling factory.

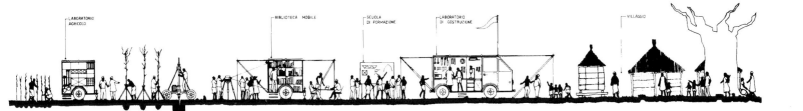

It is easy to discern the influence of our experience in Otranto on this solution. But the reality was very different. A matriarchal society held sway in the whole of that area. When the young men grew up, they emigrated to Dakar and started to earn some of money. The first son to succeed in the city used to send a pile of corrugated iron to his mother to fix the roof of the hut.

Naturally, while roofs made of plant fiber offered some protection from the heat and humidity, huts with corrugated-iron roofs were an inferno: scorching hot in the summer, they made so much noise when it rained that you couldn't sleep. Worse; the wooden hut underneath started to rot away, since there was no natural evaporation. After a while all that remained were the sheets of metal, and these sheets, first shiny and then rusty, had become a symbol of modernity for the people, a sign of inexorable progress.

In those years I started to work with Paul Henry Chombard de Lawe, a sociologist of the Parisian school, who helped me to understand this mechanism better. You may feel that a problem is not real, but if it is part of the aspirations of a community, then you have to treat it as if it were: The roof is scorching hot in the summer, it's true, but it is a proof of the success and affection of my son: I have a son who has gone to the city, and my neighbors can see it, because he has rebuilt my house. I don't want this to be grist for cynical, or even racist attitudes toward underdevelopment, for exactly the same thing goes on at home. In collaboration with UNESCO again, we started a project on the island of Burano, near Venice, where there used to be a tradition of repainting the houses in beautiful colors every year. But we found that the traditional lime plastering had been replaced by cement rendering, and that synthetic paint was being used instead of lime-based paint. Of course, this meant that the colors were brighter, more "modern," and didn't have to be repainted every year. The result is that the wall cannot breathe any more, the damp rises by capillary action, and the wall is even more hygroscopic, since it is loaded with salt. And in the end there is no alternative but to knock it down and rebuild it.

Just like in Senegal, the real reasons have nothing to do with technology or construction, but with the complex world of dreams.

The island of Burano (above); typical painted houses, the subject of a study carried out for UNESCO (right).

The Molo Vecchio, an old quarter of Genoa, the subject of another UNESCO reclamation study. The upper stories become public places and are interconnected.

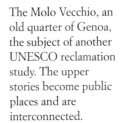

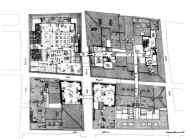

**A program of an educational character made by RAI, the Italian state television network. A series that set out to make the techniques of construction comprehensible and accessible, through an examination of past experiences and different cultures.**

There were moments in the past when the profession of architecture was more adventurous than it is now. We have used the Old West as a metaphor for adventure; the settlement of the West was itself one of those times. Pioneers loaded their wagons with planks of wood, nails, and a hammer. The planks were numbered, and the whole thing could be seen as a sort of prefabricated house. When they got to the place where they wanted to stay, the pioneers built their house. They were all architects.

Another heroic example is the construction of the Gothic cathedrals. Certainly, the architect tried assembling the beams on the ground first. But if they were going to fit together on the day the structure was erected, then it was necessary to ensure that the level of humidity was the same. Otherwise the jigsaw puzzle wasn't going to come out right. Intellectual work was not enough: to realize the dream the designer needed an interdisciplinary team that would be able to draw on the know-how of hundreds of craftspeople. This organization of work had a social consequence of incredible significance: the cathedrals were the first example of the modern labor market—the craftspeople freely offered their skills to the master builder, and negotiated their own pay. The "Habitat" program (made for RAI in 1979, and directed by Giulio Marchi to a script by Magda Arduino) gave me the chance to present to the general public these and other considerations of mine on the subject of architecture. In some ways, it was like repeating the experience of Otranto on screen.

"Habitat" was aimed at non-specialists, and so set out to render intelligible: the principles of construction, a few simple experiments on structures and materials, and other topics. Perhaps the most interesting aspect was that we linked all this to the social history of architecture, using examples drawn from other cultures as well, such as the yurt, the Mongol tent first described by Marco Polo. I also tried to get a little message across: don't be overawed by architecture. This century has produced impressive structures because it has developed fantastic machinery for building. But innovation in process does not necessarily entail high technology in construction. There is very little, today, that can bear comparison to the structural and formal research that went into a fifteenth-century church.

Sequences from the program. The model of a cathedral under construction was used to explain the method and the means of building.

Renzo Piano between
Nori Okabe and
Shunji Ishida.

Magda Arduino, who
wrote the script
(above); Giulio
Macchi, the director
(right).

# 1981 **Montrouge** (Paris) France

## Schlumberger Facilities Restructuring

Construction: 1981–84

**Part of the Schlumberger establishment, on the outskirts of Paris, was converted into offices and laboratories. A large park was laid out in the area cleared by demolition of the old plant, covering a parking facility with space for a thousand vehicles. The project was subtle interaction between old and new, between the built and the natural.**

The factory before the intervention.

The historic center is the heart of a city. In an industrial city (and that is what all of Europe's metropolises have been at one time or another) there is a more recent history: that of the development of industrial structures. This has led to the rise of other centers, now historic themselves, made up of factories rather than townhouses and based on the logic of industry rather than that of residential planning. This history too is worthy of respect—first because it is part of our civilization, and second because some of the buildings it has produced are very fine.

Schlumberger at Montrouge, on the outskirts of Paris, was the first of a series of projects in which I have worked on the architectural reclamation and reutilization of industrial areas. I set aesthetic and functional rehabilitation on the same plane, for they are different sides of the same coin: it is impossible to redesign an abandoned site without reconsidering its function, its use, and its social purpose.

Schlumberger is an electromechanical engineering company specializing in measurement systems, especially for fluids—from water meters to devices that detect the presence of oil underground. This last area has gradually become the company's main business. At the time we were asked to intervene (by Jean Riboud, who was also the moving spirit behind the firm's cultural policy), Schlumberger was on the verge of a radical transformation: the mechanical systems made by the company were progressively being replaced by electronic ones.

It was not just a question of spatial dimensions, but also of their quality: the assembly of electronic components requires a very clean and protected environment. Furthermore, the proportion of the workforce engaged in research and development was destined to grow considerably. One of the main reasons behind the company's decision to restructure its existing establishment, instead of building a completely new one, was its desire to maintain a continuous presence on the site. The area, a right triangle, was bounded on two sides by a series of five-story constructions that were to be renovated. The workshops located in the middle, on the other hand, were to be demolished.

Some of the measuring equipment made before the restructuring of Schlumberger: electric, gas, and water meters.

Jean Riboud.

Aerial view after the restructuring.

Opposite: The end of one of the buildings after the restructuring.

One small detail is perhaps worth mentioning: works of this kind, abroad at least, are always subject to competition. I don't want to give the impression that the client called us up and asked if we would like to work with them. Schlumberger consulted more than twenty architectural studios and then gradually cut the number down to a short list of three, which was submitted to Jean Riboud. Riboud came from an illustrious family (he was the brother of Marc Riboud, the photographer, and Antoine Riboud, the great patron of Danone). He was a man of great authority. One day he called me in for a meeting and said, "Okay, I've chosen you, but I don't understand why you have chosen me. You have done things that are very new. Why are you now interested in an old and disused factory?" I explained, or tried to explain, that I believe in the relevance of the past to the present, the sort of things that I discussed earlier on, and he answered: "All right, I'll be straight with you. I had no intention of offering you the job, it was a lie. I hadn't made up my mind yet. Now I have." And so we started work on the Schlumberger project. Supervision of the job was entrusted to Alain Vincent, who subsequently left Schlumberger to join my studio (where he remains today).

One unusual aspect of this project was the fact that people carried on working while the restructuring was underway. The factory did not close: one part of the complex—what they called the incubator of new Schlumberger activities—remained in operation. The company was very active in the field of innovation. It had recently registered several new patents and three or four enterprises had been set up to exploit them. Before being given their own facilities and complete autonomy, these subsidiaries were located in the incubator. For a year or two they carried out product tests, made trial production runs, and prepared their machines for installation on customers' premises. In a way it was like restructuring an inhabited city, like working in a house without driving out its occupants—something we had already experienced with UNESCO.

The tall buildings along the perimeter, with their imposing and austere character, had strong links with the historic identity of the quarter. So we decided to preserve their original external appearance, restricting major interventions to the interior, where many modifications were needed to bring the facilities up to the required standards. In the central space that had been cleared by demolition of the workshops, we decided to create a park, in collaboration with Alexandre Chemetoff. The plants were selected so that they would provide changing scenery and different colors in different seasons: the cycle of nature juxtaposed with the cycle of technology.

Moreover, we decided to use the greenery in an intrusive way. Access to Schlumberger is along paths laid out in the garden. From here a bridge extends to the first floor of the central nucleus. A lake is set under the glass wall and at the base of the stairs. Ornamental plants and creepers enliven the stairs, the

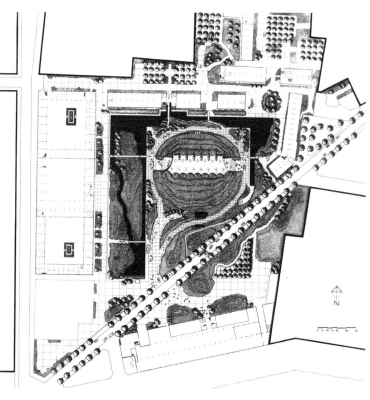

Overall plan of the intervention showing the layout of the park that has taken the place of the preexisting workshops.

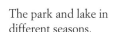

The park and lake in different seasons.

Opposite: The new staircases in the main building show that nature is present inside, as a continuation of the park; section through the new staircases.

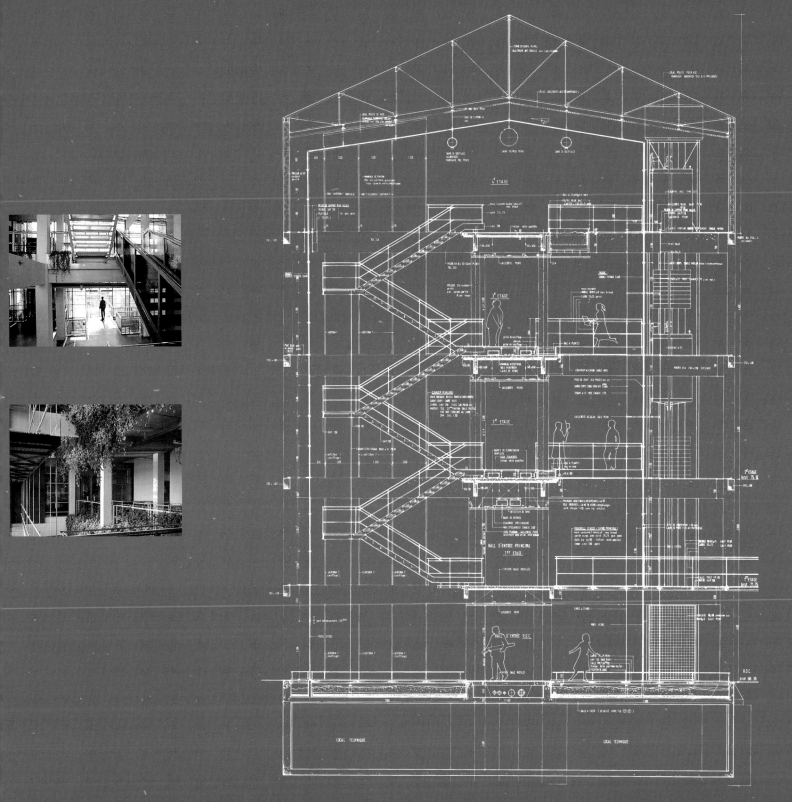

corridors, the landings—they even make their way into the offices. There is no definite borderline, no point where nature comes to a visible halt. Even the area known as the "forum," to be used for services (restaurant, bar, bank, travel agency, gymnasium, conference hall) is partially covered by an artificial hill, with a route for pedestrians cutting through it. A tensile structure of Teflon shelters this area from the rain and the sun.

In addition to balancing the imposing character of the old buildings that surround it, the park provides pleasant scenery both for the staff of the Schlumberger Company and for passersby on Avenue Jean-Jaurès (the third side of the triangle). This oasis of greenery helps to improve the quality of life in the quarter and the factory's relationship with the urban fabric.

The decision to use nature as architecture is certainly not an original one, but it takes on a new value in this context. It is no accident that we talked about the vegetation "taking over" the construction. This does not mean that nature has had its revenge: Schlumberger still exists, and many people go to work there every day. It means that nature has penetrated the walls of industry (literally), restoring a balance of values that had previously been weighted heavily in favor of technology. I would like to see Schlumberger as the metaphor for a new and cooperative relationship between technology and the environment, between the use of resources and their conservation.

The renovation of the buildings has left the original structure visible, drawing attention to the changes made to the curtain walls and to the new plant.

The tensile structure which shelters the cut in the hill at the center of the park, makes the space of the "forum," to be used for the company's services, the element of cohesion between the park and the office and workshop buildings.

General view of main building B with the lake in the foreground and the forum with its tensile structure at right.

Internal views of the offices and workshops.

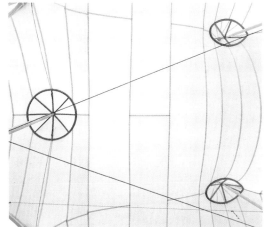

Details of the tensile structure with the characteristic struts that determine its shape.

# 1982 Turin Italy

## Alexander Calder Retrospective Exhibition

Realization: 1982

**The restructuring of a space, the Palazzo a Vela in Turin, so that it could be used to stage a retrospective exhibition on Alexander Calder. A work on light, space, and the location of works of art.**

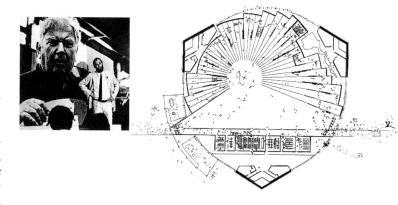

Calder's mobiles are an exercise in irony and great craftsmanship: a refined juggling of weights, forms, spatial relationships, and movement as well as a real game played according to the laws of mechanics. Out of this have come some of the most interesting objects that the art of this century has associated with technology. These are some of the many reasons that attract me to Calder, that make me feel close to him.

In 1982 the critic Giovanni Carandente proposed that I design the setting for the largest exhibition of Calder's works ever to be staged, in Turin. It is not easy to put these mobiles on display. In the traditional setting of a museum they would have lost their irreverent quality. So what we were looking for was a "non-museum." We found it in the Palazzo a Vela, located in the park of the Italy '61 exhibition—a reinforced-concrete building in the shape of a sail, with only three points of support at the sides and an enormous open space of fifteen thousand square meters. It was an open space that gave us total freedom yet was not designed to house events of this kind, and therefore needed to be completely reshaped.

We decided to work chiefly on the immaterial aspects of the space. We covered the seven thousand square meters of glass with reflective panels of aluminum, painted dark blue on the inside. The ceiling of this great space was also painted dark blue. The darkness masked the immensity of the hall, while the gaze of the visitor was directed toward the works by blades of light.

Next we turned our attention to the temperature, not only to prevent damage to the pieces, but also because a cool and dark environment helps to instill a sense of absorption (as the architects of the great cathedrals were well aware). The exhibition was planned for summer, and Turin in the summer can be like an oven. By improving the ventilation system and letting water flow over the roof, we were able to lower the temperature by about six degrees centigrade. Thus we produced an unexpected "space," a microcosm that was related to the artist's own vision: it was a materialization of Calder's great "Circus." The sculptures were set at different heights and arranged in a sunburst around a central focus, where three works of large size were placed, along with a number of smaller ones. The location of this focus, slightly off-center with respect to the axis, helped to accentuate the sensation of movement.

Plan of the exhibition.

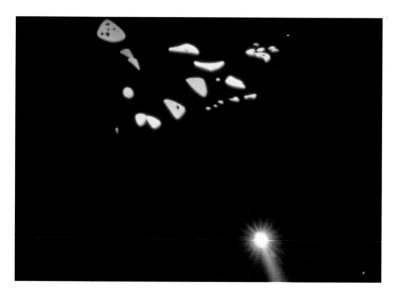

One of Calder's mobiles.

Calder's great
"Circus" materializes
out of the half-light.

# 1982 **Houston** Texas

## Menil Collection

Construction: 1982–86

**This museum houses the Menil Collection, made up of more than ten thousand works of primitive and modern art. Only some of the works are on display at any one time, in rotation, in a setting illuminated mainly by natural light. The others are stored in a "Treasure House." The museum is a complex space, enriched by the pattern of multiple planes and the invasion of nature. It embodies the idea of a "museum village."**

John de Menil was an oil magnate who had found his oil in Texas. His wife, Dominique, a French noblewoman, had followed him to Houston. Mme. de Menil is now a very lively ninety-year-old with a great passion for art. For many years Mme. de Menil cherished the idea of a museum to display her collection. This led her and her closest collaborators, Paul Winkler and Walter Hopps, to contact us.

Mme. de Menil had developed some very clear ideas about architecture and about the form her museum should take. She wanted nothing to do with the rhetorical modernity of downtown Houston. What she wanted was an experimental museum, one that would function simultaneously as a restoration center, exhibition site, and village. She had a great love for light, and wanted us to work on the theme of natural illumination. Mme. de Menil wanted the light in her museum to be bright, throbbing, as variable as the day—so as to permit everchanging perceptions of the colors in the works.

In addition to light, the most interesting aspect from the technical viewpoint was the conservation of the works of art. We took an interdisciplinary approach, as with the acoustic chambers of the IRCAM: we were given the help we needed by several acknowledged experts in conservation science. With them we studied the questions of relative humidity, temperature, and lighting: each of these factors had a threshold that could not be exceeded without damage to the exhibited works.

At a certain point the problem of lighting became entangled with that of the abundance of material. As sometimes happens, the overlapping of two problems provided us with the solution. Ten thousand pieces are really a lot, and it would have been difficult to put them all on display at once while giving each the space it deserved. This led to the idea of the Treasure House, and it was Mme. de Menil who came up with it. Why not, she asked, create a protected and secure place, in which the climate could be kept under strict control, separate from the area open to the public, and put the works on show in turn, for short periods of time? The Treasure House represented the squaring of the circle: it allowed the project to take a com-

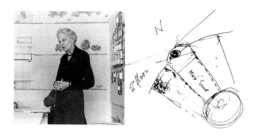

Dominique de Menil.

Initial sketch made by the client, representing the idea of the Treasure House.

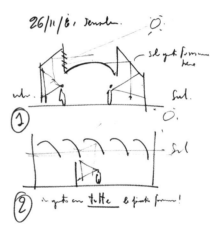

The concept of natural light diffused from above, in a sketch made by Renzo Piano in Israel.

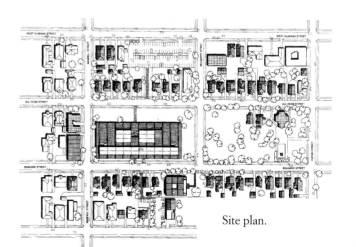

Site plan.

pletely new approach to the problem of conservation. The works can be exposed to a level of light higher than they would normally be able to tolerate because after a while they are removed and returned to safety. In compensation, as long as they are in the rooms open to the public, they can be seen under much brighter lighting conditions. This was just what we were after.

It is easy to say: natural light. But paintings cannot be exposed to ultraviolet rays, so we had to study the different methods that have been adopted to eliminate them in an attempt to find the one best able to maintain the brilliance, subtlety, and vibrations of the light. Pontus Hulten advised me to visit Israel, which is at more or less the same latitude as Houston. In the Tel Aviv Museum I found excellent systems of illumination based on double reflection of light, but perhaps the example that proved most useful was the tiny museum of a kibbutz close to the Sea of Galilee, where the light entered through a sort of square skylight oriented toward the four cardinal points.

The heart of the Menil project is the roofing of the exhibition spaces, based on the repetition of a modular element. The unit, which was immediately christened a "leaf," is made up of a very thin section of reinforced concrete integrated with a steel lattice girder. The leaves are lightweight and yet capable of performing the functions of roofing, ventilation, and control of light in an efficient manner.

The soft and natural curve of the section is the outcome of the use of highly sophisticated mathematical models: starting out with an external level of illumination of 80,000 lux—that of a springtime sky—we carried out computer simulations to find out what would provide a level of 1,000 lux inside. The results obtained were used to define the form of the leaf. Peter Rice made a major contribution to the whole of this process. Peter was not just my structural engineer, he was my traveling companion. The best ideas came out of wild discussions with him. Together we worked on the idea of the leaves, refining the concept before using systems of calculation to determine the actual form. We both felt that the leaves could perform a structural function as well, becoming an integral part of the roof frame.

Once the design was completed, we built a section of the roof at a research center in the desert, near Dallas. Then we started to mistreat it, simulating the worst calamities imaginable. We used the engines of propeller-driven aircraft to fire jets of water at the structure at two hundred kilometers an hour. We simulated vortices of water and even a tornado. The leaves, made in England and transported by sea to Houston, passed all the tests.

The Menil Collection is located in a park in the center of Houston. Alongside it stand examples of traditional American architecture—wooden houses like those of the pioneers, con-

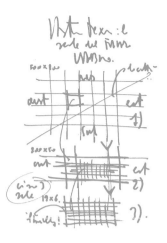

The Menil Collection was designed to be a "museum village." It fits seamlessly into the orthogonal urban grid of its surroundings. The construction is no higher than the nearby small houses. The aerial view shows the link with the open spaces.

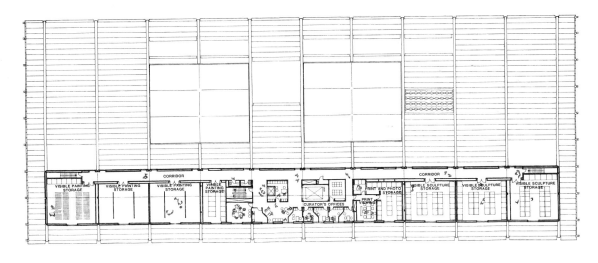

Second-floor plan with the Treasure House and the offices of the curator.

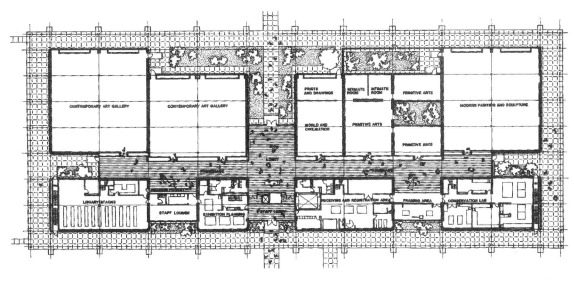

Ground-floor plan with galleries and service areas.

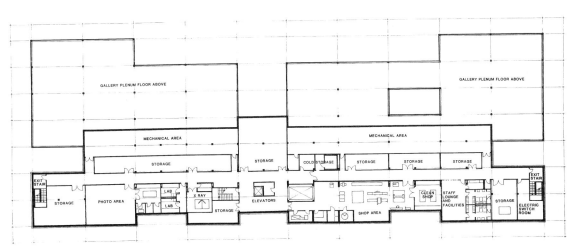

Basement plan with equipment rooms, storage, and workshops.

structed on the balloon-frame principle. They are period constructions and represent the history of local building much better than the surrounding skyscrapers. The insertion of the museum into this context was made the object of a careful study.

We used construction materials and techniques typical of the area: the walls are built out of planks of wood attached to a metal framework. In a hot and humid climate like that of Houston, this ensured that the building breathed properly. The construction is large but not monumental, and rises no higher than the nearby small houses. The museum is made up of several buildings—it is a "museum village" and as such fits without a break into the orthogonal urban grid of the surroundings. The strong link represented by the vegetation of the park helps to make this connection seamless.

This homogeneity with its context allows the museum to act as a sort of missing link for Houston: the historic center of a city that has no history. Whereas Centre Pompidou took a polemic attitude toward the unbearable weight of the past and the monuments of Paris, the Menil Collection was born out of a completely opposite need. In Houston, a city without memory, the problem was one of imparting a sacred character to the museum. Both were museums—but Beaubourg sought to create the social atmosphere of the square, whereas here the theme was that of the ritual character of the place of contemplation.

Paradoxically, the Menil Collection, with its great serenity, its calm, and its understatement, is far more "modern," scientifically speaking, than Beaubourg. The technological appearance of Beaubourg is a parody. The technology used for the Menil Collection is even more advanced (in its structures, materials, systems of climate control), but it is not flaunted. It exists because it is useful, and therefore is visible only as effect, not means. The result is a place with an incredible atmosphere, inducing a sense of peace and quiet and encouraging contemplation. The passage of the overhead light through the leaves gives the interior a unique character. Reyner Banham has written of its "ethereal beauty," of a "place that puts the magic back into functionalism." The Menil Collection succeeds in creating the feeling of a sacred place. To achieve this, we gave a richness, a complexity to the space that goes beyond the actual volumes, the pattern of repeated components, and the multiple planes. We have tried to bring immaterial elements such as transparency, lightness, and the vibration of light into the architecture. All this forms part of the composition.

I believe that essentiality of forms should not be confused with poverty of space. The scantiness of the roof, the linearity of the walls, and the white exterior are choices of expression. The intention was to foster a sense of absorption, rather than astonishment. Simplicity is the result of great, demanding, and painstaking labor: it appears to be a point of departure, but in reality it is a point of arrival.

East facade.

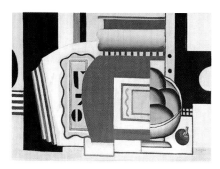

Fernand Léger.

Idols from the Cyclades.

The cabinets of the Treasure House.

Etruscan art.

Benin bronze.

Oceanic art.

Pablo Picasso.

Medieval icon.

Coptic portrait.

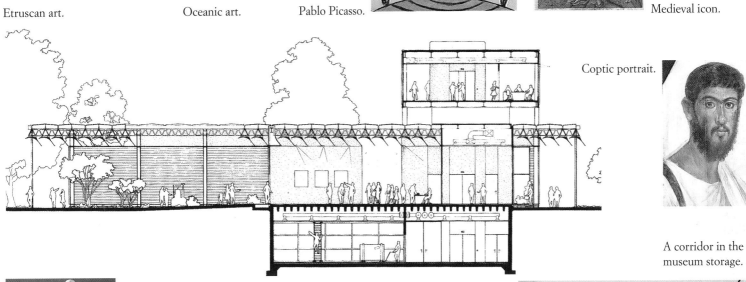

George Segal.

René Magritte.

A corridor in the museum storage.

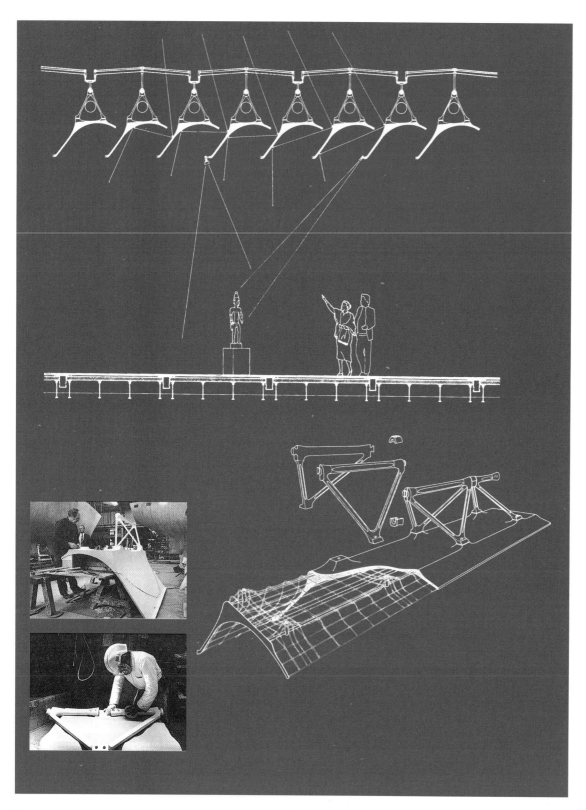

The study of natural light from above led to the design and construction of "leaves," very lightweight elements that filter the light, drastically reducing the level of lux. The model on the site (above); construction of the leaves (photos left).

View of Tropical
Garden. On the
second floor, an
exhibition hall for
primitive art; on the
third floor, the garden;
on the fourth floor,
another hall for
primitive art; finally,
on the fifth floor,
another garden. The
space is dilated by
means of planes of
multiple transparency.

Dominique de Menil wanted a variable light, which would reflect the moods of the weather. And she wanted a museum setting that, while accepting the leading role played by the works of art, would not result in an excessive neutrality of the space.

The different layouts
of the art galleries.

The restoration
workshops viewed
from the outside and
the inside.

# 1983    IBM Traveling Pavilion

Realization: 1984–86

**A temporary "building" designed to house an exhibition on the future of information processing staged in the parks of various European cities. Forty-eight meters long, twelve meters wide, and six meters high, it is made up of thirty-four arches, each consisting of six pyramidal elements of polycarbonate. The other materials used are laminated wood and cast aluminum. It is a transparent and immaterial pavilion, immersed in nature.**

At the end of this century, the watchwords in scientific innovation are "high technology" and "high sensitivity." With the passing of the era of mass production, based on the movement of people, materials, and machines, the economy has found its new motor in the impalpable flow of information. While repetition and mass were the distinctive features of the industrial city, the immateriality of communication is the emblem of the wired city.

The IBM traveling exhibition was created to take the marvels of the technological future to twenty cities of Europe. The theme was a very interesting one, because it had to convey a fundamental message: telecommunications eliminates distances, and therefore makes the physical location of the workplace irrelevant. This is a fact that has enormous repercussions on the organization of the territory. In fact, it has rendered obsolete the traditional concept of "center," which has hitherto guided the development of commercial and financial services in our cities.

In keeping with this approach, the exhibition was not to be presented in existing buildings, but to have a pavilion of its own, to be set up each time in an urban park. The exhibition and pavilion were to travel in containers, and so another requirement was ease of disassembly and reassembly, just like a circus tent.

Ever since my earliest works, I have maintained a great interest in temporary buildings: the absence of the need to make them last removes many constraints, and allows more wide-ranging experimentation. For the IBM exhibition we decided to use a fairly unprecedented cocktail of old and new materials: laminated wood for the crosspieces, cast aluminum for the joints, and polycarbonate (an extremely light and transparent product) for the elements of the pyramid-shaped roof. These components were self-supporting and, when joined together, formed the structural arch of the pavilion.

We also took advantage of an opportunity provided by modern chemistry: special adhesives made the joints between parts of different materials incredibly strong. I remember that, to re-

London.

Like the big top of a circus, the transparent pavilion has been set up in different cities. It is a circus intended to present the communications technology of the future, but also a transparent greenhouse to be placed in various parks.

Lyons.

York.

Rome.

Opposite: Milan.

move any last doubts, I went to the IBM offices in Paris (where Gianluigi Trischitta, coordinator and inventor of the project, had organized a meeting) with one of these pyramids and a sledgehammer. The first time someone questioned its resistance, right in the middle of a meeting, I took the sledgehammer and struck the pyramid a very powerful blow. It made a terrible noise, but the pyramid was not even scratched. I don't know whether it was the experiment that convinced them, or the rather intimidating nature of my action, but they approved the project the same day.

For architects today, chemistry has the same innovative value as welding had for architects of the last century. The new adhesives have extraordinary properties, and it is no accident that they are extensively used in the aerospace industry. Technological process, the promotion of new materials, and the study of new forms that are suited to them: this is the most appropriate way to show respect for the great European building tradition. The imitation of familiar forms, on the contrary, is a purely cosmetic exercise: it is stealing the outward show of the past, not its soul.

Out of our project came an almost immaterial pavilion that someone described as a greenhouse of information processing: a container for the new generation of technologies, from microelectronic hardware to artificial-intelligence software, which from a distance looked like a winter garden. Set in a park, the pavilion became an almost provocative blend of advanced technology and nature. It was such a light building, in its transparency, in its fragmentation into a thousand small details, that it could fit in anywhere and adapt itself to any of the cities in which it was erected. Its connection with the place was provided by the natural surroundings of the park.

The Traveling Pavilion was a great success: the exhibition was seen by a million and a half people. In the container, visitors could read the contents: the pursuit of the ancient human dream of immateriality.

Assembly of an arch prototype on the beach close to the office in Genoa.

Phases in the assembly of the pavilion.

Details of the joints between the various materials.

The interior space.

The structure is made up of self-supporting arches. Each is structurally independent and consists of different elements that are a cocktail of old and new materials: laminated wood for the basic structure, pieces of cast aluminum for the joints, and pyramids of transparent polycarbonate for joining the structure.

85

# 1983 Venice and Milan Italy

## *Prometeo* Musical Space Design

Realization: 1983–84

**A wooden structure that can be dismantled, designed to house an orchestra and an audience of four hundred. At once a musical instrument and ship, with ribs and frames of laminated wood and a secondary structure of metal. A space was conceived with the work.**

*Prometeo* was my second experience of architecture in the field of music. The group that developed the idea was a very high-powered one—or a band of madmen, depending on how you look at it: Luigi Nono, Claudio Abbado, Massimo Cacciari, Emilio Vedova, and myself. I had met Luigi Nono many times in Paris. It was he who proposed that I create a musical space for a work that he was composing, *Prometheus, or the Tragedy of Listening*. The world premiere was organized by La Scala in Milan and staged in the church of San Lorenzo in Venice, in collaboration with the Biennale.

The idea was to turn the traditional layout of the concert hall on its head. The audience was to be placed in the middle, with the musicians set at different heights all around it. Moreover, the music was supposed to interact with the space, emerging from points that would change continually. In part this effect could be achieved by electronic means, but the musicians were also to shift around during the performance, moving from place to place along staircases and gangways. In essence, this meant designing an object that would be at once stage, scenery, orchestra pit, and sound box.

The project was fascinating, but also extremely complex, and not just for acoustical reasons. The first problem was posed by the conductor. Under the conditions of the piece, it was difficult for Abbado to be visible to all eighty members of the orchestra and choir at once. His collaboration was invaluable, and allowed us to devise a system by which he could conduct by means of strategically placed monitors. Cacciari worked on the texts. Vedova was supposed to design a show of colored light and images, but at a certain point politely withdrew, reducing his contribution to a few variations in lighting. He did not wish to interfere with the real protagonist of the work, which was the music.

The whole setting was designed as a gigantic musical instrument, naturally made of wood for its acoustic properties. We brought together the skills of the instrument maker and the shipbuilder, for it is only maritime technology that has the know-how required to construct objects out of laminated wood on such a scale.

*Prometeo* was an extraordinary experience, for the space was born with the work and for the work, and was therefore part of the same process of creation.

Renzo Piano and Luigi Nono.

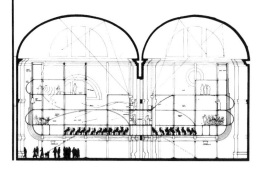

Section of the space for *Prometeo* set up in the church of San Lorenzo in Venice.

The musicians move around during the performance of the work.

Luigi Nono, Massimo Cacciari, and Renzo Piano.

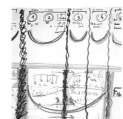

Scores by Luigi Nono.

The audience is at the center of the structure.

The structure set up inside the former Ansaldo plant in Milan (near right); various stages in the assembly.

# 1983 Genoa Italy

## Subway Stations

Construction: 1983–91

**These six stations differed according to their context but were all constructed out of a prearranged kit of components, so as to maintain a recognizable common identity. In this way the component elements could be made in sufficient quantity to obtain good quality at reasonable costs.**

Anyone who has been to Genoa knows that it is a long and narrow city. All the lines of communication (national highway, expressway, railroad) are concentrated in a strip of land between the mountains and the sea, and for much of their passage through the city, must be run below ground or raised above it. This struggle for space means that all the existing structures are fully exploited. And in fact, when a subway system was created in Genoa, it made use of tunnels that had been built at the beginning of the century for streetcars. Consequently, not just the rolling stock, but also the stations, have had to adapt to the constraints imposed by the context.

The design of the stations was commissioned from us by the city through Ansaldo, the general contractor for the subway. Three stations were built. The prototype was the one at Brin, which, among other things, was the only one situated aboveground. The different locations of the structures meant taking different approaches to the architecture of the links with street level. But an attempt was also made to give a uniform appearance to the stations as far as design of platforms, points of access, and the signage.

In the case of Brin, the body of the station is enclosed in a gallery with a transparent covering that protects the platforms from the weather and the surrounding houses from the noise of the trains. It is a large structure laid on top of the track for the trains. It is laid in the sense that it is connected with the city in the same way as a train that is connected: it is an extraneous body and accepts that fact, without hypocrisy.

All the cities of the world have always built subways that look like subways. To be honest, I cannot understand why one would want to disguise them. Indeed, in this case we took completely the opposite approach to the form. Realizing that it was impossible to make the station blend in with its surroundings, we attempted to create an identification between train and station. This led the container to resemble the contents. The fluid and aerodynamic architecture of Brin, with its semielliptical form and colored ribbing visible through the transparent covering, belongs to the world of transportation. Brin is more train than city.

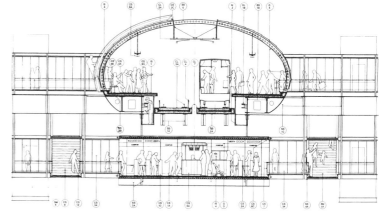

Brin station under construction; section.

Brin Station in
operation.

# 1983 Turin Italy

## Lingotto Factory Conversion

Construction: 1988–95

**A project for the conversion of an automobile manufacturing plant into a multifunctional center (trade fair and congress center, offices, auditorium, hotel, stores). Two hundred and fifty thousand square meters of floor space with vast public areas: a genuine piece of city.**

Ramp leading to the track on the roof, one of the characteristic features of Lingotto. The reinforced-concrete structure, though strictly functional, becomes a work of art.

Five hundred meters long, five stories high, and an unmistakable appearance due to the presence of the test track on its roof, Lingotto was the first example of a modular construction of reinforced concrete based on the repetition of just three compositional elements: pillars, beams, floors. In the 1920s, when it was built, it held two additional records: the largest factory in Europe to be used for mass production and the first example in Italy of a completely integrated assembly line for automobiles.

"You will find that it looks like the side of an enormous steamer viewed from the edge of the dock. And you will be stuck there with your nose in the air staring up at it and perhaps reflecting." This is how a reporter described Lingotto in the 1920s. And Le Corbusier, in his book *Vers une architecture*, said that it was "undoubtedly one of the most impressive sights offered by industry."

I sincerely believe that the great monuments of manufacturing are as deserving of loving restoration as any great work of architecture, and Lingotto is one of these monuments.

Lingotto is the name of the district of Turin in which the complex stands. The same name was given to the establishment in which Fiat, at the end of the First World War, placed its hopes for future growth. Matté Trucco, the engineer entrusted with its design, drew his inspiration from North American industrial architecture, borrowing two concepts: the vertical layout of the assembly line (one floor above another) and the spartan modularity of the basic components, which ensured rapidity and reliability of construction. The resistance of this huge building was put to a severe test during the Second World War. But as Fiat's president Gianni Agnelli likes to recall, "Not even bombs were able to knock it down."

Lingotto makes no attempt to conceal the reasons for which it was built. While there is a certain amount of decoration (such as the beautiful ramps of reinforced concrete), it is the quintessence of factory. To the east it is flanked by a group of buildings that are neither too high nor too close, and to the west by the railroad: thus it looms over the city like a medieval castle.

At the beginning of the 1980s, after sixty years of uninterrupted activity, Lingotto was sent into retirement, its place taken by new and more modern factories. This left Fiat and Turin

Vehicles on the rooftop test track.

The old Balilla assembly line.

Opposite: Interior of the auditorium, conceived as a musical instrument lined with solid cherry wood.

with the great opportunity (or great problem) represented by a quarter of a million unused square meters.

Lingotto was the first project in which I tackled the theme of urban space in a systematic manner. My previous experiences had been circumscribed, experimental and much smaller. Nonetheless, they represented an important store of knowledge from which I could draw. For in the end, the challenge was the same: to work on an existing structure without betraying it, without destroying its soul, without turning it into a travesty of its former self.

All projects for the reclamation of former factories have to face the fact that no function today requires as much space as industrial production. But the problem posed by Lingotto went further: it was not just a question of architecture and city planning. Before deciding what to do with the walls, it was necessary to re-create an identity, a relationship, an image that would meet the city's expectations.

Both the public authorities and the management of Fiat were aware of the extent of this problem. Consequently the discussions over the fate of Lingotto were from the outset carried out at the highest level. In 1984 twenty architects were invited to contribute projects to an international exhibition. In the end my proposal for the reutilization of the building was chosen: it was based on its transformation into a multipurpose center devoted to the service industry and innovation—a piece of city, with all its complexities and subtleties.

The entrance to the trade fair center from the inside and the outside.

For all intents and purposes, Lingotto was such a piece of city in terms of its size, its impact on the territory, and its economic role. Thus it was inconceivable to replace it with a garden, a condominium, or a simple block of offices. The people of Turin looked to Lingotto for employment and growth.

At the same time, Lingotto was different from the Schlumberger restructuring for many reasons. First, Schlumberger remained private property after its conversion, while much of Lingotto was destined to become a public place. Second, the disappearance of Schlumberger would not have threatened the collective identity of Parisians. The elimination of Lingotto, on the other hand, might have had just this effect on Turin. Against a background of profound changes in the city's economy, it was necessary to find not just a new use for the former factory, but also a new role; not just an urban function, but also a symbolic one. Once again, just as in the 1920s, Lingotto was expected to indicate the way forward for the city.

Turin is science, technology, industry, in other words, it is the culture of doing (and in this I feel a close affinity with the city). Until recently, however, this "doing" meant "manufacturing," and today that is no longer sufficient. It was necessary to promote the transition from the culture of production to that of exchange. Turin's reputation could no longer be based solely on a material product, but on the immaterial product contained within it: knowledge. So Lingotto, having abandoned its single func-

The courtyards have become public spaces with different characters: a luxuriant Mediterranean garden, a place for open-air concerts, the courtyard with Shingu's fountain.

The restructuring of Lingotto sought to maintain the monumental architectonic character of the building and its social and economic significance for Turin. Thus a range of public and private functions was inserted, turning it into a piece of city.

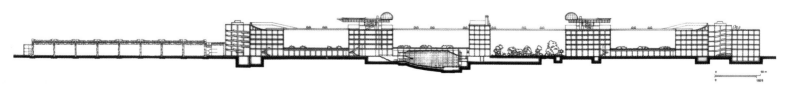

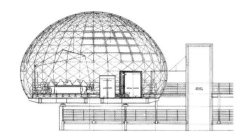

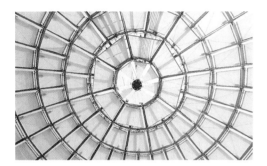

The "bubble": a very special meeting room, suspended above one of the courtyards, which counterbalances the helicopter landing pad. This, along with the auditorium and the small botanical garden embedded in the building, is one of the three unexpected "guests" that announce to the outside world that the functions of Lingotto have changed.

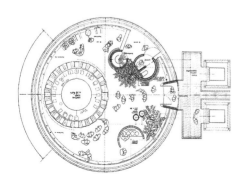

tion of manufacturing automobiles, was to be given a multifaceted future: center of technology and trade fair, incubator and university, park and auditorium.

The choice was not a simple one. Feelings within Fiat ranged between enthusiasm and perplexity. I recall a long meeting at the offices on Corso Marconi with Gianni Agnelli, Cesare Romiti, managing director of Fiat, and Alberto Giordano, then president of the Lingotto company. It was at that time that the decision was made, among other things, to give the main hall the twofold function of an auditorium and a hall for conferences.

By the time the municipality of Turin had also given its approval to start work, only a few months remained before the event that was supposed to launch Lingotto in its new role: the automobile show of 1992. Having passed under the yoke of approval, we faced a race against time. We finalized the project, commenced the restructuring, and completed the first phase in record time—and in time for the show. It was quite stressful, but helped us to meld the team led by Maurizio Varratta and Susanna Scarabicchi, who were to carry on the work later with Eddy Magnano.

Innovation is the guiding thread of Lingotto's new functions. Faced with predominance of technology, we were initially tempted to let nature "take over," as we did with Schlumberger. In the earliest drafts of the project this was a very strong element: we planned to create an area of greenery in front of the main building, enlivened by artificial hills. Then another approach gained the upper hand: that of underlining, rather than opposing, the force with which Lingotto imposes itself on the urban landscape.

Today there is a large open space in front of the building, the equivalent of the parvis of a cathedral: a very strong, inorganic courtyard. The part facing the railroad will, on the other hand, be dedicated to greenery and nature, an urban park open to the public. The exchange of ideas I had with Lawrence Halprin proved very useful to the development of the park concept. In making this choice we wished to show complete respect for the straightforward character of Lingotto, and to avoid masking its lines, so like those of a great ship.

Such a rigorous structure needs to be interrupted by the unexpected. Matté Trucco was well aware of this, and gave his ramps an extremely refined shape. This concern of a formal character is linked with a more general theme of the project: as well as keeping faith with its original spirit, Lingotto had to convey a strong signal of change. I wanted this signal to be one of joy. This was another point in our program: imparting a sense of joy to a place whose function has always meant that it was perceived in an austere and somewhat punitive manner.

In order to achieve this, we, like Trucco, decided to insert a number of "unexpected guests" into the body of the building. The first of these is a large and sheltered garden in one of the four internal courtyards. The work on this was done by my

Section through the auditorium.

Claudio Abbado.

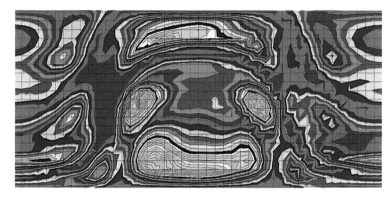

Computer diagram of the flows of sound in the hall.

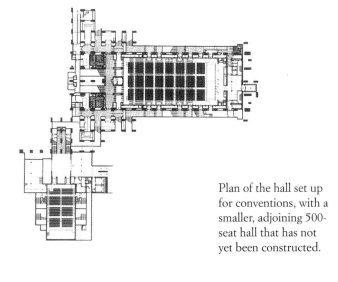

Plan of the hall set up for conventions, with a smaller, adjoining 500-seat hall that has not yet been constructed.

nephew Daniele Piano, son of my brother, Ermanno. The greenery that is missing from the parvis has been given refuge inside the building, in the form of a small botanical garden. The vegetation is not typical of the Turin region. On the contrary, exotic plants dominate: a homage to the Mediterranean, to the Ligurian Riviera, so familiar to the people of Turin.

The second unexpected guest is the bubble on the roof: it is a room for high-level meetings (in a literal sense, given that it sticks out from a structure crossing over the track). Totally transparent, on clear days it offers an incredible view of the landscape on all sides, with the Alps to the north and west and the hills of Turin to the south and east. The bubble is visible from a distance, and has quickly become another distinctive feature of Lingotto. Mark Carroll made a major contribution to the construction of this object, with the help of the young people of Meccano, including my son Matteo and Stefano Arecco.

The third is the auditorium. Stemming from the realization that Turin did not have a concert hall capable of housing two thousand people, it was initially intended to be an object wholly extraneous to the building, a sort of wooden shell to be set under the second internal court. In the end, however, we decided that this object, too, should conform to the rigorous formal logic of Lingotto: the surprise would have to lie in the beauty of the hall, in its technical and acoustic qualities, and not in its incongruity with the context.

The design of the concert hall had a point of reference as prestigious as it was demanding: the Berlin Philharmonic. The orchestra was scheduled to inaugurate the auditorium. Claudio Abbado, whom I had gotten to know at the time of *Prometeo*, had just been appointed its conductor, and a close collaboration developed. We went to Berlin with the model of the hall to explain its characteristics. For his part, Abbado recommended Helmut Müller as the best source of advice on acoustics, whose study had already been started by Arup Acoustics. It would be superfluous to point out how invaluable my earlier experiences with Berio, Boulez, and Nono proved to be on this occasion.

Let us return to Lingotto as a whole. What is often missing from schemes for the reutilization of industrial zones is the richness of urban interchange. This cannot be said of Lingotto: it is not a monument uprooted from its context, but a piece of city, with its candor, its memory, and its character.

I learned that the city takes a long time to react, that it has a slow kind of metabolism. Now Lingotto is practically finished, and is beginning to produce its first effects on its surroundings. An example: the 1996 meeting of European heads of state made it necessary to reorganize the access routes. It's not much, but it's a first step. The city needs twenty or thirty years to generate (or regenerate) a district. But the process is now under way at Lingotto, and nothing will stop it.

# 1984 Montecchio Maggiore

(Vicenza) Italy

## Lowara Company Offices

Construction: 1984–85

**The building is set in front of the preexisting establishment, which manufactures electromechanical components, and is 150 meters in length and 15 meters wide. It has a constant section, generated by a large catenary roof that increases to a height of 7.2 meters, starting from a height of 2.4 meters. It is a continuous and open space, made up of compressions and expansions of the volume.**

The offices of the Lowara Company at Montecchio Maggiore are the outcome of a sort of dare: I received a call from Renzo Ghiotto, an industrialist from Vicenza, proposing that I design a building for his company. In a way that, I must admit, warmed me to him from the start, he told me, "Mind you, it's going to have to be dirt cheap." He went on to explain that he had the money, but didn't like the idea of building something elegant when all that was needed was a functional construction: "I'd feel like a snob, and I'm not." At that point he came up with his dare: "I could call in any old architect and tell him to build me two thousand square meters of office space. Can you do it for the same price?" On the one hand, I felt that I ought to turn down a job with such tight budget restrictions. On the other, however, I was intrigued by the challenge.

I thought: the client is right. I'm also bothered by the idea that quality depends on what you pay. Why spend twice as much to obtain honest industrial quality, something that ought to be taken for granted in any product? I took up the gauntlet.

In collaboration with Maurizio Milan, we designed a structure as taut as a sail, very simple and very light. Naturally the curve of the sail was no mere aesthetic exercise, but the result of a structural calculation that allowed us to use the four walls of sheet metal typical of an industrial shed in a way that was neither obvious nor disagreeable.

Looking back, I now think that if Ghiotto had said to me, "Do what you want, spend as much as you want, but give me a memorable office block," it would have frightened me off, because, even as an architect, what would be the sense of it, for a job like this? Once again, I found that constraints stimulated me more than a blank check. The client turned out to be a good judge of character: he had played just the right hand.

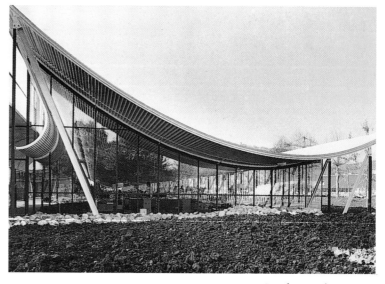

Roofing, with its characteristic catenary shape.

Section showing the location of the new office building in relation to the existing structure.

The interior space.

## Novara <sub></sub> Italy

### Institute for Research into Light Metals

Construction: 1985–87

**From a project for a continuous curtain-wall system, as a prefabricated component, came this building, to house the research center of the Aluminia Company. The facade is made up of elements measuring 7.2 by 3.6 meters, assembled in the factory and equipped with glass units fixed with silicon.**

This project fits well into a series of works characterized by research into the potential of materials. The Aluminia Company had decided to set up the Institute for Research into Light Metals in Novara to investigate new applications for aluminum and new methods of working the metal. Naturally they wanted to use the material in which the company specialized, wherever possible. We ended up suffering from a real overdose of aluminum.

In fact, the initial commission was not for the design of a building. Aluminia had called us in to design a multipurpose curtain wall that could be mass-produced and -marketed as a prefabricated component. We questioned how this product could be tested under real conditions, and the possibility emerged of constructing a building in which the curtain wall could be used. That was how the project got under way.

Out of it came a modular building composed of two main elements: a system of glass and aluminum facing, and a structure assembled out of standardized concrete components. The relative heaviness of the dry-mounted structures was required to ensure the building's stability against vibrations caused by machines in the workshop. Thanks to its modular character, the complex was erected in a very short time: just four months.

The famous modular facing elements, with which the whole thing had started, were the result of a combination of extruded and cast aluminum. Basically, the uprights were extruded, the reinforcing elements were cast, and the links with the structure were made out of concrete. The panels were entirely factory made, including the expanses of glass, made structural by the use of sealants. The internal components were also the outcome of experiments carried out with pressed, cast, or extruded aluminum: this material was used for the handrails, balustrades, and even the supports for the steps of the stairs.

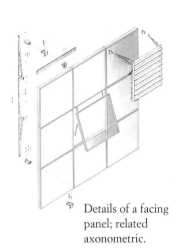

Details of a facing panel; related axonometric.

Street facade.

# 1985 Cagliari Italy

## Credito Industriale Sardo

Construction: 1985–92

**A building born out of the desire for a close integration of private and public uses. The building housing the bank proper consists of three blocks, and features the use of local stone.**

This job came out of our participation in the competition "A Square for Cagliari," organized by the Credito Industriale Sardo, directed at the time by Paolo Savona. The real scope of the competition was the construction of a new head office for the bank in Cagliari. To underline its key role in the city and in civic life, the building was to be set on a large pedestrian square. Until just a few years ago, companies and institutions tended to build their headquarters in protected, inaccessible places, symbolically underlining their distance from the public. Now, however, insertion into the urban fabric is increasingly fundamental to their plans. I feel that I have made a contribution to the emergence of this new trend.

The square called for in the competition has been created by setting the bank back from the street front. Beyond an entrance reinforced by a canopy projecting into the square, the public area continues in a series of covered and partially covered courtyards. In addition to these courts, an auditorium with two hundred and fifty seats has been placed at the city's disposal for conferences and performances. It is a highly versatile space: each part of the floor can be raised or lowered, allowing the seats, stages, and screens to be arranged in different ways.

The structure is made up of three main blocks built out of reinforced concrete: two are set on the long sides of the perimeter, and one, taller than the others, crosswise. Perhaps one of the most interesting elements is the use of stone as a facing, which creates a kind of link with the context. The sun screens at the ends of the corridors and stairways are also cut from stone.

In the case of a bank, openness to the public conflicts with objective security requirements. The problem was solved by creating a hierarchy of access based on level: the ground floor is used for communication with the world outside; the upper floors house the management facilities of the Credito Industriale Sardo. In the middle are offices and public service activities.

The main facade on Viale Bonaria was set back to create the pedestrian square.

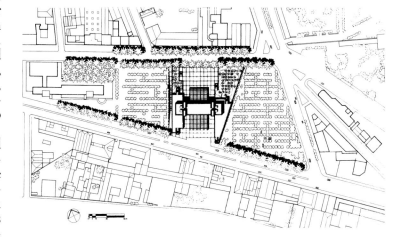

Overall plan.

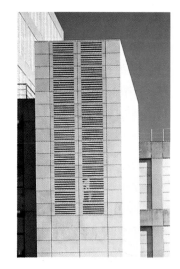

The building is faced with slabs of local stone. Some of the slabs are perforated to create an effect of transparency.

Details of the stone facing.

At the entrance to the building a canopy extends over the pedestrian square, creating a semiprotected area.

Section through the entrance zone and the auditorium.

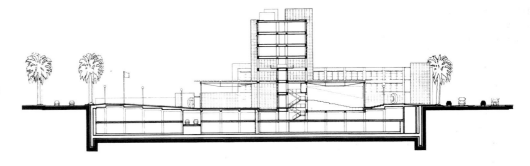

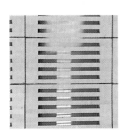

The auditorium was located so that it forms an extension of the entrance canopy. It is a flexible space of variable configurations.

# 1985 Genoa Italy

## Columbus International Exposition

Construction: 1988–92

**The urban reclamation of the old port of Genoa included the restructuring and restoration of a number of buildings: the Cotton Warehouses (built at the end of the nineteenth century), the four bonded warehouses (from the seventeenth century), and the Millo (another, more recent warehouse). Several new constructions were added: the aquarium (now one of the most popular attractions in Italy), the harbor office, and the Bigo, a gigantic derrick that was the symbol of the Columbus Exposition and now serves as a powerful reminder of the return to the city of one of its most important areas, the ancient port.**

In 1992 the municipality of Genoa organized a major international celebration to commemorate the five-hundredth anniversary of the discovery of America, and I was asked to make a contribution to it. A great cultural or sporting event can result in damage to the city that hosts it. This happens when precious resources are diverted into works of short-term value (Italy is full of ghost villages, half-empty sports facilities, and dilapidated structures). But it can also represent a great opportunity, a concentration of efforts and energies that makes it possible to carry out the sort of intervention that would normally require decades in just a short span of time.

My project for the Columbus Exposition was based on a very simple philosophy (in a way an expression of the traditional Genoese aversion to waste): that of carrying out works of permanent value to the city, of making interventions that would still be useful when the lights of the celebrations were turned off. To me this attitude seemed to be the proper response to the crisis faced by Genoa. The funding for the exposition was a great opportunity to rescue the historic city from decay, and it was necessary to make the best possible use of it. Yet it was not just a matter of economics. There was also the question of respect. Why show visitors a bogus face, when Genoa's real one is so beautiful? Why create peripheral entertainment facilities outside the urban fabric that are destined for rapid obsolescence? Why not offer visitors the city itself, its monuments and its history?

In my proposal the ephemeral character of the exhibition was to be dignified by a lasting intervention of urban reclamation in the area of the old port. This idea had an important precedent. Back in 1981, at the request of the city, I had drawn up a project for the rehabilitation of the Molo Vecchio, one of the oldest quarters of Genoa. Like almost everywhere else in

Genoa and its port in 1937.

The marble terraces: port warehouses built between the city and the harbor in 1835.

The old and incredibly dense city is built all around a gulf surrounded by mountains.

Opposite: Between two seventeenth-century harbor buildings is seen the back of the Millo coffee warehouse, built at the beginning of this century.

the historic city, the lack of space on the Molo Vecchio, or Old Wharf, had forced people to build ever higher over the course of the centuries: up to seven or eight stories. The streets that separate the buildings are very narrow, with the result that there is little light and almost no movement of air. The damp and stagnant environment that this produces was considered unhealthy even in the seventeenth century.

Our project, once again based on the logic of "weak construction," did not envisage any demolition, just a reorganization of urban space "in layers." Flying footbridges were to link the buildings at different heights, permitting pedestrian circulation at several levels. One interesting aspect lay in the idea of turning the upper stories into public levels. Residents on their way home would have to head down, and not up. A system of vertical public transport would be provided to meet these needs: the elevators were not to be private, or even jointly owned, but at the service of the district. This would make it possible to keep their numbers to a minimum (we planned to install no more than three in the block chosen for the pilot project).

The problem of illumination and ventilation of the lower layers would be tackled simply by updating the "gentle" methods that have always been used by the local inhabitants: reflective screens, solar chimneys, and so on. I have always been attracted by the unpretentious combination of such modern devices with the antiquity of the urban setting. In particular we experimented with a system of mirrors that reflected light from the roofs, sending beams of sunshine down into the dark alleys.

The project for the Molo was never carried out, but in a way it represented the seminal research on which we based many of the ideas that were applied later in the Columbus Exposition.

For me, working in Genoa is like climbing into a postcard from the past. What I was being asked to do in the old port was a complex operation of open-heart surgery. And the heart was that of Genoa, my own city.

There is a thread linking this project with those of Lingotto, Otranto, and Burano. It is the development of a methodology for analysis and intervention in urban space. Taken as a whole, the old port is a disused factory, like Lingotto. The difference is that it was not built over the course of five or six years, but over a period a hundred times as long. All the centuries, from the fourteenth up to our own, are represented. The wharves, for instance, were rebuilt further forward every time the existing ones became obsolete: the ones now closest to the sea date from the nineteenth century, while the ones near the Ripa are half a millennium older. Any earlier wharves were made out of wood, and time has erased all trace of them. So we were dealing with a much greater complexity than in any other scheme of reutilization: a complexity of styles, techniques, and meanings. The port is a factory spread over space and time.

Around it have been built the city's most important histori-

Aerial view of the old port before the intervention.

Aerial view of the area after the intervention. It shows the restored buildings, the new aquarium building, the road along the seafront known as the Via del Mare, and the Bigo, symbol of the exhibition.

Details typical of the port of Genoa: cranes, mooring rings, the treatment of walls, etc.

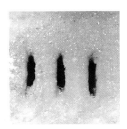

Archaeological remains of a seventeenth-century wharf uncovered during the work.

Overall plan of the intervention.

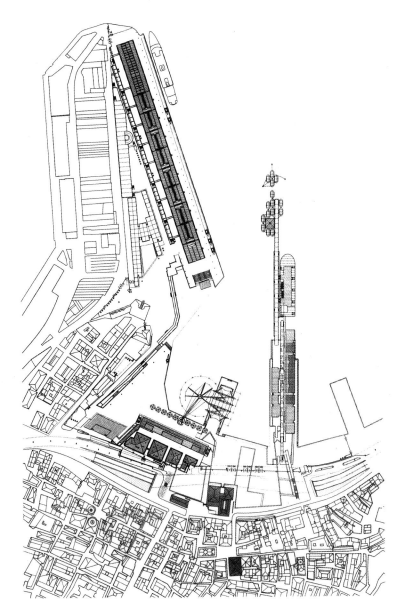

Elevation showing the basic concept of the project: to tie the old city to the harbor.

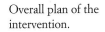

105

cal monuments, such as the Ripa and Palazzo San Giorgio. The latter marked the birth of the banking institution in the modern sense: it was the first "City" of international finance. In 1835 direct contact between the city and its harbor was interrupted: infrastructures for the customs offices and warehouses were built in front of Palazzo San Giorgio. These were demolished at the end of the century to make room for the first railroad line. In 1965 an elevated roadway for fast traffic was built alongside the line. It is still in operation, with an extremely busy urban street running underneath.

This digression is intended to show how obvious, immediate, and natural it was to link the old city and its port back together. And this was the basis of our project. Clearly, the ideal option would have been to get rid of the elevated road, replacing it with an underwater tunnel passing beneath the mouth of the harbor. This was rejected for reasons of cost. However, at the suggestion of the Harbor Trust, a plan was drawn up to move part of the road system underground, for a short stretch in front of Palazzo San Giorgio. This decision, the fruit of delicate juggling of needs of the city and port, later turned out to present great problems, owing to the presence of important archaeological remains. Nevertheless it was carried out, at the expense of the preservation of several significant ancient wharves.

Above this tunnel is Piazza Caricamento. *Caricamento* means "loading," and this used to be the place where ships were loaded and unloaded. Not far away stands the Stock Exchange. Finance and trade: this was the focal point of Genoa's public life, the fount of the city's wealth. The new Piazza Caricamento stretches from the porticoes of the Ripa to the waterfront, and leads to the new structures that have been created near the sea. It is a first, small step toward linking the harbor and the city.

The Columbus Exposition allowed us to recover and revitalize several wonderful historic buildings on the wharves, such as the Cotton Warehouses. Built in the nineteenth century by English designers, they have the typical characteristics of British industrial architecture of that era. They have been converted into exhibition spaces while retaining the original structure with its cast-iron columns. At the end of the construction closest to the sea, which is more recent, we have built a congress center, with two identical, mirror-image halls seating eight hundred people.

The Millo, another warehouse—in the free port area—was a building of very large dimensions but with less architectural value. We chose to reduce it in size so that it would not become the dominant element of the whole space. Two stories were eliminated and the front part of a third set back, creating a large terrace.

Behind the Millo and parallel to it are four bonded warehouses dating from the seventeenth century. They are proba-

Set for the performance of *Moby-Dick*, with Vittorio Gassman, under the tensile structure of the square of festivities.

Meeting on the construction site.

The Bigo: system of arms that supports a panoramic elevator and the tensile structure of the square of festivities.

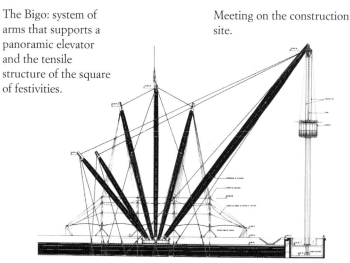

The Columbus Exposition provided a great opportunity for the reclamation of the old port. The philosophy of the project was to use the temporary event as an opportunity to carry out permanent works that would be at the disposal of the city once the exposition was over. Existing port buildings such as the Cotton Warehouse, the Millo, and the seventeenth-century bonded warehouse were restored and rehabilitated, and new structures were built, such as the aquarium and the Bigo.

The port shortly before work started.

The port when work was almost complete.

Details of the Bigo.

The aquarium is one of the newly designed buildings. Set on the existing bed of the Spinola Bridge, it consists of a series of raised tanks, in which are the exhibition spaces, aquatic and otherwise. The unusual configuration means that the architecture is somewhat reminiscent of the form of a ship.

Right: City elevation; section showing the characteristic configuration of the building; elevation along the wharf of the Spinola Bridge.

Opposite: Section of the former Cotton Warehouse, a totally rehabilitated port building dating from the beginning of the century. The restoration was careful to respect its original characteristics while introducing new distribution and plant systems suited to its new function.

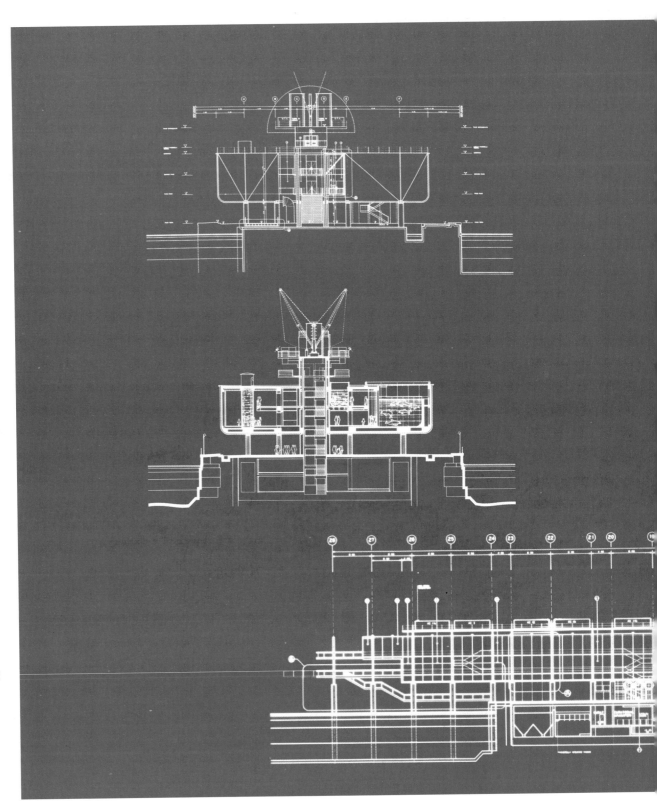

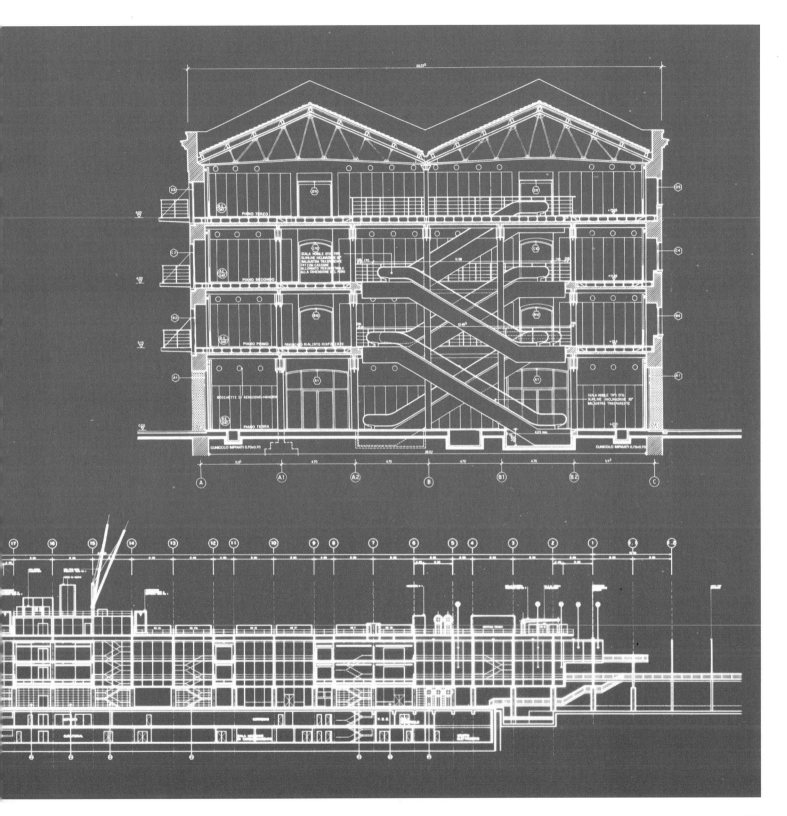

bly the earliest example of a free port in history. The buildings themselves, the fine internal fittings, and the trompe l'oeil frescoes on the facades have all been carefully restored.

Perhaps the most characteristic of the newly created structures is the Grande Bigo, chosen as the symbol of the celebrations. *Bigo* is an Italian naval term for a derrick. It consists of several arms of hollow steel that open out from a common base set at sea level. In the case of our Bigo, the main arm supports a panoramic elevator, which turns slowly on its axis to present a complete view of the city and harbor. Two more arms support a tensile structure used to cover an entertainment area: the square of festivities. During the exposition a performance of Melville's *Moby-Dick* was staged here (with Vittorio Gassman in the lead role). We collaborated on the set design, with Giorgio Bianchi in charge of our contribution.

In the context of the port, the great tent over the square is somewhat reminiscent of the sail of a ship. The form of the aquarium also alludes to the sea: in fact, it looks like a ship in dry dock. The aquarium is raised on circular concrete columns, and floats above an old wharf. This is a rather curious feature, as the columns seem to be trying to keep the fish out of the water. The main tanks are designed so that visitors can see into them from two different levels: depending on their point of observation, they receive an effect of underwater immersion or a view of the surface, illuminated by natural light entering through the transparent roof. For the technical and curatorial aspects we turned to the American studio Cambridge Seven Associates, which specializes in the design of aquariums. The plant engineering was handled by Italimpianti, while Mark Carroll supervised the project on our behalf. Underneath the two stories of this structure, the quay of Ponte Spinola has been turned into a covered pedestrian precinct, where services are located.

It is difficult to evaluate the project. Many things that we would like to have done proved impossible. During the excavations for structural work, archaeological finds of incredible importance were made all over the port area. Haste prevented us from taking advantage of these riches, which were buried again to protect them until a more suitable moment. By bringing this material back to light, Genoa would be able to offer visitors the most significant maritime archaeological site in the whole of Europe. At this very moment we are working, in collaboration with the Monuments Service and at the behest of the city of Genoa, on the master plan for this area. Venanzio Truffelli is working on the project with Daniele Piano and Vittorio Tolu. At the time of the Columbus Exposition many of the Building Workshop's architects were on the front line: Shunji Ishida, of course; Venanzio Truffelli along with Olaf de Nooyer, who worked on the Bigo, Giorgio Grandi (the bonded warehouses and the service spine), Donald Hart (Congress Center), Musci Baglietto (Italian Pavilion), and Claudio Manfreddo (inner harbor and harbor office).

The old port warehouses from the seventeenth century were decorated in the Genoese traditional manner. It was possible to salvage the old decorations.

Far right: Aquarium and Via del Mare; Cotton Warehouse facade along the Molo Vecchio; the Bigo, the Millo, and the historic city in the background.

Interior of the meeting center in the Cotton Warehouse.

Interiors of the Cotton Warehouse after restoration.

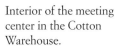

The Bigo elevator and the mobile sculptures of Susumu Shingu.

# 1986 Rhodes Greece

## Ancient Moat Rehabilitation

**A project, designed for UNESCO and the Greek government, that proposed using the two-and-a-half-kilometer moat that runs around the walls of the city to create a garden containing all the varieties of vegetation to be found on the island as well as a place for open-air cultural events.**

Rhodes was an interesting project, even though it was never realized, since it brought together the aspects of historical revaluation and environmental rehabilitation. The aim of the project, which was one of those carried out on behalf of UNESCO, was to reclaim the moat around the historic city of Rhodes. Over the centuries this moat had been filled with detritus, which had to be removed. The next problem was what to do with the long circular promenade that this would leave the city.

Studying the site, we discovered that the island of Rhodes has been spared many of the great epidemics of the plant and animal worlds. At the end of the last century, for example, all the vines in Europe were killed by phylloxera and had to be replaced with American varieties. But on Rhodes the European vines still survive. So on this island it is possible and legitimate to create a natural park for the original flora and fauna of the Mediterranean. The moat provided a perfect environment: circular, and therefore exposed to all cardinal points, it contained an extraordinary sequence of microclimates, simultaneously offering sun and shade at different points. In addition, at the points with a southern exposure, the great walls acted as heat exchangers, providing a warm climate even at night.

The idea of the natural park was complemented by another consideration. A moat lined with masonry provides excellent conditions for the reverberation of sound. These acoustic effects could be exploited to create listening points. This opened up the possibility of using the moat for a complete range of cultural activities—concerts and theatrical performances, shows and street music—in a gentle Mediterranean climate, surrounded by luxuriant vegetation that dates back centuries and cannot be found anywhere else in the world.

Overall plan of the old city showing the moat.

Views showing existing conditions inside the moat.

Typical section of the moat illustrating the project.

# 1986 Valletta Malta

## City Gate

**This was another UNESCO project that tackled the theme of the historic center of an ancient city. The reduction in size of the gate and the bridge leading to it would have restricted it to pedestrian, and therefore more respectful, use.**

Aerial view of Valletta with the city gate in the foreground.

Valletta, capital of the island of Malta, is a small city dating from the sixteenth century. It stands on a promontory, ringed by fortifications that protected it from invasion by the Turks. The main road, Republic Street, runs through the center in the direction of the sea. At the point where it meets the walls stands the historic entrance, the city gate.

The project commissioned by UNESCO (the coordinator was Salvino Busuttil) and the government of Malta envisaged two levels of intervention: a reclamation of the monumental part (gate and walls), and the establishment of a link between Valletta's past and its modern urban expansion (in essence, Republic Street). The city gate has been rebuilt several times over the course of the centuries. The present one dates from the 1950s. A large bridge suitable for vehicles links it to a traffic circle where the bus terminal is located.

Our proposal was based on reducing the mass of the gate, at present excessively large, and replacing the road bridge with a wooden footbridge. The design of the latter, gently curved and kept in tension by a tubular structure of steel and by tie beams, was intended to allude to the idea of the drawbridge. The whole project was designed to create an impression of impermanence and lightness, in deliberate contrast to the solidity and mass of the walls.

Passing over the bridge, visitors would have been able to look down on the gardens set in the moat, and even to make their way down to them by stairs set on both sides. Beneath the gardens, a system of underground car garages on two levels would have compensated for the limits placed on automobile circulation, permitting easy access to the whole of the historic center. Both the city gate and the walls of the ramparts at the side of the moat were to have been constructed out of local stone, which is a very pale and bright limestone.

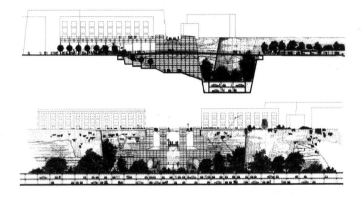

Section and elevation with the proposed new access to the city.

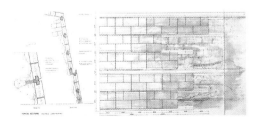

Details of the stone facing.

# 1986 Lyons France

## Cité Internationale

Construction: 1991–95

**This modular project allows the complex to be built in different stages. So far, office buildings, conference centers, and the museum of contemporary art have been realized. A hotel, casino, and multiscreen movie theater are under construction. The composition is a piece of city between a centuries-old park and the Rhône River. It is the first application of a "double skin" for buildings.**

Lyons is the third largest city in France, after Paris and Marseilles, and is linked to both by the TGV (the French high-speed train). Its central position, not just in France but in Europe as a whole, makes it a natural location for trade fairs and conferences, such as the meetings of the G7, which brings together the seven most industrialized countries in the world. The meeting held in the spring of 1996 represented the complex's baptism; it was still incomplete but already in operation, thanks to a strong topographical layout in which the building can be executed in modular units.

In 1985 Lyons held a competition for the restructuring of the Foire Internationale (International Fairgrounds), a large site covering fifteen hectares of the city alongside the Rhône and adjoining the park of the Tête d'Or. The urban significance of the intervention and the importance of the relationship with the river and the public gardens were evident from the outset. We thus drew up the project in collaboration with the landscape architect Michel Courajoud, and won the competition.

The program for the Foire of the future envisaged a variety of uses, not limited to that of the trade fair: consequently the name was changed to "Cité Internationale." It was to become a multipurpose center, a true urban microcosm. Thus in Lyons, too, I tried to propose the "humanistic" city model that I have been cultivating for years, and I did it essentially by operating on the spaces for communal use, in this case the internal road.

In interventions of this kind the risk of banality is very high. It can overtake even the most attractive of architectural modules. The scale of the reproduction is such that the result is a luxurious ghetto. We wanted to divide the complex into homogeneous units, but to preserve the image and specific function of each; to guarantee the necessary formal unity, but not to fall into the trap of uniformity. To achieve this we had to adopt a unitary element that would have its roots in the location.

The buildings of the Foire, constructed in 1918, follow the curve of the Rhône, opening up in a fan between the park and the road that runs along the river. Unfortunately they had an unfavorable orientation: each faced onto the plaster front of

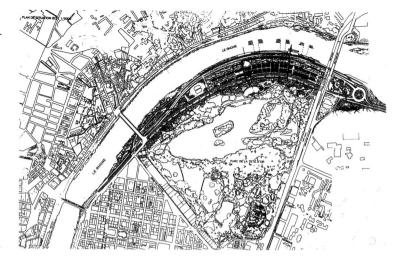

Overall plan.

Perspective showing the internal road (above); congress and office center (below). Opposite: The internal street.

the next, without offering a pleasant view of the park or of the river. A cost-benefit analysis yielded negative results: the commercial desirability of the buildings was compromised by their position, and even a drastic restructuring would not have been sufficient to make them an attractive proposition. So we decided to demolish them. All that we spared was the entrance pavilion, known as the Atrium.

The most important legacy of the old Foire was the road, a strong feature that ran across the site parallel to the river. Here was the unitary element. The placeform was there; it just had to be followed.

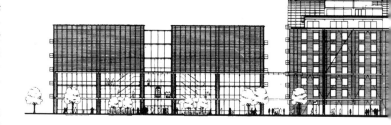

The new buildings of the Cité Internationale are being erected in pairs at the sides of the road that used to mark the limits of the area. Their siting, at right angles to that of the previous buildings, offers their occupants a view of the surrounding nature. In addition, the blocks are arranged so that they do not interrupt the communication between park and river; between the constructions run routes perpendicular to the axis of the road.

The road itself has been turned into a pedestrian promenade. It no longer creates a barrier; instead it is a link with the Tête d'Or park. This avenue follows the same radius of curvature as the Rhône and external main road, thereby underlining once again the distinctive feature of the site's geography. In this way it takes on a twofold centrality: from the viewpoint of the architecture, it is the backbone of the area; from the perspective of its urban role, it is a place of meeting, exchange, and interaction that is important to the social life of the whole city of Lyons.

The avenue is 750 meters long, thus a true piece of the city. However, it is totally immersed in greenery, friendly and secluded, silent and pleasant, since it is cut off from automobile traffic. Traffic on the section of the outer road that runs alongside the site, between the Churchill and Poincaré Bridges, has also been slowed. Cars are now halted at frequent traffic lights to make it easy for pedestrians to cross the road. This was a little masterstroke by Paul Vincent, the architect in charge of the whole project. It was he who persuaded the municipal authorities to make alterations to the city plan and the road system. This was no easy task: it entailed reducing the speed of traffic along one of the main arteries leading into the center, a decision that no administrator takes lightly. (Of course, a very fast stretch of road in urban traffic only means that more cars will come to a stop at the first bottleneck. Changing the order of the factors that affect traffic flow does not change the real length of the journey. But the fact is that time is measured by the mind of the driver, not by the clock.)

In addition to Paul, I have to express my gratitude for the cooperation of Henri Chabert, the councillor responsible for city planning, who was the tenacious crafter of the project. All three Lyons mayors over this period have made valuable con-

Plan of the first phase (below); the buildings right after construction (bottom).

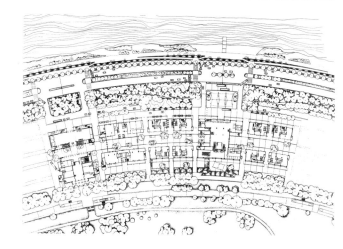

Elevation of the
buildings in the first
phase.

The Museum of
Contemporary Art,
created by the
restructuring of the
entrance to the former
trade fair building.

An interior view of the
museum.

tributions to the Cité Internationale project, but Henri was the person who, holding his post for the longest time, has been involved continuously.

The first part to be built consisted of the five blocks that extend from the old Atrium to the east. The Atrium has been turned into a museum of contemporary art, and a multiscreen movie theater will be placed in front of it. This will be followed by a luxury hotel and a casino. Office buildings and the convention center were built during the first phase of the project.

Other buildings will follow in the same pattern of "pairs": each will be constructed at the same time as its twin on the other side of the road. In some cases, such as the convention center and the hotel, the pair will form a single block. Both of these will straddle the central road. The largest halls in the convention center are located underground, which allows them to expand sideways, in the direction of the neighboring blocks. Cultural and entertainment facilities are an integral part of any contemporary trade center. Their presence is an attraction for occasional visitors and also a permanent benefit for residents. The same can be said of parks and gardens.

The Cité Internationale is located alongside the Tête d'Or, a centuries-old park with tall trees. The whole area between the avenue and the river has been landscaped by Michel Courajoud. In addition to providing a pleasant view of natural scenery, the vegetation will help to create a strong connection between the existing park and the river. Various types of trees and shrubs are being planted in the part nearest the outer road: from the side of Churchill Bridge, for example, thickets of willows will run down to the banks of the Rhône.

In Lyons the "placeform" has not been shaped by the human hand; the architect has followed nature. The main road, the tree-lined avenue, and the boundary of the park simply echo the curve of the river. Here the bas-relief does not model the site: it is the site. The construction yields to this hierarchy just as the road follows the bend in the river. It is a lightweight creation that rests on the park without cutting into it, without damaging it. If we want to find an allusion, then once again it would be the greenhouse. This analogy also holds for the natural mechanism of light and heat regulation that we have created by giving the buildings a "double skin."

The protective finish is provided by a terra-cotta covering that, as well as responding very well to the local climate, bestows a warm color and delicate texture on the buildings. The outer layer of the facing consists of glass panels. Some of these panels can be opened, turning on pivots like a skylight. This increases the depth of communication between interior and exterior. Between the two surfaces, a gap acts as a heat exchange, reducing energy loss.

The use of glass and terra-cotta derives from the need for thermal efficiency and from an expressive choice: the combi-

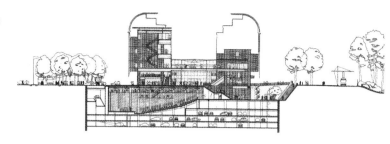

Section through the congress center (above); the "moat" running alongside the congress zone toward Tête d'Or Park (below).

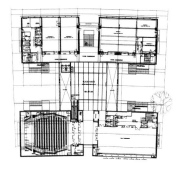

Plans and views of the hall and of the three-hundred-seat hall of the congress center.

nation of the two materials produces a surprisingly blurred effect—a light and permanent vibration. The reflections in the glass shell cause the appearance of the constructions to change completely with variations in the strength, color, and direction of light. All the buildings in the complex, whatever their function and size, will be faced with these materials, and this will give the Cité Internationale the unity (but not uniformity) that is necessary for the place to have a strong and distinctive character.

The double-skin facade: prototype (left); detail drawing of the opening system (right); the facade (opposite).

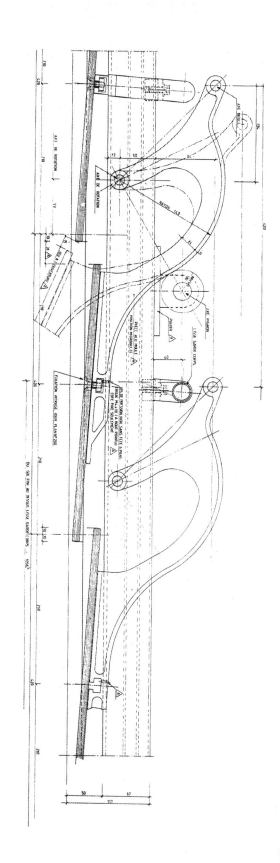

# 1987 Bari Italy

## San Nicola Stadium

Construction: 1987–90

**This stadium for sixty thousand people has tiers of seating built out of 310 prefabricated concrete elements. Twenty-six "petals" provide access to the upper rows of seating, solving the security problem. Two important themes were the use of a single material and lightness.**

I am not a great soccer fan. When I was asked to build the stadium in Bari, I tried to remember the last time I had seen a soccer match. Thirty years had gone by. Peter Rice, on the contrary, had a passion for soccer. He had dreamed of designing a stadium for years, and tried every way he could to get us to do it together. Throughout the work, my detachment was balanced by his enthusiasm, and vice versa, and this dialectic greatly enriched the project.

Being a non-specialist helps you to take a broader perspective, to consider solutions that have never been tried before. This was my role. Peter, a longtime soccer fan, helped me to design a structure that would meet all the spectator's requirements of participation and safety. He was thoroughly familiar with these needs, having gone to watch his team, the Queen's Park Rangers, in half the stadiums of England.

A stadium is by definition a container: a space to be filled with events and the people who watch them. So the stadium in Bari (named after St. Nicholas, patron of the city) is a project where space plays a highly significant role. It has been treated in two ways: as the tension between solids and voids, and as the tension between the form of the construction and the form of the place. In a way, this project is an investigation of the expressive properties of empty space: the stadium is characterized by cuts, compressions, and expansions that give the void a leading role. As we shall see, a variety of factors have contributed to this choice. One of the most important was safety.

Another extremely important theme is the relationship between the form of the constructed object and the form of the place, between impermanence (not just of the architecture, but also of the event that it houses) and the permanence of the topography. The stadium stands at the center of an artificial hollow, reminiscent of the crater of a volcano. The soccer field is an incision, even in physical terms: in accordance with the tradition of the Greek theater, the arena is sunk into the ground (the field is set two meters below ground level). The upper part of the stands is poised above the crater like a crown. From a distance only this part of the stadium can be seen: a raised structure that comprises the uppermost sectors and the semitransparent roofing.

The stadium in Bari was built for the World Soccer

The large concrete volumes of the upper tiers skim the ground without touching it, creating a spatial tension between the compressed zones of the space and the expansive ones, on the outside.

Championships of 1992. The initial project envisaged the soccer field alone, and would have permitted a stronger relationship between the spectator and the event. Subsequently the municipality of Bari decided to include a running track as well.

The years immediately prior to 1990 had seen some of the greatest disasters in the history of soccer, and so there was a strong and widespread awareness of the problem of safety. It was one of the main factors that the design had to take into account. Once again it proved helpful to combine the intuition of the layperson and the experience of the supporter. Thinking it over together, Peter and I became convinced that the greatest danger did not lie in the excesses of the hooligans, but in the irrational reactions of the crowd that prompted them. Thus we laid down a number of general principles of what might be called an "ergonomics of panic." First: never concentrate too many people in a single sector. Second: each sector should have an escape route of its own. Third: there should be no extraneous objects along these escape routes that might hamper the movement of the crowd. Fourth: the greater the visibility, the less danger there is of triggering mechanisms of collective hysteria.

Applying these principles to a sports facility means reckoning with an enormous capacity, in this case sixty thousand people. This required a creative effort that in the end contributed to the aesthetics of the building. The majority of stadiums are made up of superimposed rings, and the horizontal divisions (i.e., the barriers that separate the supporters of rival clubs) consist of dangerous gratings. In our case, the upper sectors are separated from the lower ones, and project upward and outward, like the petals of a flower. Between one petal and the next there is a gap of eight meters, into which the access staircases descend, lowered like drawbridges. Thus each sector has an independent escape route. The very devices that are used to divide the fans into groups of a manageable size impart a sense of openness and lightness to the structure. The solution to the safety problem has produced an elegant formal result.

The area around the stadium, from the base of the staircases to the parking lots, is completely empty and slopes slightly downward. The absence of obstacles allows the stadium to empty rapidly, even under emergency conditions. The slope ensures a very wide field of vision: of all the measures designed to avert panic, this is one of the most effective. Nothing creates as much anxiety as an inability to assess the danger.

The stadium was built out of one basic material, concrete, and here the contribution of an engineering studio in Bari, run by the Vitone brothers, was essential. The shape of the stands and the beams clearly reveals the modularity of the structure. The entire ellipse of the stadium is made up of twenty-six petals, each assembled out of 310 crescent-shaped elements, prefabricated out of concrete on site. Beneath this level, each sector is supported by just four pillars. Although these supports are fair-

Castel del Monte, like the stadium, seems to emerge from the landscape.

A powerful landscape, in which stone dominates.

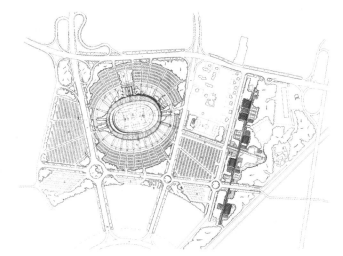

Site plan (above); the stadium at night (below).

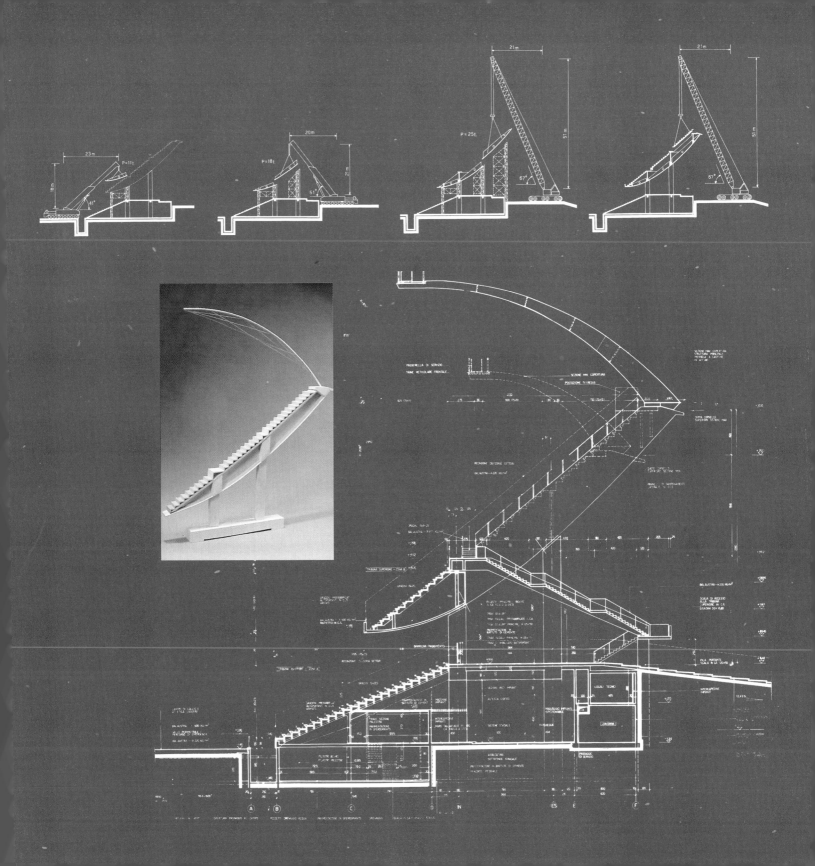

ly massive, the curvature of the elements lends impetus to the structure, and makes the petals rise above the banked ground as if they are floating.

The access staircases are extremely simple, all made out of concrete in one piece. The same material is used for the banisters and handrails on the stairs and in other parts of the stadium. The facilities for the teams (changing rooms and infirmaries, laundries and offices) are located underneath the bottom ring and are served by an underground route to which authorized people can gain access by car from both ends of the stadium.

At the height of the crater rim (and therefore behind the ring of the lower tiers and under the pillars that support the petals) a broad passageway has been created, linking all the systems for spectator circulation. It is here that people pass on their way in or out of the stadium or to the lavatories, and it is here that kiosks selling food and drink are set up during matches. From here, the playing field, the sky, and the surrounding countryside are visible. The feeling of greatest openness is at this point.

The gaps between the petals let the light and color of the landscape into the stadium, giving the tiers an extroverted character. Concave structures, especially when crowded with people, tend to induce claustrophobia. I believe that the transparency achieved with the vertical cuts reduces this effect. The lightness of the space contributes to the tranquillity of the environment, and in this case, perhaps, to a more relaxed enjoyment of the sporting event.

The canopy that shelters the public from the sun, rain, and strong winds of Puglia is a tensile structure of Teflon and steel. This roofing also covers the fissures that separate the petals and thereby reasserts the unity of the whole. The ends of the structural elements of steel, extending out from the top of the stands, house the floodlights used to illuminate matches played at night: this has eliminated the need to install additional framework. Seen at night, with the lower part of the petals lit up and the roofing of translucent Teflon, the stadium looks like a flying saucer or an enormous tropical flower.

Puglia is a region of plains and gentle hills. Amid this soft scenery stands another intruder, another spaceship: Castel del Monte, the hunting lodge of Frederick II Hohenstaufen. Immodestly, we took our inspiration from this incredible construction. Like the fourteenth-century architect, we worked on a form that was closed and protected but had to provide excellent lines of visibility. And the result has been somewhat similar: an extraneous body, but one that has very close ties with the topography of its location.

Like Castel del Monte, the stadium in Bari seems to emerge out of the landscape, and at the same time not to touch it. It is a monolithic building, made entirely of concrete, sunk in the ground and yet apparently just grazing it.

The construction site at the start of work; the laying of the pieces of prefabricated concrete; the stadium under construction.

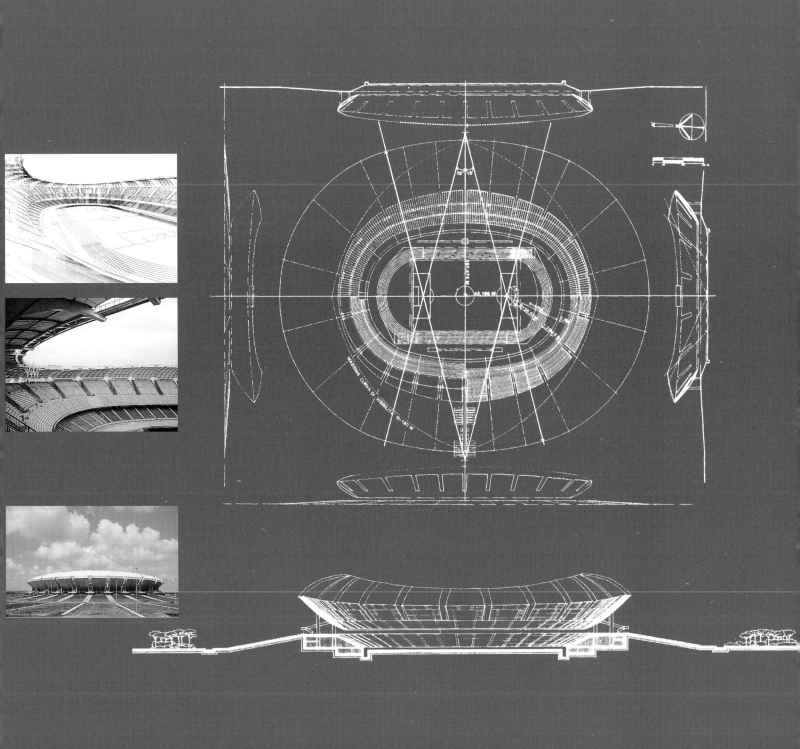

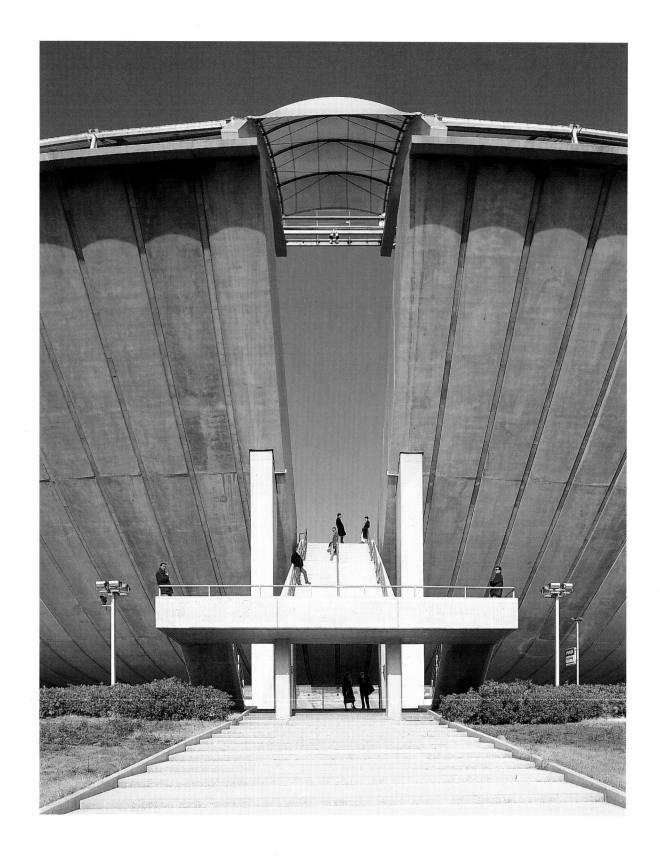

Even the empty spaces play a leading role. The vertical cuts that separate the "petals" impart lightness and transparency to the space.

# 1987 **Pompeii** (Naples) Italy

## Intervention in the Excavated City

**An improvement scheme that tackled the problem of routes of access and of how to make a visit to the archaeological remains an enjoyable experience, by allowing people to share in the fascination of the excavations. A way of preserving the finds.**

View of one of the main axes of the ancient city.

The volcanic eruption of 79 A.D. made Pompeii immortal thanks to an exemplary process of preservation. First is a layer of small, solidified pieces of lava known as *lapilli*, i.e., a sort of expanded clay: here the air could circulate, so that the objects in it remained perfectly dry. Then is a good coat of ashes, which reacted with the rain to form an impermeable layer. This would have been sufficient to protect Pompeii from any form of decay for all eternity—except that, two centuries ago, the city was discovered, and the spell broken.

During the Fascist era there was even an irresponsible director of the excavations who did not understand why it was taking so long to finish the work. Ashamed of the state's slowness, he decided to put on a good show of efficiency and sent bulldozers right into the middle of the *insulae*. He smashed everything, but demonstrated that you can do a great deal in a very short space of time.

The project for Pompeii, born out of a collaboration with Federico Zeri and Umberto Eco, started out with exactly the opposite intention: to do things very, very slowly. Archaeology is a matter of excavation; it is the act of searching. When you dig up an object, the search is over, and the technical problems begin: conservation, restoration, interpretation. Experts, careful and meticulous people who need peace and quiet and a lot of time for their work, take over.

In order to enjoy Pompeii for as long as possible, the idea was to divide the space still to be excavated into fifty sites, each to be investigated over a period of twenty years. This meant making the excavation of Pompeii last for a thousand years. Then it would be time for someone else to think about it. Instead of being in the open air, each site would be covered with transparent panels when opened; it would thus be sheltered from the rain and from ultraviolet light, and yet remain visible to the public. The result would have been a mobile museum that could follow the excavations around.

Pictures of the preeminent archaeological city.

The idea met with a negative response from many interest groups, especially tour guides and grave robbers. They had different motivations, I believe, but they were equally adamant in their opposition. Needless to say, our idea came to nothing.

Overall plan.

Plan of the roof of one of the "spheres" that house educational activities for the public (below); axonometric of the roofing system for the excavations (bottom); sections of the system of presentation and protection (below right).

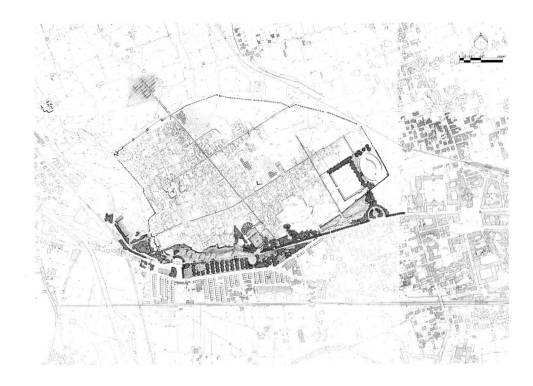

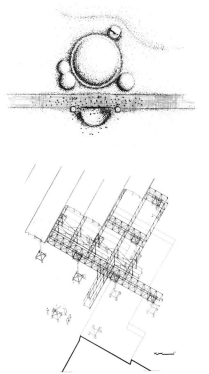

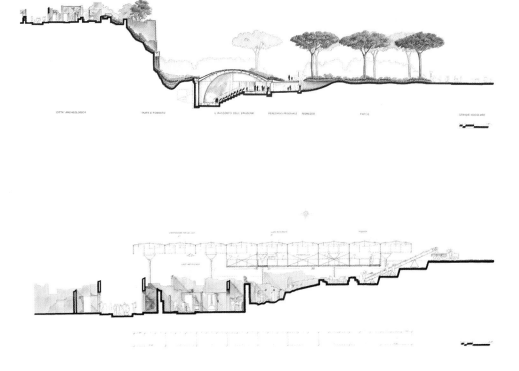

# 1987 Matera Italy

## Restoration of the Sassi

**The basic idea of the project was to tackle the problem of restoration in the manner of a workshop while providing basic services: accommodation, restaurants, bars, and public meeting places. It involved a scheme for the revival of ancient techniques and a sense of participation.**

In the twentieth century in a "civilized" country, the idea of people living in caves seems absurd; but it happens (or happened until just a few years ago) at the Sassi in Matera. The Sassi are the outer face of a network of caves that extends into the slopes above the Gravina. They were built in the sixteenth century over an underground settlement of very ancient origin, dating from approximately 2000 B.C. They served a fairly rich agricultural economy: animals, foodstuffs, and reserves of water were kept in the caves. The environment was healthy, thanks to its exposure to the sun and good natural ventilation.

During the last century, the slump in local agriculture impoverished a large number of peasant families, who took refuge in the Sassi. But the caves did not have sufficient light and air, and the overcrowding caused serious health problems. The use of the caves as dwellings, for which they were in no way suited, destroyed the previous ecosystem.

When we became involved in the scheme for the restoration of the Sassi, the population had already been moved into more suitable housing. Small numbers of people were, however, beginning to return. We were asked to study solutions for the reclamation and rehabilitation of the area, which is of great historical value. Obviously, the problems were enormous: the absence of sanitary facilities, communication systems, and services.

Plan of the zone (above); the Sassi (left); sections and plan of proposed intervention (below and opposite).

Clearly, one of the reasons behind the choice to bring us in was the experience we had gained with the workshops in Otranto and Burano. In Matera, too, an attempt was being made to reconstruct the history of the place in order to understand just what had allowed the system of the Sassi to function for centuries. Again it was necessary to intervene using gentle and, for the most part, conservative techniques. Here too the local community had to be involved if the use of the area for habitation was going to be at least partially revived. Our approach was based to a large extent on education. The theme was a stimulating one, and it looked like a good plan to us. But, having reached this stage, everything came to a halt.

What can I say? I have gradually come to realize that interventions of this kind are the most difficult of all. They require a great deal of subtlety and very, very long periods of time, the sort of time needed by homeopathic medicine rather than by surgery. And it is very rare for the administrations of cities and their patience to last that long.

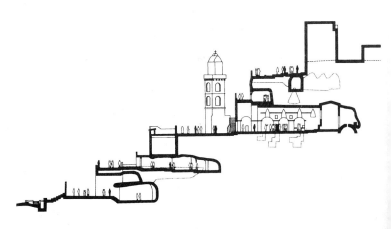

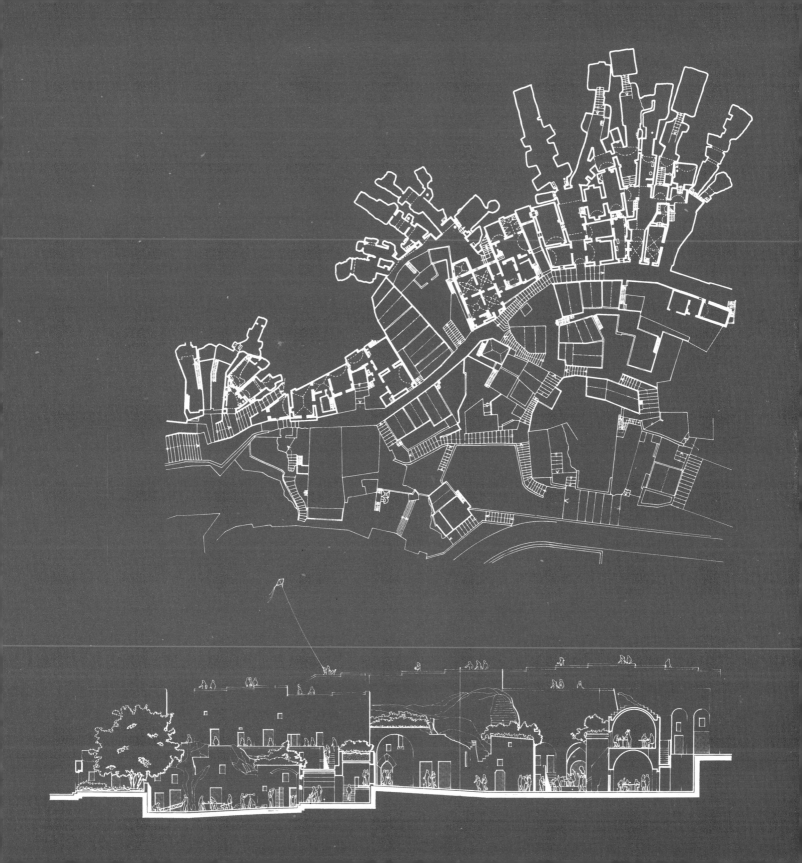

# 1987 Charenton le Pont (Paris) France
## Bercy 2 Shopping Center
Construction: 1987–90

**The form of this shopping center derives from its context: an expressway interchange. The roof is made of twenty-seven thousand panels of perforated stainless steel, in thirty-four different sizes. It is an example of the application of new methods of construction.**

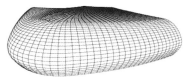

The expressway junction at which the shopping mall has been built. The form was strongly shaped by the place, even though there is a vague reference to an airship.

I tend to picture the *genius loci* as a benign spirit, but this is not always the case. Viewed from the air, Charenton le Pont, to the east of Paris, is a tangle of spaghetti junctions. The Bercy 2 Shopping Center is right there, at the intersection between the Boulevard Périphérique and the A4 expressway. Thousands of people drive past the place every day. The theme of the project was to attract their attention, to stir their interest.

The work did not get off to a good start. We inherited it from another architectural studio: the client thought that the design for the roof was too conventional. At that stage of the project, though, many of the basic choices had already been made: structural grid, access, position of the services and parking facilities. All these things had been agreed with the local authorities of Charenton, and were therefore fixed by the urban development scheme for the area. We accepted these constraints in the same way you accept the presence of houses, roads, or factories on a site: as the legacy of previous human experience. There is simply no such thing as a blank page. The obligations of the context are the essence of architecture.

The client had a clear objective in mind, and this is always a good starting point. Bercy was a shopping mall, and therefore, above all, had to be visible. It had to attract the attention of potential customers, not fade into the urban background. A degree of effrontery was necessary and even demanded.

In spite of its futuristic appearance, Bercy is a fairly conventional building on the inside, the outcome of laborious discussions with experts on retail outlets. There are laws that govern the layout of spaces and circulation in shopping centers, and they are shown even more respect than the law of gravity. The potential for creativity on this front was limited, so we worked mainly on the form of the exterior and the appearance of the facing.

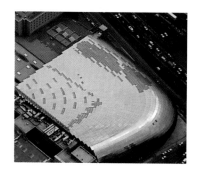

I believe that the themes of movement and speed are naturally suited to a place like this. At Charenton, the *genius loci* travels by car. So we modeled the building around the curve of the bypasses, just as at Lyons we had taken our inspiration from the bend of the river. Even here the building was generated by the forces acting on the site: the complete opposite of a gratuitous gesture.

Opposite: The roof of the building with the city in the background.

Tackled in this way, the structure began to soften, to grow rounded, until it unexpectedly took on the appearance of a giant meteorite. From this point on the project acquired a growing technical interest. It was a question of establishing a relationship between the supporting structure and a complex three-dimensional profile. Above all, it entailed designing a roof that would be in keeping with this form.

The simplest solution would have been to use sheets of zinc, very widely used on Parisian rooftops, but in the end it was decided to employ stainless steel instead, for reasons of durability. The advantage of using thin sheets of metal is that they can be modeled on the spot, into any shape. But Peter Rice put a bug in my ear: why not use preformed components? It was an interesting challenge, because it presupposed a close link between the geometry of the whole, the geometry of the piece, and the study of production methods. Perhaps I saw an analogy with my early works in this; the fact is that I accepted. Once the geometric rules for the section had been determined, we developed a mathematical model to work out the optimal shape for the roofing panels. The modular facing of metal (this too a tribute to the futuristic character of the surroundings) now gives Bercy the appearance of a gleaming airship with the ramps of the expressway furled around it.

Under the roof we find the idea of the double skin again. The principle is the same as at Lyons: a layer of air will slow down the exchange of heat with the outside. There it was applied to the walls; here to a roof with a surface area of almost two square kilometers. The metal panels are not just decoration: in fact, they reflect the rays of sun in an efficient manner, helping to keep the cavity underneath cool. Thus the roofing elements are made of stainless steel with a satin finish, so that their opacity varies with their position and the light. This gives the shell a variegated appearance that produces an unusual contrast with the industrial standardization of the panels.

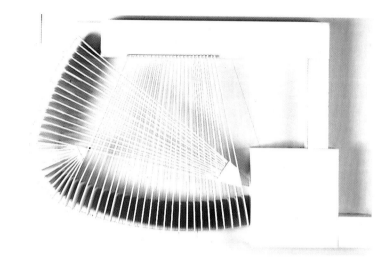

Study model (above); numbering and positioning of the perforated stainless-steel panels (left).

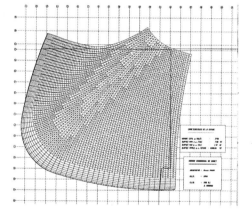

Laminated-wood beams for the roofing structure.

Joining the panels.

Details of the roofing
(below); view of the
interior (right); section
(below right).

# 1987 Paris France

## Rue de Meaux Housing

Construction: 1987–91

**These two hundred low-cost apartments are in a heavily populated area of the 19th arrondissement of Paris. The inner garden is the central element and provides access to all the apartments. It is another development of the application of the "double skin" and terra-cotta. The relationship between the peace and quiet of nature in the courtyard and the city outside and the idea of immaterial space were central.**

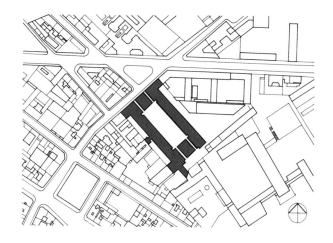

I have talked about the Lowara project, and the rather masochistic enthusiasm with which I took on the task of constructing an office building at industrial costs. On Rue de Meaux, in Paris, I tried my hand at low-cost housing instead. The underlying motivation was the same. I claim that quality in architecture does not depend solely on cost. When someone asks me to prove it, I feel obliged to accept the challenge.

The ugliness of the modern city does not result from a lack of money, but from a senseless use of resources. The impoverishment of urban life is due to reasons that are almost always outside the control of architects: overcrowding, traffic, absence of services. But architects certainly have to take their share of the blame as well, and their crimes can be seen on every street corner: obsessive repetition, indifference to the surroundings, lack of taste and character. What fascinated me on Rue de Meaux was the idea of going beyond "shelter, comfort, and functionally usable space": I wanted to show that even the limited funds available to public building are enough to produce houses filled with light, greenery, and ornament.

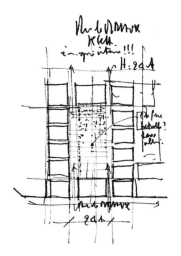

Site plan (top); sketch by Renzo Piano (left);. Rue de Meaux facade (above); garden facade (below).

Rue de Meaux is in the 19th arrondissement, a working-class district in the north of Paris. The client for this project was the municipality, or rather the "Régie immobilière de la Ville de Paris," headed by M. Lombardini. The goal was to build a low-cost housing complex of 220 apartments.

Initially the program envisaged a public road running through the middle of the site. On my advice, a different solution was adopted that showed more respect for the privacy of the home: setting the houses around the edges of a rectangular garden planted with trees. The short sides of the rectangle are interrupted by two vertical cuts, dividing the facade into three elongated blocks that are in proportion to the surrounding buildings. These cuts are the means of access to the interior. The contrast between the noise of the road and the silence of the court is a pleasant surprise. Two large flower beds have been laid out in the garden. We filled them with grass, low shrubs, and white birch. The foliage of the birch trees is visi-

ble through the openings in the facade as you approach the complex.

Access to all the apartments is from this central court. The housing units have two fronts, one facing the garden and the other facing the city, and their size varies according to position. The standard unit has a fairly large living room oriented in a north-south direction, with a balcony on both sides and a sleeping area. On the upper stories, the front is set back to make room for a terrace: on this level, as on the ground floor, some apartments have two stories. On the street side, the lower floors house commercial activities. The access roads for service vehicles and the entrances to the underground garage, which extends underneath the entire area, pass beneath the ends of the blocks.

The buildings are very simple in form. The constraints of a low-cost housing scheme do not prevent the architect from doing good work. They simply make it necessary to concentrate resources. Instead of working on a more complex structure, we decided, together with Bernard Plattner, the patient custodian of this project, to invest in the finishing and ornamentation of the facades. We did this because we felt that they were the elements that would make the greatest contribution to improving the urban environment.

Thus we adopted a solution that had already been used several times before: the double-skin facing. The visible element of the inner facades is a square panel of about ninety centimeters on a side, detached from the wall by thirty centimeters. The gap between the two surfaces ensures good ventilation of the wall. The panels do not cover the entire surface: behind the open modules, protected by the bars of the supporting grid, are traditional windows with white frames and yellow shades. On the long side of the garden, the same shades are used to screen the more exposed parts of the balconies as well.

The element that projects from the wall consists of a frame of GRC (concrete reinforced with glass fibers). Inside this are mounted first a layer of insulation and then a facing material: GRC again or terra-cotta tiles in their natural color. In the case of the complex on Rue de Meaux, terra-cotta is not just a homage to the context: the tiles are four times the size of normal bricks, and, anyway, the majority of the neighboring buildings are finished with plaster. The aim was to impart a variety of color and texture to the surface, creating a pleasing contrast with the rigorous geometric pattern of the facade. The richness of form that results is not common in low-cost buildings. Another quality of this facade is that it will grow old gracefully, for the patina of time tends to soften it. On the side facing the street, the pattern and color of the facade are the same, but there is no double skin: the facing is attached directly to the primary structure.

The combination of extremely modern materials (such as GRC) and traditional ones used in an innovative fashion (ter-

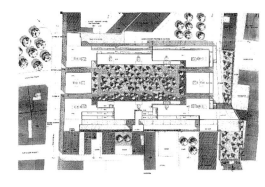

Overall plan (above);
typical floor plan
(below).

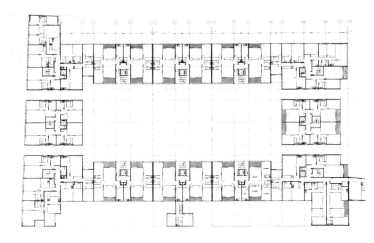

Typology of an
apartment.

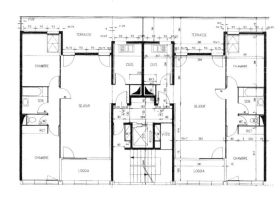

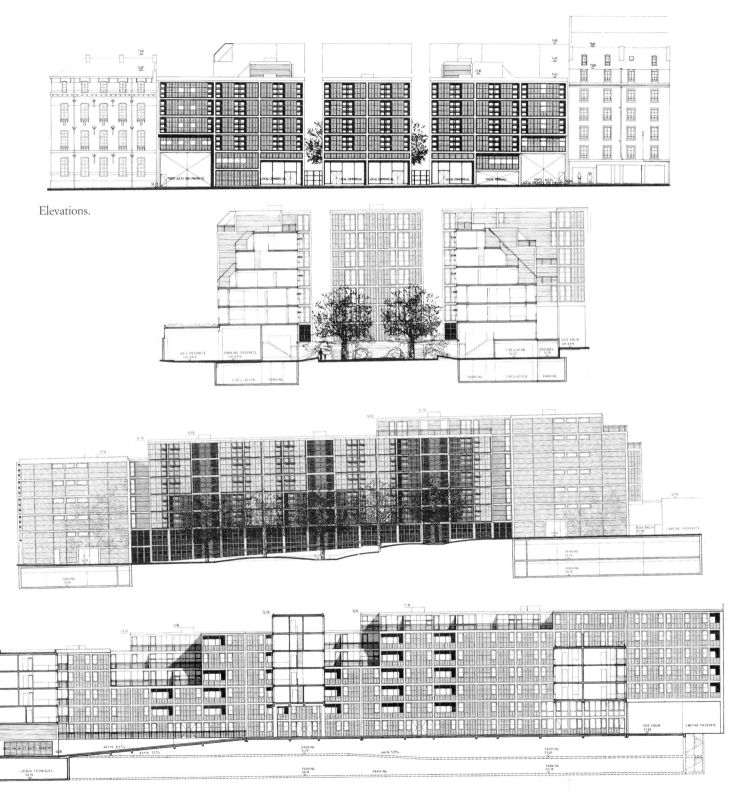

Elevations.

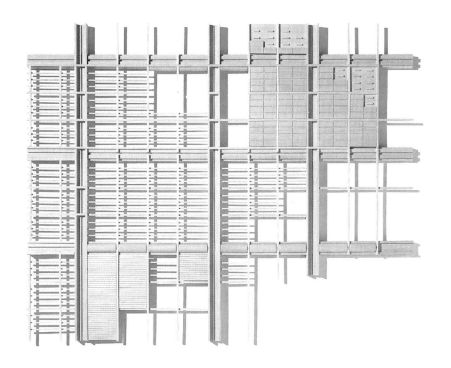

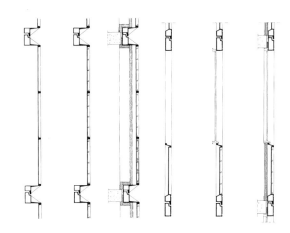

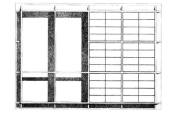

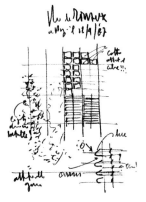

Model of facade
detailing (above);
sections of various
typologies (right).

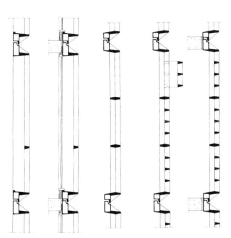

ra-cotta) is a frequent feature of my work, as is the presence of nature, a vital element of decoration in the urban fabric, in deliberate tension with the surrounding constructions. On Rue de Meaux the foliage of the birch trees, a soft green in color, contrasts with the technological gray of the GRC and the red of the terra-cotta. This chromatic contrast, the texture of the materials, and the proportion of the facades are all elements designed to induce a slight optical vibration, an imperceptible iridescence that fills the air with reflected colors. Here we are dealing with a theme that has always been essential to the architect: space.

The structure of Rue de Meaux is as elementary as can be imagined from the viewpoint of the disposition of masses. At the same time, anyone entering the court perceives a change of space, a dimension different from the one outside. It is like leaving the city and going into a silent, secluded, and protective space. This means that the perception of space is more complex than the perception of volume. It involves not just cultural factors, but also those that are physical (such as sound and light) and psychological ones (such as intimacy and participation). The spatiality of the immaterial is one of my favorite lines of research and Rue de Meaux provided an important area for its exploration.

There is something else I would like to say about the court: it is a joyful setting, but also a "private" one and, in this sense, different from the square and the street. The original terms of the program called for a public road to run through the middle of the complex. We put up courteous but firm opposition to the idea. The home should be a refuge of peace and quiet. Does this mean that the quality of social life and the possibility of participation have been reduced? Quite the contrary. The true sociability is here, in this communal courtyard where all the residents can go to stroll, read, and talk.

Entering the garden of Rue de Meaux, you get not only a sense of protection but also one of belonging, of belonging to the community of people living in the building. The court is an open-air living room shared by all the residents.

The space inside the courtyard creates a marked difference in noise from the road. The light is colored by terra-cotta and is made to vibrate by the minute and fragmented detailing of the facades.

# 1988 Saint Quentin-en-Yvelines

(Paris) France

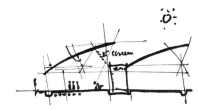

## Thomson Optronics Factory

Construction: 1988–90

**This modular solution was designed to compensate for the fact that it was impossible to tell in advance how much space would be needed by this electronics company in its new plant. Through the use of tall modules, 14.4 meters wide, the facilities can be located on a grid of 3.6 meters. The strong presence of greenery and the use of natural light are important.**

I have said somewhere that the architect never starts out with a blank page, that there is always a program of use, a context, and a set of rules to point the way. Usually that is the case, but there are exceptions, and Thomson Optronics was an extreme one.

Thomson had to build a new manufacturing plant in the area of Saint Quentin-en-Yvelines, near Paris. A site had already been designated on which there were no constructions to reckon with; the environment itself was flat, shapeless, and not characterized by any particular vegetation. Even more unusual, there were no precise indications on the part of the client. Thomson is an electronics company: in this field, the process of miniaturization of components is so rapid that companies must continually redefine their needs for space. Thus it was necessary to devise a very flexible and evolutionary plan. We found ourselves working with Paul Vincent in charge of the project with only one constraint: time. The factory in Paris had been sold, and Thomson had undertaken to leave the premises within eighteen months. It was a fine exercise in creativity, for we introduced our own constraints. It was not possible to predict the division of functions with any accuracy; it was not even clear just how big the complex would eventually be, so we had to create a completely open space, a theme with which we were thoroughly familiar.

In this case, the basic module is a large arched element with a span of almost fifteen meters, which produces buildings with soft, curved lines. The interiors provide pleasant working conditions, thanks to the presence of greenery (the work of Michel Desvignes) and the extensive use of natural light. In addition, a number of special places for meeting and socialization were created inside.

The landscape responds to the fluidity of the construction with the rigor of an orthogonal grid defined by lines of trees and other plants. Thus the buildings are given a logical setting by the "frame" of the vegetation, as if they were placed on a checkerboard. The integration of architecture and nature is based on a respect for the same formal rules: future enlargements will need to do no more than follow them.

Sketch by Renzo Piano (top); the roofs protruding from a field of maize (center); the first phase after construction (above).

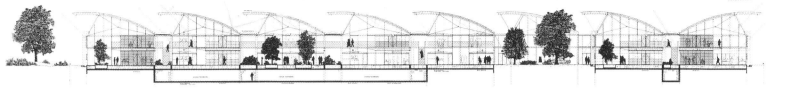

View of an end wall of
glass, at night, and the
surviving greenery.

# 1988 **Paris** France

## IRCAM Extension

Construction: 1988–90

**This is the building into which the offices of Pierre Boulez's Institute of Musical Research, attached to the Centre Pompidou, were moved. Consisting of nine floors, six of them above ground, it has a tiny plan due to the fact that it fills the angle left between two existing buildings.**

The need for the greatest possible soundproofing led IRCAM to excavate a protected space underneath Paris. The need to provide its offices and research structures with a public face suggested the creation of an extension on the surface, to which the project gave the form of a proper tower. Previously all that IRCAM had revealed to the outside world was a glass ceiling and a few elements of the ventilation system. Today its outward expression is a clearly visible urban landmark, sharply defining the corner of Place Beaubourg and Place Stravinsky.

The extension is made up of nine floors, six of them above ground. There were three reasons for the decision to build upward: the limited size of the area available; the need to underline the link with the nearby Centre Pompidou, of which IRCAM forms part; and the desire to emphasize the institute's role and image after years spent in the catacombs under Place Saint Merri. The tower is taller than the adjoining buildings, and its height is reinforced by the vertical thrust of an opaque section and two transparent sections (a row of windows set one above the other and the elevator shaft).

A great deal of care has been taken over the insertion of the tower into the context. The reference to Beaubourg is evident not only in its height, but also in the exposed steel structure at the top of the elevator shaft and the grid of aluminum supports for the panels of the facing and windows. The opaque section, which marks the corner of the square, is the same red color as the adjacent buildings; in this case, however, it is not that of an unplastered wall, but of terra-cotta facing panels. These panels are hooked onto concealed bars and separated by aluminum elements, which constitute the only visible part of the supporting framework. The elements of the facade naturally resemble brick in their texture and color. This effect has been accentuated by making horizontal cuts in them to create the same impression of size, a small example of attention to ornamentation, which helps strengthen the relationship with the context.

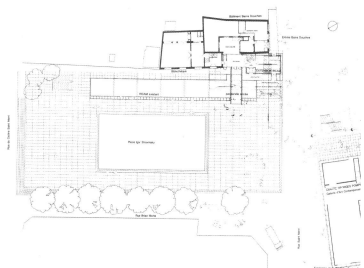

The IRCAM Tower viewed from the square (top); plan (above).

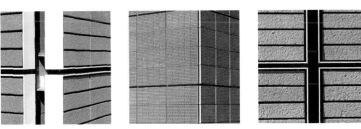
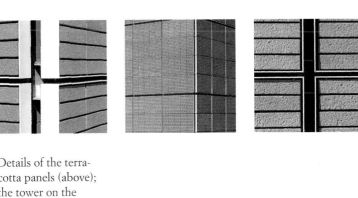
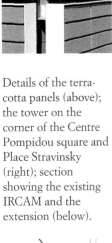

Details of the terra-cotta panels (above); the tower on the corner of the Centre Pompidou square and Place Stravinsky (right); section showing the existing IRCAM and the extension (below).

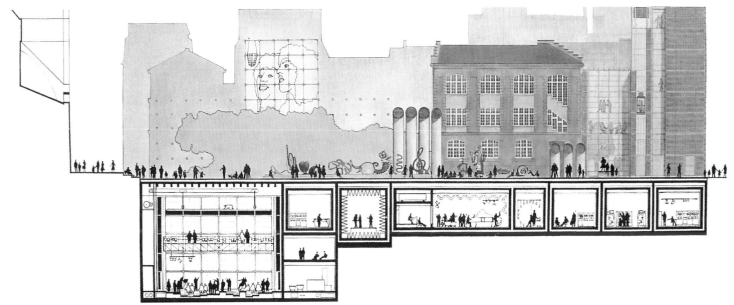

# 1988 Osaka Japan

## Kansai Air Terminal

Construction: 1990–94

**The airport offices and facilities are located on an artificial island that is 1.7 kilometers long and can handle 100,000 passengers a day. The roof is made up of 82,000 identical panels of stainless steel. The form was suggested by the internal flows of air; the structure had to be able to resist an earthquake . . . which then occurred. Without damage.**

The context has to be understood, absorbed, and interpreted: this is always the beginning of the adventure. Sometimes it is rich in suggestion, like the historic center of a city; at others it is poor, like a large field of maize; or it is even poorer—wind and sea, as at the Kansai Air Terminal. Nevertheless, very strong points of reference.

Before entering the competition for Kansai, I asked the client what I always ask in these cases: to visit the site. There was a moment of embarrassment, because there was none. Japan is a very crowded country, and Osaka had no room for a new airport, so the relevant authorities decided to build it in the sea. An artificial island was constructed—not a "floating" platform (as I have heard it described), but one set firmly on the bottom, and stabilized by piles driven deep into the seabed. This island is an impressive work of civil engineering, and was created in a surprisingly short span of time. At the moment I asked about the site visit, it did not yet exist.

But Japanese courtesy has no limits. The client took the three of us, Peter Rice, Nori Okabe, and myself, on a boat trip that lasted an afternoon. "Where is the airport going to be?" asked Nori, who was in charge of my studio in Osaka at the time. "Here," answered our guide. We were in the open sea.

Castaways adrift on a raft—at least that was how we felt. We were lost in the infinite, drunk on space. So we started to look for something to hold onto outside the physical context: in the collective unconscious, in memory, in culture.

Architects are creatures of the land. Their materials rest on the ground. They themselves belong essentially to the world of materiality. In this sense, I feel atypical, perhaps partly because of my youthful passions: the harbor, temporary structures, loads suspended from cranes, reflections in water. Aboard that boat we tried to think in terms of water and air, rather than land; of air and wind, elongated, lightweight forms, designed to withstand the earthquakes to which the area is prone; of water, sea, tides; of liquid forms in movement, energy, waves. Many of the ideas that shaped the project were born that day on the sea.

Writing such a description will surely get me labeled an ar-

The approach to the airport (left); the gallery leading to the planes (opposite). The space is boundless and the sensation of being unable to see the end is accentuated by the curve of the roof, which descends from a height of twelve meters at the center to one of four meters at the end of the vista.

chitect of the organic again. Perhaps it is time to return to land, where we find Tom Barker, my longtime collaborator on questions of plant and environmental engineering. With him I commenced a fascinating investigation of jets of air, from which the form of the terminal's roof was to emerge. From poetic intuition (letting ourselves be guided by the air) we moved on, as always, to the patient work of the craftsperson.

In cross section, the roof is an irregular arch (in reality, a series of arches of different radii). It has been given this shape to channel air from the passenger side to the runway side without the need for closed ducts. Baffles resembling blades, not set in pipes but left open to view, guide the flow of air along the ceiling and reflect the light coming from above. In this way all the elements that would have prevented people from seeing the structure have been eliminated. We regulated the movement of air by creating a ceiling that is aerodynamic, but the "other way up," for the flows we are interested in are on the inside, not the outside. We did this by entrusting the work of calculation to excellent designers and the computer, which gave us the speed and precision we needed. If there is a "naturalistic" element in this, it does not lie in the imitation of a wave, but in reducing the components required to a minimum: a theme typical of Kansai, which we will encounter again when discussing the roof.

Kansai is a precision instrument, a child of mathematics and technology. It forms a strong and recognizable landmark; it has a clear and simple shape that declares itself without hesitation. But it is also an extraordinary spatial experience. One critic has commented that Kansai succeeds in being modern without being childishly futuristic. I find this a very fine compliment.

It is a structure with undulating, asymmetrical lines, and yet the exposed beams are repeated with the regular pattern of a filigree. It is laid out on several levels, which unexpectedly give rise to a single large atrium at the center. It is a construction where vegetation penetrates from the outside, invading the passenger arrival areas: the first welcome to Japan.

The airport spreads over the island like a glider; the archetypal flying machine, the missing link between ground and airplane. In the absence of other constraints, the only factor that has shaped its volumes is the space taken up by the aircraft and their maneuvering. The planes determine form, function, and extension; they are the true masters of the island. We have paid homage to these local divinities with a departure area that has forty-two passenger loading bridges and extends for 1,700 meters. Kansai Air Terminal is one of the largest buildings ever constructed: three Lingottos in a row.

The shape of the glider is clearly visible in the plan. Access roads delineate the two large tail fins. The main block is the fuselage. The embarkation terminals are wings that spread out to embrace the island, in a sort of symbolic clasp.

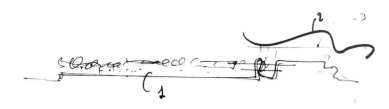

Sketch by Renzo Piano; the creation of the artificial island.

Renzo Piano and the director of the airport, Takeuchi.

Nori Okabe.

The ceremony of "breaking" the ground.

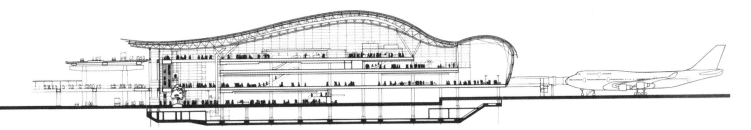

Section.

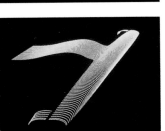

Detail of the structure
that supports the roof
of the terminal.

The airport from
above: a glider resting
on the ground.

Computer images.

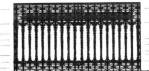

The gymnastics carried out by the workers every morning before starting work.

Renzo and Milly Piano;
the foremen of the
construction site.

There is an anecdote about these wings: they were nearly clipped. At the beginning of the 1990s, Japan was hit by a serious economic downturn, which led to severe cuts in all the country's budgets, including ours. We were asked to adjust to the new limits on expenditures. It was a serious problem, for the project was at an advanced stage. It would not have been possible to eliminate one element without disturbing the balance of the parts. So, somewhat provocatively, we decided on a drastic mutilation: cutting off the wings. It was obviously an absurd proposal, but our bluff achieved the desired effect. Six months after the work had started, the budget was restored.

The basic organization of the terminal derives from a functional study carried out by Paul Andreu for Aéroports de Paris. The main block that houses and sorts the passengers is higher on the runway side, which helps to direct the flow of people. Its asymmetrical structure provides them with clear orientation at any point.

The system of transport along the wings, given the distances involved, is based on a shuttle service. The routes that lead to the embarkation gates are located on different levels, and converge on a very tall atrium filled with vegetation, which we nicknamed the "canyon."

The enormous three-dimensional trusses that support the roof are over eighty meters long. Their asymmetrical profile is the fruit of the same calculations that made it possible to channel the invisible flow of air. These structural studies inspired us to look for a mathematical model that would permit the maximum standardization of components. The results turned out to be extraordinary. The 27,000 facing panels used in the Bercy 2 Shopping Center were in thirty-four different sizes, and this was already an excellent ratio. In the Kansai Air Terminal (thanks in part to the overall size of the building, which made it possible to absorb curves into small tolerances), all 82,000 stainless-steel panels are identical. The primary elements were all made from the same mold, and only in a few cases did they require slight adjustment. The secondary structural elements are also identical.

Even the tapering curves of the wings are the result of the application of a rigorous rule of calculation: they were defined on the basis of a toroidal geometry. Conceptually, the wings represent the upper part of a ring of 16,800 meters, with its radius tilted at an angle of 68 degrees to the horizon, passing though the ground and emerging on the island. In reality the curvature is almost imperceptible, but was necessary to improve lateral visibility from the control tower.

The airport was the last project I designed with Peter Rice, who never had the satisfaction of seeing its inauguration. All of these structural masterpieces are his work: Kansai represents the most complex fruit of our collaboration. The project was handled locally with the collaboration of Nikken Sekkei, one of the largest design studios in Japan.

The construction of Kansai was a great adventure too. It took thirty-eight months and required six thousand workers, rising to ten thousand at some points. I recall this great crowd of people at dawn, before starting the day's work. They were all doing gymnastics together on the naked platform that the artificial island was at the time: nothing but a great expanse of gravel, which then took shape day after day, turning into the object we had pictured in the drawings. At Kansai I learned the meaning of the expression "fertilizing the desert."

In Japan there is even a ritual for talking to workers. The architect has to show a concern with one thing above all: their safety. The formula used is very beautiful: "I have conceived this dream. I thank you, because you are making it come true. Do it in safety, be careful." The architect is the artist: he or she decides what has to be done, but does not physically do it. And so the architect asks the workers not to run risks, expressing a hope that they will not be hurt.

It is well known that insurance companies use statistical tables to predict the number of accidents on a particular construction site. They are used to calculate the risk, and thus the premium to be paid. At Kansai the tables were proved wrong, for there were very few accidents and no deaths. The Japanese incantation had worked.

When the platform for Kansai was created, Japan grew by fifteen square kilometers, as Takeuchi, the director of the airport, liked to point out. Coyly, he used to add that all the books on Japanese geography would have to be reprinted on his account. Kansai is also the island that vanished for a day. This is an amusing story, but to tell it I shall have to explain a few technical matters.

I've already said that the platform is a great work of civil engineering. It is supported by over one thousand piles, which go down through twenty meters of seawater and twenty meters of mud and are then driven firmly into forty meters of rock. The first problem is that the layer of mud settles; the second, that the settling is not even.

The solution found was extremely complex. Special sensors detect when the settling has exceeded the maximum permitted tolerance (ten millimeters) at a particular point. Each pile is equipped with a system of calibration that operates by means of powerful hydraulic jacks: when the alarm "goes off" (in a manner of speaking, for such developments are fully provided for and totally under control), the pile that signals the displacement is adjusted and then locked into the new position. This regulation will continue for ten years, and then the jacks will be fixed into place.

In the early phase the phenomenon occurred on a considerable scale: the island settled by fifty centimeters between 1992 and 1996. Information on this process was given out periodically, and journalists had great fun with it. Articles came out with the title "Kansai has sunk by $x$ centimeters." One day

Opposite: Lateral glass wall of the terminal (above); wooden model of a joint (below).

The check-in area for international departures, situated on the fifth floor, has a view of the panels that reflect the light and guide the flow of air. This movement is made visible by a lightweight work by the artist Shingu.

the authoritative *Japan Times* carried the dramatic news: "Kansai has sunk completely." This caused a great stir, in part because the report was taken up by other media outlets. Not everyone noticed the date: April 1, 1990. It was an April Fool's trick.

I would like to make one last comment on lightness. During the briefing stage, we had long discussions with the client's representatives over the building's "quakeproofing characteristics." These were calm, serene, and fatalistic discussions. When I heard about the earthquake in Kobe, in January 1995, I was reminded of them. At that moment I understood what it means for a people to coexist with earthquakes.

Kansai was exactly the same distance from the epicenter as Kobe. The intensity of the shock was the same. And yet our work, so immaterial and apparently frail, was able to resist: the building registered no damage, not even broken glass. The fury of the elements toppled the oak, but did not break the light and supple reed.

Departure wing.

Opposite: Entrance hall of the airport, known as the "canyon."

# 1989 Kumamoto Japan

## Ushibuka Bridge

Construction: 1989–95

**A 900-meter-long bridge following a curved path and using continuous beam frames with a length of 150 meters, which addressed the study of wind and respect for the environment.**

Another project with close ties to the sea is the Ushikuba Bridge, which links three islands of the Amakusa archipelago. Nine hundred meters long, it was built to improve communications between the harbor and the southern districts of the city. Ushikuba is in the Kumamoto prefecture, in the south of Japan. Its principal resource is fishing. Hsokawa-san, governor of the region, commissioned the bridge. The descendant of a local noble family and a man of great culture, he had also been prime minister of Japan for a brief period, in the years 1994 and 1995.

Essentially two problems were posed by the project: the preservation of a very beautiful natural setting and the safety of people using the bridge, especially pedestrians and cyclists. Winds in this area can reach very high speeds. In order not to disturb the formal balance of the bay, we decided that the response to the context had to be very clear, very clean. So we linked the three promontories together with a curved path: a single very strong sign in the shape of a bow, rather than a broken line made up of straight segments. For the same reason we reduced the number of supporting piers to a minimum, using continuous beam frames with a length of 150 meters.

Two provisions were made to deal with the wind. The lower face of the bridge is curved, which reduces the pressure of the air, and special baffles, tested in wind tunnels, are set at the sides of the roadway to protect people on foot or bicycle. These two elements create an unusual optical illusion: the rounded lower part does not seem to touch the supports, and this creates an impression of great lightness, which is accentuated by the reflections of the baffles, thus decorating the girders with a pattern of light and shade.

To some extent all Japanese bridges use a technique of this kind. By working on the structure they avoid the impression of clumsy bulk. By reducing the scale they set the object delicately on the placeform.

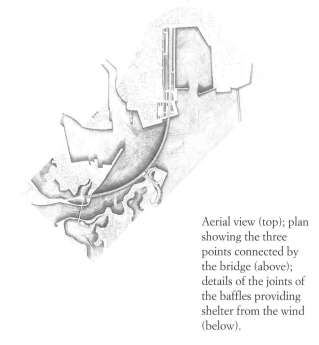

Aerial view (top); plan showing the three points connected by the bridge (above); details of the joints of the baffles providing shelter from the wind (below).

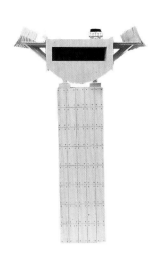

Wooden model (above); wind-tunnel test (below).

# 1989  Punta Nave (Genoa) Italy

## UNESCO Laboratory and Workshop

Construction: 1989–91

**Built completely out of glass, with the roof structure of laminated wood, it stands on the ancient terraces of the Ligurian coastal region. It has research links with UNESCO and the European Union.**

The studio on the Punta Nave is my own interpretation of a "scene of an interior with people at work." This is something that I understood when working on the project for Constantin Brancusi's studio. He saw his atelier as a "scene of an interior with works and works to be."

The difference is that my studio is more of a metaphorical harbor than a metaphorical wood: people coming, people going, objects staying. These objects have a history (a bamboo plant is Nouméa, a lamp is Lingotto, a terra-cotta tile is Berlin), and together they tell a story.

Brancusi felt that his studio and works were one and the same thing, and thought that the presence of earlier works inspired and guided the creation of new ones. I feel much the same way. I walk around the tables, look at the new designs, see pictures and drawings of the ones that have already been built. By so doing, I see the world.

The UNESCO Laboratory and Workshop is an obvious tribute to my homeland. Made almost entirely of glass and transparent to the sunlight and reflections from the Gulf of Genoa, it looks like a greenhouse, one of many scattered over this stretch of the Riviera. It is poised between the mountains and the sea, a bit like the Ligurians themselves. It stands on a terraced slope, and has respected the characteristics of this land carved by human hands, even echoing the same stepped structure in its interior. Yet the origins of this building, so closely bound to the *topos*, lie in Senegal.

Our experience in Dakar, carried out with UNESCO, ended in a twofold disappointment. On the one hand we had not been able to win the unequal struggle with sheets of corrugated iron. On the other, we were obliged to break off extremely interesting research into the properties of plant fibers and their use in architecture: a subject that at first seemed to have only local significance, but that then became a passion for us. The fibers turned out to have surprising potential, not just as facing materials and thermal insulation, but also as structural components.

We would have liked to carry on with the research. So someone (perhaps Peter Rice) had the idea of proposing to UNESCO a study of the application of natural materials in construction. Alongside the experimental cultivation of plants that have proved particularly promising, there would be a research

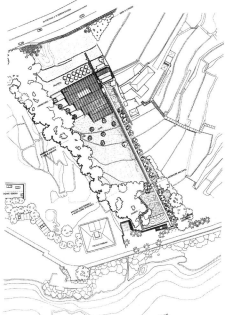

The site in its original state (above); external and internal views of the workshop (below and opposite). The space of the building is immaterial, made up of transparencies, vibrations of light, and constant alterations in the scale of the details.

and development center, to be used jointly by ourselves and UNESCO. UNESCO accepted. It funded the cultural and educational program, on the condition that we would finance the construction of the workshop in its entirety.

The work was carried out by my brother Ermanno's building firm. It was the first time we had worked together since my earliest experiences of construction, since the time of my youthful studies of temporary structures. The two spirits of the family—architect and builder—were reunited for the occasion. Our father would have been happy.

This first joint project has led to others. At the moment we are working with UNESCO on two fascinating themes, particularly dear to us: the influence of climate and the use of natural light in architecture. We have also carried out two programs with the European Union, which concern systems of roofing with a high thermal inertia, and are aimed at reducing energy consumption and increasing the lifetime of building materials. With Ove Arup & Partners, we are also investigating a subject that has already cropped up in several of our works: the construction of roofs with a double lining, where the chamber of air in the middle acts as an insulator between the inside and the outside.

At the Scoglio Nave, greenery is an essential component of the space. The place itself derives its morphology from the requirements of cultivation: the site has been patiently banked and terraced by farmers in order to exploit a hostile terrain. The local vegetation, together with the cliffs, provides us with the placeform. The exotic crops, on the other hand, are an essential part of its function.

The plants surround and penetrate the construction, blending into the work spaces and appearing clearly through the glass walls. Working here, it is possible to attain a special form of absorption, linked to the sensation of being in contact with nature, the climate, the seasons. It is an immaterial element that has been captured by the architecture. Today specimens of bamboo, cane, and agave are grown in the laboratory and on the adjacent terraces. In the near future, specimens of marine flora will also be planted along the shore.

The UNESCO Laboratory and Workshop extends upward from the top of the rock with an inclined elevator. The work areas follow the slope and are set on different levels. In addition to creating a suggestive sequence of spaces, this solution permits a view of nature and sea at every level. Through the windows facing toward Genoa we can watch the spectacle of ships entering and leaving the harbor. All these "steps" are illuminated by sunlight coming through the pitched roof. We work all day with natural light, its level automatically adjusted by photosensitive skylights.

Artificial light, even from the most beautiful lamp, imparts a coldness that has no sense of time. Our light is a natural clock: it changes with the hour of the day and the weather, giving dif-

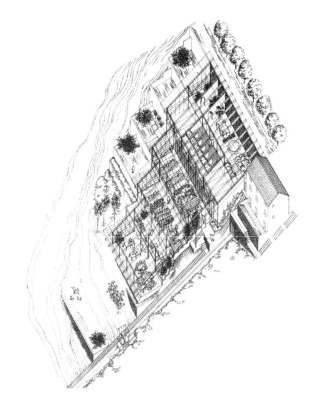

Axonometric; views of the facade facing the sea.

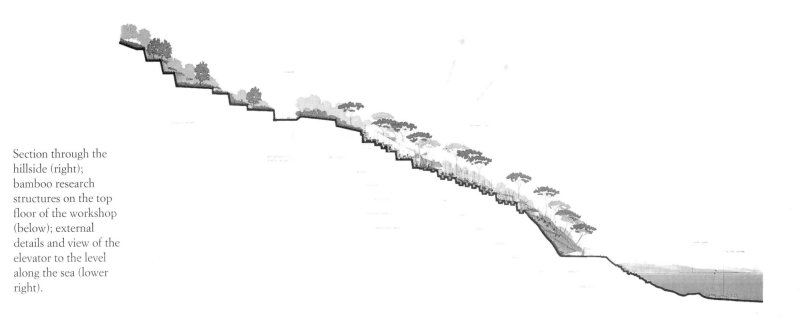

Section through the hillside (right); bamboo research structures on the top floor of the workshop (below); external details and view of the elevator to the level along the sea (lower right).

ferent colors to the walls, the worktables, the drawings. The louvers on the roof create blades of shadow, lending a variable texture to all the surfaces. Perhaps Mario Fazio, writer, journalist, and old friend, is right when he says that the light from overhead is the true protagonist of this space.

In a transparent building, the very concept of inside and outside changes. There is no rigid separation. There is no wall between me and the world, but an impalpable diaphragm. That is how it should be. An architect kept in a box tends to go off, to give him- or herself a trademark, develop a label, offer a product that is always the same.

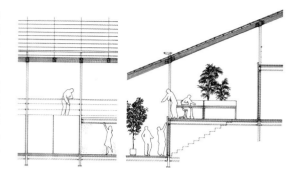

The studio has a spectacular route of access. The ascent from the road at sea level (the Scoglio Nave) up to the cliffs where the greenhouse-laboratory is built is by means of a transparent elevator. This runs under the open sky along a very steep track: a sort of gorge that follows the profile of the mountainside. About halfway up, the topography of the ground forces a sudden change of slope, producing a roller-coaster effect. The child in me really enjoys it, and he's not the only one. The elevator climbs up amid the vegetation, and the view of the sea gradually broadens until it takes in the entire horizon. At this point our greenhouse appears.

The construction extends like the wing of a butterfly. The side next to the elevator track is straight and has a staircase that runs along the inside of the glass wall and connects all the levels. The opposite side has a stepped profile, decreasing from the top to the bottom and offering a broad view.

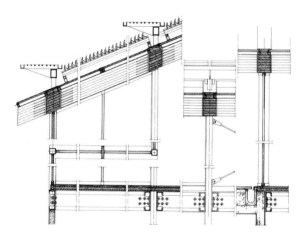

The visible element that dominates the construction is the frame of the roofing, made out of beams of laminated wood. The whole structure is supported by slender uprights of steel. The coupling elements are also made of steel. The walls, on the other hand, are made out of glass panels with no frames, held in place solely by thin tongues of the same material. The outer wall has been faced with rough stone on the outside, finished with plaster and painted on the inside. The pale pink color that we have used is typical of local buildings.

The regulation of light is carried out by a system of intelligent venetian blinds: sensors with solar cells cause them to close when the level of light outside increases. At dusk the lamps come on; these project from the walls and are directed toward reflective screens on the ceiling—thus even the artificial lighting comes from above.

All their lives architects build houses, factories, and offices designed to meet the needs of other people. Here I have made a garment to my own measure, to meet my own needs and those of the whole Building Workshop. I said earlier that the Punta Nave is a refuge, a response to the excess of information. This has nothing to do with a rejection of the city (an attitude that I neither preach nor practice). Rather I like to think of this place as a post-urban workshop.

The play of light, emphasized by the slats and drapes.

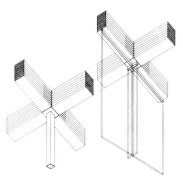

Details of the
connection and
support of the beams
and flooring.

The studio is made of space, sunlight, and nature, in accordance with the theories of Le Corbusier, but it is linked to the whole world, through instantaneous telecommunications. It owes a great deal to Reyner Banham's studies of the "well-tempered environment." In fact it places technology at the service of humanity, and not the other way around.

The Punta Nave is the architectural form assumed by my method of working: participation and reflection, technique and thought, love of tradition and continual search for the new. But there is something more: it is a building that expresses an ethic, my ethic, our ethic.

The machines that it uses do not destroy nature, but help us all to live with it in a better way. The space has no hierarchy: it is designed to provide everyone with the same pleasant surroundings in which to work. In the same way it has no barriers: architects, researchers, clients, technical staff—all are united under the same sloping roof, in sight of one another at the various levels of the building.

# 1991 **Nouméa** New Caledonia

## Tjibaou Cultural Center
Construction: 1993–

**The center is composed of ten "houses," all of different sizes and with different functions intended as a celebration of Kanak culture: it is a genuine village, with its own paths, greenery, and public spaces, located outside and in direct contact with the ocean. The project addresses the exploitation of currents of air and the difficulties of finding a way of expressing the tradition of the Pacific in modern language, and embodies the decisive contribution of the anthropologist.**

The Kanak are a people found all over the Pacific, but in particular concentration on New Caledonia. The island, with Nouméa as its capital, is a French territory, now set on a peaceful course toward autonomy. During the negotiations for independence, the local authorities asked the government in Paris to fund a major center devoted to Kanak culture, and their request was granted. The center, named after their leader Jean Marie Tjibaou, whose life came to a dramatic end in 1989, had a wide-ranging program: permanent exhibitions devoted to the community's traditions as well as events that would bring them back to life. For example, dance is very important in Kanak culture. In addition, the center was supposed to provide a bridge between tradition and modernity, between the past and the future of the Kanak people. An international invited competition was staged for the realization of this project, and that was how my adventure in New Caledonia started.

When we say "culture," we usually mean our own: a fine soup blended from Leonardo da Vinci and Freud, Kant and Darwin, Louis XIV and Don Quixote. In the Pacific it is not just the recipe that is different, but the ingredients as well. We can approach their soup with detachment, bringing our own cutlery. Or we can try to understand how it was born, why it has gone in certain directions, what philosophy of life has shaped it.

This was exactly why I won the competition: I didn't bring my own cutlery. All I brought were my skills and those of the Building Workshop: the techniques needed to create spaces and construct buildings. My proposal had made the effort to be born there, thinking Kanak. Working in the antipodes, with a people whose existence was almost unknown to me just a few months earlier, was a wonderful challenge. Moreover, it was not a tourist village that I had to build. I had to create a symbol: a cultural center devoted to Kanak civilization, the place that would represent them to foreigners and that would pass on their memory to their grandchildren. Nothing could have been more loaded with symbolic expectations.

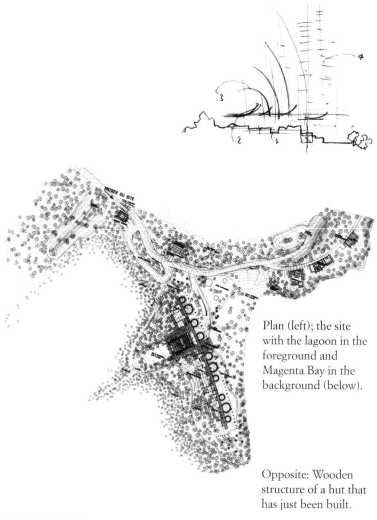

Plan (left); the site with the lagoon in the foreground and Magenta Bay in the background (below).

Opposite: Wooden structure of a hut that has just been built.

The spirit of the Pacific is ephemeral, and the constructions of the Kanak tradition are no exception. They are born out of unity with nature, using the perishable materials it provides. The continuity of the village in time is not based on the duration of the individual building, but on the preservation of a topology and a pattern of construction. When drawing up the project, we worked on both planes. We sought a strong link with the territory, which would embed the center in the geography of the island. From local culture we stole the dynamic elements, the tension that would serve to bind the construction to the life of the inhabitants.

The cultural center stands on a promontory to the east of Nouméa, in a natural setting of great beauty. The expression of an age-old tradition of harmony with nature, the center is not (and could not be) enclosed within a monumental structure. In fact it is not a single building: it is an assemblage of villages and open spaces planted with trees, of functions and routes, of solids and voids.

Surrounded on three sides by the sea, the site is covered with dense vegetation. Footpaths wind through the greenery to the villages: clusters of buildings closely linked to the context, whose semicircular layout defines open communal spaces. These spaces are used to exhibit elements from the life of the Kanaks, and periodically to revive ancient ceremonies.

Along the ridge of the promontory, a gently arched covered passage connects the different parts of the complex. The visual link between these and traditional Kanak villages is made very explicit: not just through the arrangement of the constructions, but through their form as well. They are curved structures resembling huts, built out of wooden joists and ribs; they are containers of an archaic appearance, whose interiors are equipped with all the possibilities offered by modern technology. These ten large spaces, each with a theme of its own, open unexpectedly onto the road running through the center, providing a dramatic passage from a compressed space to an expanded and unforeseen one.

The staves of the outer facing are of different widths and spaced in an uneven manner. The optical effect of slight vibration that this produces strengthens the affinity with the vegetation stirred by the wind. The wood chosen is iroko, which requires little maintenance and, in the way that we have used it, evokes the intertwined plant fibers of the local constructions.

One of the characteristics of the project is an investigation of the texture of materials: we have used laminated wood and natural wood, concrete and coral, aluminum castings and glass panels, tree bark and stainless steel, always in a quest for richness and complexity of detail. In spite of the uniformity of the basic model, the spaces inside can have very different characters. The huts that house exhibitions are covered with panels that have white inner faces, while the ones used as schoolrooms incorporate bookcases, and so on. Where the hut's function

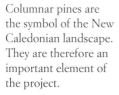

Columnar pines are the symbol of the New Caledonian landscape. They are therefore an important element of the project.

Dance and song represent an important part of Kanak culture.

Overleaf: A traditional village; detailed section through the base of the perimeter of a hut; elevation and two sections showing the competition project; section through the multimedia library.

177

requires, the roof and sides are transparent. The panels of glass are screened by external skylights.

Thanks to the strong formal analogy with the traditional vegetation and indigenous settlements, the huts unify the project. They are also the dominant element: there are ten of them, all of different sizes. Some are fairly small, while others are on a scale that matches the surrounding tall trees. The largest forms a clearly visible landmark with its twenty-eight meters of height, as tall as a nine-story building.

These constructions are an expression of the harmonious relationship with the environment that is typical of Kanak culture. The link is not just aesthetic, but functional too: exploiting the characteristics of the New Caledonian climate, the huts are equipped with a very efficient system of passive ventilation. Once again, a double roof has been used: the air circulates freely between two layers of laminated wood. The openings in the outer shell have been arranged to exploit the monsoon winds coming from the sea, or to induce the desired convection currents.

The flows of air are regulated by skylights. When there is a light breeze they open up to favor ventilation. As the wind grows stronger they close, starting with the ones at the bottom. The system was designed with the aid of computers and scale models tested in a wind tunnel. This system for air circulation also gives the huts a "voice." Together they make a distinctive noise, a sound: it is that of the Kanak villages and their forests.

Access to the cultural center is provided by a footpath winding along the coast, which marks a sort of change of dimension: starting at the parking lot, it wends its way through the thick native vegetation, leads to the stairs that climb the promontory, and finally reaches the courtyard of the entrance to the center, where the reception services are located.

The center is organized into three villages. The first is dedicated to exhibition activities. In the hut next to the entrance, a permanent show introduces visitors to Kanak culture. The buildings devoted to the history of the community and the natural environment of the island are located further along. Not far off is a space for temporary exhibitions. This village also has a partially sunken auditorium with seats for four hundred. At the back of the auditorium is an amphitheater for open-air performances.

The second village contains the offices used by the center's historians and researchers, curators of exhibitions, and administrative staff. The huts in front of the offices house a conference hall and a multimedia library. On the lower level, specimens of the island's traditional crops are grown on a series of terraces.

The village at the end of the path, set slightly apart from the flow of visitors, is devoted to creative activities. The huts house studios for dance, painting, sculpture, and music. On one side there is a school, where children are introduced to the local art forms.

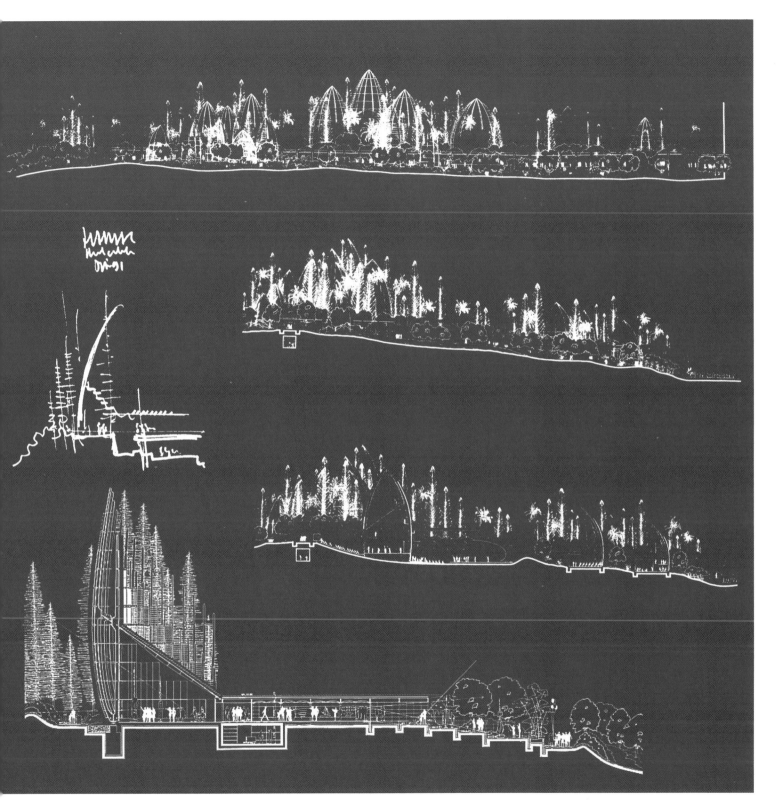

179

Another route has been laid out between the edge of the lagoon and the tip of the promontory, this time thematic in character. It was conceived with the aid of Alban Bensa, the anthropologist who worked on the project with us from beginning to end. It is called the "path of history." The Kanak representation of human evolution makes use of metaphors drawn from the natural world. Creation is seen as a water lily surrounded by flowering trees. Agriculture is symbolized by the terraced fields typical of the island, on which sweet potatoes and other food plants are grown. Themes such as the environment, death, and rebirth are illustrated in similar ways.

A true acceptance of the challenge inherent in the program took courage: it meant taking off the mental clothes of the European architect and steeping myself in the world of the people of the Pacific. In a discussion with anthropologists this seems a simple thing, and saying it makes a good impression. But it is very difficult to express the same concept in your own words at a Kanak banquet, where nothing is familiar: neither the language, nor the ritual, nor the food, nor the way of eating it.

The project for the Tjibaou Cultural Center, carried out in collaboration with Paul Vincent, was the most reckless of my many ventures into other fields. The dread of falling into the trap of a folkloric imitation, of straying into the realm of kitsch and the picturesque, was a constant worry throughout this work. At a certain point I decided to tone down the resemblance between "my" huts and those of local tradition, by reducing the length of the vertical elements and giving the shells a more open form; in the final version, in fact, the staves no longer meet at the top as had initially been planned. The wind tunnel proved me right, showing that this produced a greater effect of dynamic ventilation.

Throughout the process I received a great deal of support and understanding: the people of the island saw the huts as a sincere attempt to enter into the spirit of the Pacific Ocean and to pay a tribute to the local civilization. The Kanaks, convinced of the project's worth, have helped me to improve it: Marie Claude Tjibaou (Jean Marie's widow) and Octave Togna have been tireless fellow workers.

It has to be said that, quite apart from good intentions, from the rejection of any form of colonialism, and from the respect due other cultures, there was no alternative. A proposal based on our own models would simply not have worked in Nouméa. It was not feasible to offer a standard product of Western architecture, with a layer of camouflage over the top: it would have looked like an armored car covered with palm leaves.

A mistaken concept of universality would have led me to apply my mental categories of history and progress outside the context in which they developed, a grave error. True universality in architecture can be attained only through connection with the roots, gratitude for the past, and respect for the *genius loci*.

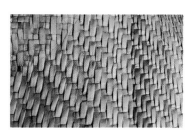

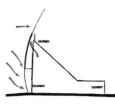
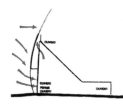
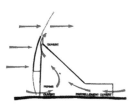
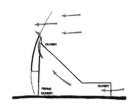

Functional scheme of natural ventilation.

Details of traditional hut construction.

Wind-tunnel test of
the huts (above);
wooden model (right).

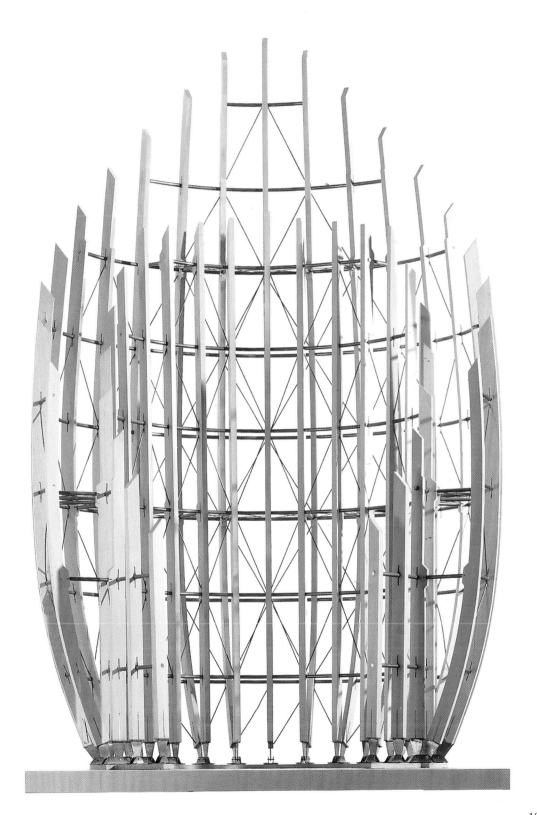

Some huts under
construction (left);
detail of the structure
of a hut (opposite).

# 1991 San Giovanni Rotondo

(Foggia) Italy

## Padre Pio Pilgrimage Church

Construction: 1995–

**The church is intended to serve the ever-increasing number of pilgrims flocking to visit the places where Padre Pio, the friar famous for his stigmata, used to live. The challenge presented by the project lies in the use of local stone as a structural material.**

The monastery at the time of the arrival of Padre Pio; a portrait of the friar.

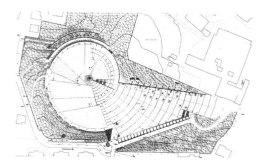

I tend to see obstinacy as a positive quality; I don't identify it with the pigheadedness of those who refuse to accept criticism, but with the legitimate conviction of those who stick up for their own ideas. Under these circumstances, persistence becomes a moral imperative, a sort of mission. This reminds me of Padre Gerardo.

Padre Gerardo is the administrator of the province with jurisdiction over the Capuchin monks of San Giovanni Rotondo, to whom Padre Pio of Pietralcina belonged. For half a century this small town in Puglia has drawn swarms of pilgrims: once to listen to the preaching of Padre Pio, already regarded as a saint in his own lifetime, and now to venerate his memory. In order to cope with such large numbers of devotees (hundreds of thousands every year) the brothers decided to build a larger church.

The ways of the creator are infinite, and so we shall never know who directed Padre Gerardo to my door, along with Giuseppe Muciaccia, the engineer now Director of the works. The request was put very courteously: would I design the temple? I hesitated, and then said no: I found the idea too intimidating. I thought that this would be the end of the story, but actually it was just the beginning.

Renzo Piano and Padre Gerardo.

Opposite: Computer images; plan; section. The large parvis and the church merge to create a single ceremonial space for special occasions.

The next morning an unusual message came out of the fax in my studio. It was a personal blessing from Padre Gerardo, a message that was repeated the following day, the day after that, and every morning for the next three weeks, until I gave in: "In your patience possess ye your souls" (Luke 11:19).

The ceremonial hall dedicated to Padre Pio will be built on top of the hill of San Giovanni Rotondo, not far from the Capuchin monastery and the existing church. It will be served by a new approach road intended to keep the vehicles of pilgrims out of the historic center of the nearby town.

Just like at Assisi, a large wall will run alongside the road leading up to the church: it will support twelve huge bells, to be used by the church to summon the faithful for services. The sound of the bells and the great size of the wall (twenty-five meters at its highest point) will make it a clear landmark from a distance. In fact the dome of the church, not very tall and

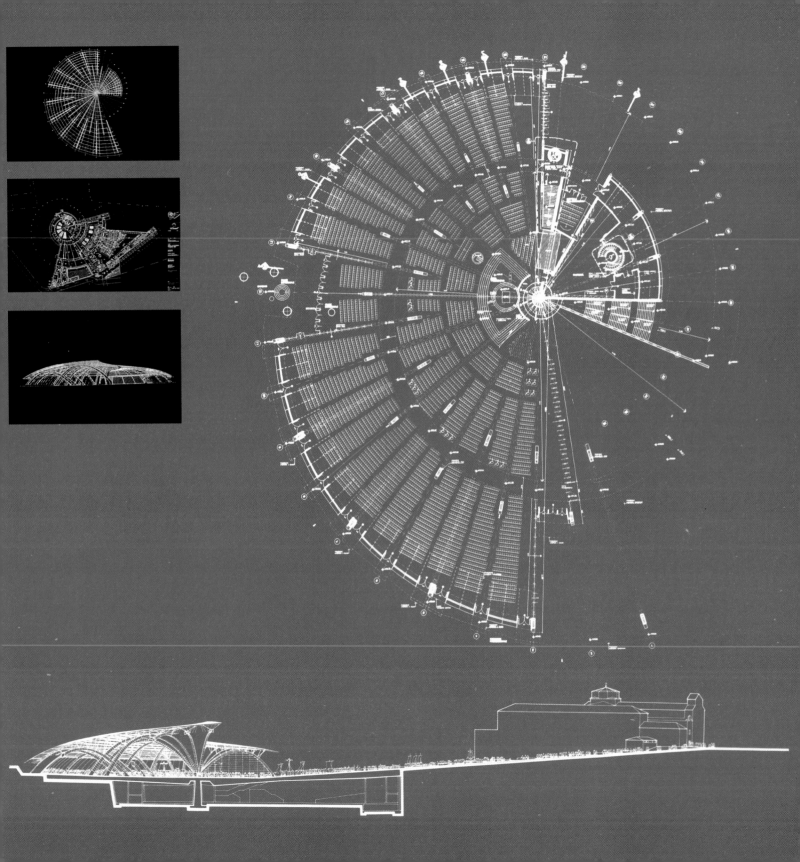

surrounded by trees, will not be visible until the visitor is close to the parvis. This triangular and gently sloping courtyard will invite pilgrims to make their way down to the church from the old Capuchin monastery. On feast days, it will be able to hold up to thirty thousand people. Room for another six thousand can be found inside the place of worship.

The aim of the project, on which Giorgio Grandi worked from the outset, was to create an open church, a building that would not intimidate the faithful but invite them to approach. For this reason it has not been given a monumental facade, but simply a glass front. The interior of the church will be visible from the square through this transparent wall. In addition, the dome will reach out toward the parvis in a friendly gesture of welcome, creating a sort of porch and stripping the entrance of all pomposity. To further minimize the difference between "outside" and "inside," the paving of the courtyard will extend into the church. The idea, as old as the liturgy itself, is that of the church as an "open house." Inside the floor will curve upward, becoming concave and creating an effect that to some extent mirrors the dome. The supporting arches of stone, just as Peter Rice had originally intended, will be arranged in a radial pattern.

Thanks to new technology (structural calculations carried out by computer and automatic cutting machines), we are experimenting with new ways of using the oldest construction material of all. In Padre Pio's church, stone will be used not just for the paving and roofing, but as a structural material as well: the main span of over fifty meters will perhaps be the longest supporting arch ever built out of stone. This is not an attempt to get into the record books; it is simply a desire to find out what can be done with stone today, almost a thousand years after the Gothic cathedrals were built. Technical virtuosity is not an end in itself, but meets the needs of a precise formal choice. The church at San Giovanni Rotondo springs out of the stone of the mountainside. Walls, parvis, supporting arches, and covering of the roof will all be made of stone. We have deliberately insisted on a single material as the expressive key to the design.

The space inside the church is rendered suggestive by the spiral form of the dome, which is high where it starts above the parvis and gradually shrinks toward the other end. This complex and articulated space will be in semidarkness. In contrast, shafts of direct sunlight will shine straight down onto the altar, creating a dramatic effect and concentrating attention on the focal point of the religious ceremony. The great "incident" of the baptismal font will interrupt the large space, dividing it up, and the same effect will be produced by the garden that will find its way into the church (an aspect on which my wife, Milly, is now working). Great importance will also be given to the presence of art: major artists have been asked to interpret the iconographic program drawn up by Monsignor Crispino Valenziano.

Computer study of the roofing.

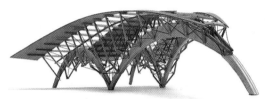

Model showing the stone arches that support the roof.

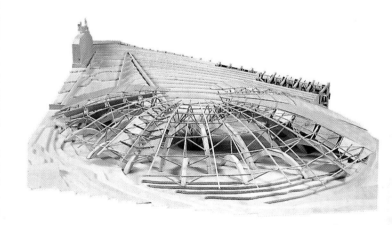

Wooden model of the structure. Stone is the main construction element of the church.

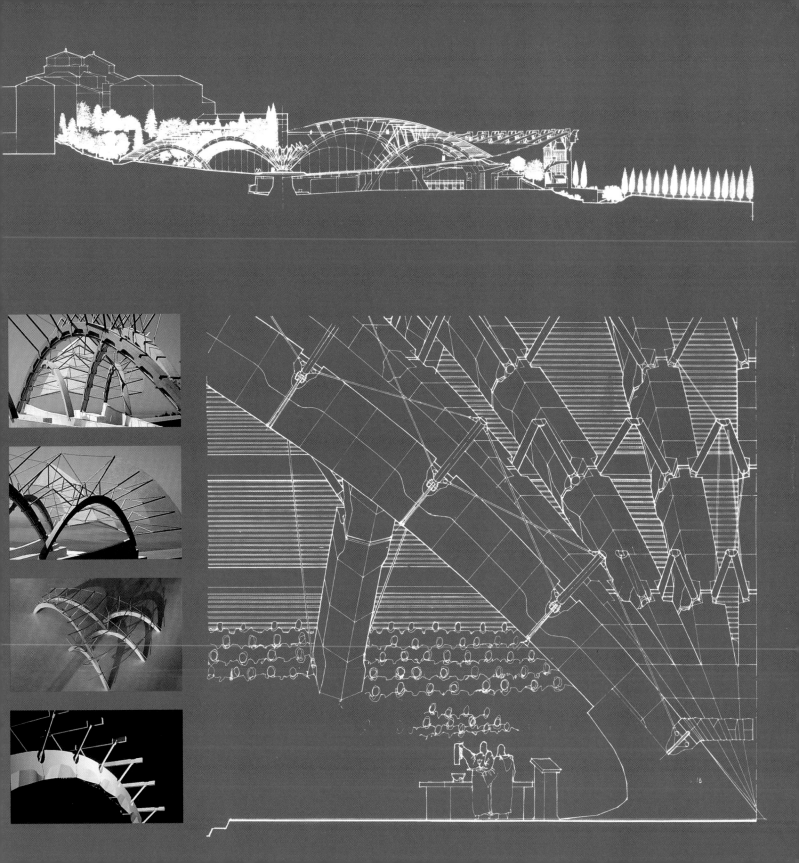

# 1991 Lodi (Milan) Italy

## Banca Popolare di Lodi

Construction: 1993–

**The new head office of this important Lombard credit institution provides the opportunity for an urban intervention that includes, along with the offices of the bank, other offices, stores, an auditorium, and public spaces immersed in greenery. In it, we further developed the theme of terra-cotta.**

Urban setting of the intervention.

This project is another one in which a company that has chosen to open up its own territory to nature and the circulation of passersby. It is a tendency that is spreading and that provides an excellent combination of the private company's need for promotion and public benefit. The "pieces of city" that are created in this way are unquestionably more pleasant than the old enclosed and protected administrative centers that had only one function.

The site on which the new headquarters of the bank will be built used to be occupied by the Polenghi Lombardo dairy plant. The idea of the project, worked out with Giorgio Grandi and Vittorio di Turi, was to reconstruct the urban block by creating a homogeneous front: almost a facade, but rendered permeable by clefts, lines of view, and passageways. Such a fragmented frontage does not represent a barrier, but is a formal device designed to allow a gradual discovery of the space inside.

The focus for the movements of pedestrians inside is a large plaza, covered by an extremely light tensile structure of glass and steel cables. The entrances to the bank face onto this plaza, along with those of the auditorium, which will also be used for stockholders' meetings: with its eight hundred seats, the auditorium is more than adequate for a small town like Lodi, and represents an important addition to the quality of urban life.

The space is characterized by several cylindrical blocks of different heights and diameters, faced with a very beautiful terra-cotta. In shape and color, they recall the typical granaries of the region. Just as farmers entrust the riches of the earth to their silos, the bank will entrust the riches of people's savings to its silos. With a sense of irony, and working with the management of the bank, we have given two of these structures the role of vaults.

This is a project that integrates and completes the city. It is a bastion, but it is also an internal public road. It is a bank—indeed, "the Bank"—but at the same time it is a square, embellished with greenery and blending harmoniously into the local building fabric.

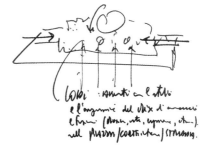

Sketch by Renzo Piano: the relationship between the square and the different functions.

Installation of a terra-cotta panel.

Terra-cotta, used as a double skin, is the unifying element of the project.

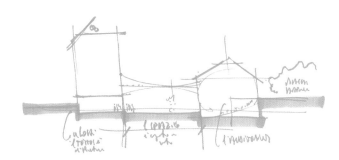

Sketch, plan, and details of the roofing of the square.

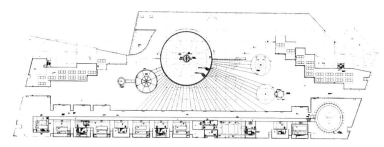

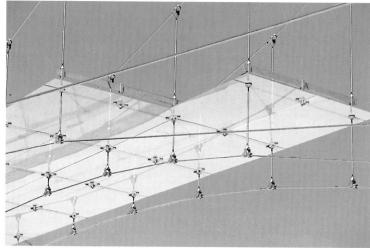

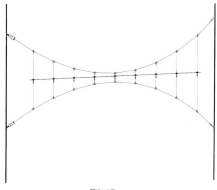

The square links the different public and private functions of the intervention, creating a strong connection with the city.

# 1992　**Berlin** Germany

## Potsdamer Platz Reconstruction

Construction: 1996–

**This project creates a "piece of city," starting from the legendary Potsdamer Platz, destroyed by war and city planners. It includes offices, housing, a hotel, stores, restaurants, a cinema, a casino, and a theater.**

Berlin brings the theme of the city to its point of greatest development and greatest tension, for in the twentieth century Berlin has experienced and represented all the excesses of which a metropolis is capable. It has been the center of cultural and social life in Europe, and the city most devastated by war; it has been the physical symbol of the division of the world into blocks, and is now the scene of the most frenzied urban development of the end of the century.

A few years ago, Berlin was a city divided by the wall. Four flags flew over its public buildings, emblems of the victorious powers of the Second World War: the United States, the Soviet Union, France, and Great Britain. There were no German flags, and in any case, all the great institutions of Germany were elsewhere. It was almost a no-man's-land, loved and respected, but somewhat neglected.

In the effort to restore Berlin to its full dimension as a city and a capital, a frenzied mechanism of property development has been set in motion. Not only public bodies but also German businesses have been "looking for a home" in Berlin. The huge influx of people and wealth has given the city the resources it needs to reinvent its future, and this is the positive side. But it has also created an enormous problem.

Potsdamer Platz, heart of the city in the 1920s, bombed and then razed by city planners and the Cold War. It was an empty space, which is now filled by this new piece of city.

Cities are beautiful because they are created slowly; they are made by time. A city is born from a tangle of monuments and infrastructures, culture and market, national history and everyday stories. It takes five hundred years to create a city, and fifty to create a quarter. We (and I say we because many other architects are involved, in the same project or in different ones) have been asked to reconstruct a large chunk of Berlin in the space of five years.

After reunification, many companies decided to allocate funds for the restructuring of various areas of the city. All the schemes were subject to international competitions: first of all, naturally, was the one for the urban development plan. On the one hand, then, was an enormous contribution from private investment; on the other were strict terms laid down by an urban development plan (drawn up along the lines set out by Hans Stimman, the city's chief architect) in order to keep property development within a framework of public utility. The first lot to be made the subject of a competition was the largest and

most prestigious area, Potsdamer Platz, straddling the line between the former East Berlin and the former West Berlin. Not far off stands the Reichstag. The bunker where Hitler spent his last days was located a short distance away, near the Brandenburg Gate.

The project envisaged not just the urbanistic reclamation of the district, but also the reconstruction of over half the buildings in it. The sponsor of the intervention was Daimler-Benz, which intended to build a new headquarters as part of the scheme of restructuring. At the time, the company was run by Edzard Reuter, son of the first burgomaster of Berlin after the war.

The competition, in which fifteen planners were invited to take part, was won by our project, perhaps because it had the most unified dimension of all those submitted. We had profited by our experience of working on "pieces of city," which had commenced with the Molo in Genoa and then moved to the Lingotto in Turin and the Cité Internationale in Lyons, and perhaps we had learned to recognize the important urban connections between the new and the existing.

One of the rules in the urban development plan (assigned to the German architects Hilmer & Sattler for the zone of Potsdamer Platz) was that of conforming to Berlin's traditional pattern of city blocks. The underlying philosophy was to try to bring the historic buildings and streets of Berlin back to life, to seek to reinterpret their models and establish a bridge with the past. This was one of Stimman's fixed points, and legitimately so. He guided us with Prussian discipline. We had two alternatives: obeying without question, or disobeying and finding good reasons for it.

The past: it is easy to say. Paradoxically, the people of Berlin venerate their past, but they also like to erase it, cultivating a (comprehensible) desire for innocence. In Berlin, you find yourself working in a place that is not just historic, but mythic. Potsdamer Platz was, in the 1920s and 1930s, the center of Berlin's social and cultural life, when Berlin was the center of Europe's cultural life, an extraordinary place, which really had everything: commerce, business, music, theater, cinema, and so on. You can look for traces of all this, but all you find are ghosts. Everything has vanished. Only the layout of the old streets is still visible. Potsdamer Platz is a desert created by the war, which destroyed the city, but completed by the planners, who swept away the shards.

Berlin suffered heavy damage from the Allied bombing raids, as did many other cities which still rose from their ruins. Even after the bombs, enough traces were left to rebuild. But in this case, the politicians wanted to forget the earlier Berlin, and the city planners wanted their tabula rasa. And so together, caught up in a frenzy, they wiped out the past.

I have noticed that this desire for innocence, for forgetfulness, has not disappeared. The Berlin Wall, for example, was

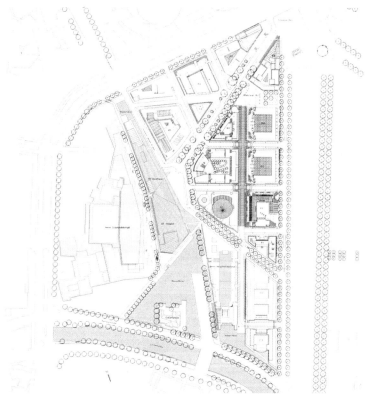

The plan clearly shows the importance of the relationship with Scharoun's National Library (the building on the left).

The square, the central element of urban attraction, links the old Potsdamerstrasse with the theater and the library behind it (right); the facades of the different buildings have varying degrees of transparency, according to their function (above).

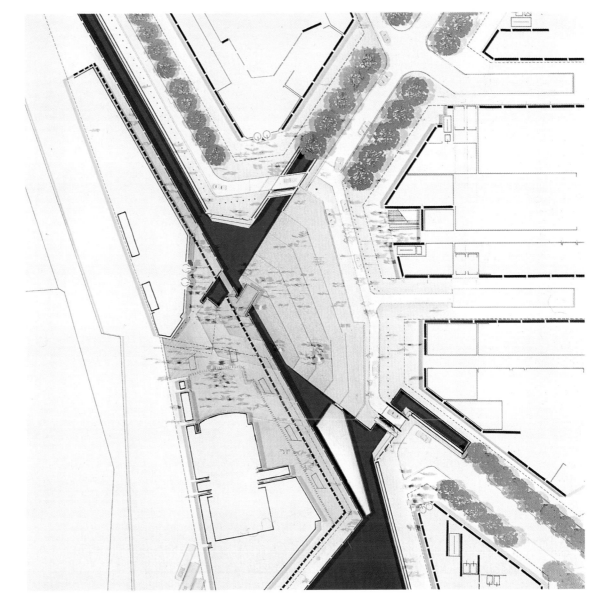

certainly not a beautiful object, but it was a monument that symbolized the history of the city for twenty-eight years. In 1989, it was time to forget again. So the wall was cleared away, demolished, removed.

The area of Potsdamer Platz comprises the great complex of the Kulturforum, made up of the Gallery (Mies van der Rohe), the Berlin Philharmonic, and the National State Library (Hans Scharoun). Scharoun's library was built in 1967, at the height of the Cold War, when it seemed obvious to everyone that Berlin was never going to be reunified. Between the two halves of the city and the two political systems that they represented were still profound feelings of ill will, which Scharoun transformed into architecture: his library treated the wall as a city limit, and turned its back on it, facing toward what it considered the center of the western city. What lay beyond the wall did not interest it; it simply did not exist. The architects of East Berlin behaved in a similar way, constructing ugly workers' housing right on the other side of the wall in the name of a misunderstood social mission on the part of architecture.

Now, a building such as Scharoun's, of such monumental dimensions and with the wrong orientation, represents no small obstacle. To call it wrong is misplaced, of course, for the architect's provocation went far beyond: it had (and has) an extraordinary inner energy, which emanates from the complex and impossible-to-grasp structure of the reading rooms. Thus we had to be careful not to betray the master, not to force his work into a presumed "urban order." Therefore, alongside the massive structure we set, as if to complete it, the equally anomalous and unpredictable volumes of the theater and casino, along with the covered square that separates and unites them.

This is no gratuitous gesture: in addition to its urbanistic role, the new complex has a precise functional ratio, for it contains the hypothesis of a second entrance to the library itself. In this way Berlin becomes once again a complex, variegated, and multifunctional urban fabric at the very point where it was once split in two by the wall. For the first time, perhaps, the Kulturforum has been integrated into the city, linking up with the densely constructed area to the east and dissolving into the Tiergarten to the west and northwest.

Several times we had tackled the problem of urban voids, of reusing spaces left empty by the transfer of industrial activities. But it was not the same thing. The Lingotto factory in Turin and the port of Genoa had lost their function, but retained a strong identity and an intense symbolic value: they were voids that gave off an incredible energy, like black holes in space. And we used this energy in their redesign.

In a way, the Berlin Wall had a function that ran directly counter to the city. Urban life is made up of social ties and economic relations. The wall represented the negation, the prohibition of both. Even after its fall, indeed even more so after its

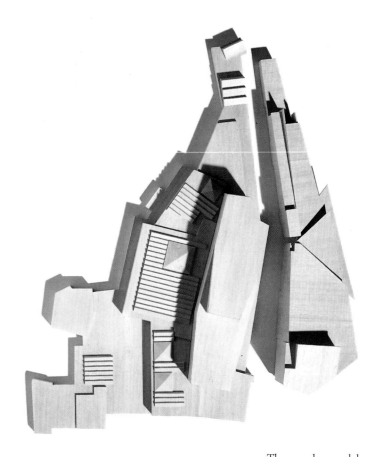

The wooden model clearly reveals the inevitable relationship between the building housing the theater and casino and Scharoun's National Library.

Opposite: Elevation; roof plan; theater plan; section.

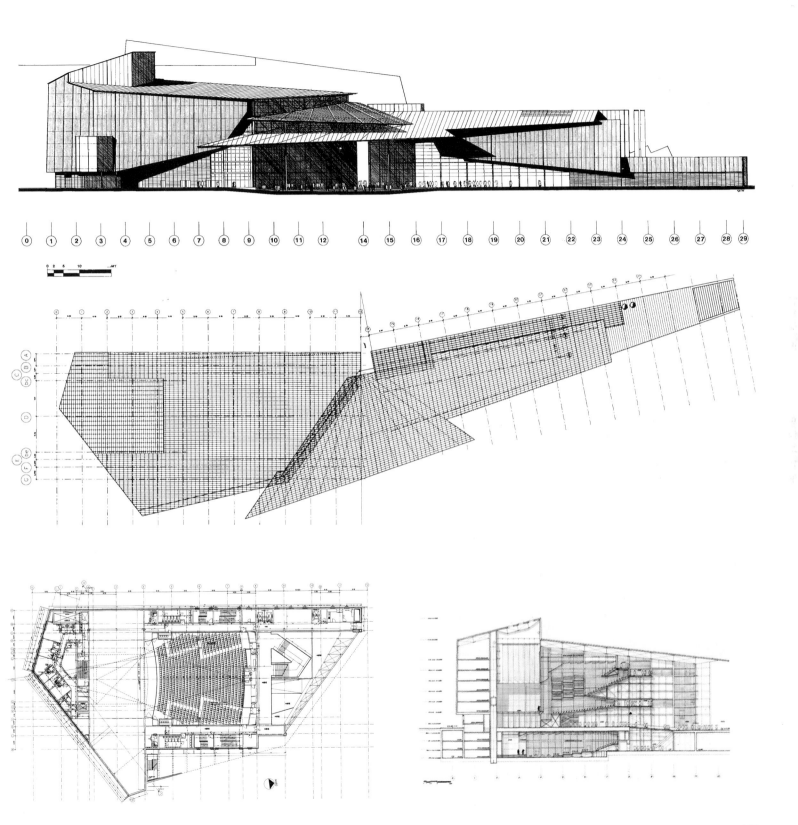

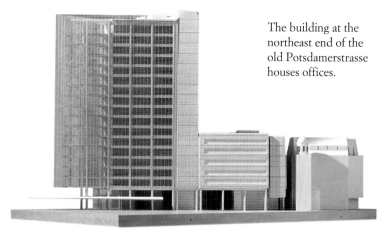

The building at the northeast end of the old Potsdamerstrasse houses offices.

In the model, the building on the right is the Weinhaushut, the only surviving trace of the splendors of the past.

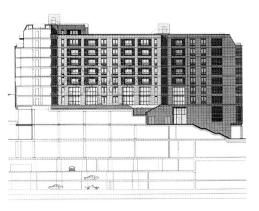

The block is made up
of a group of
apartments laid out
around an internal
garden.

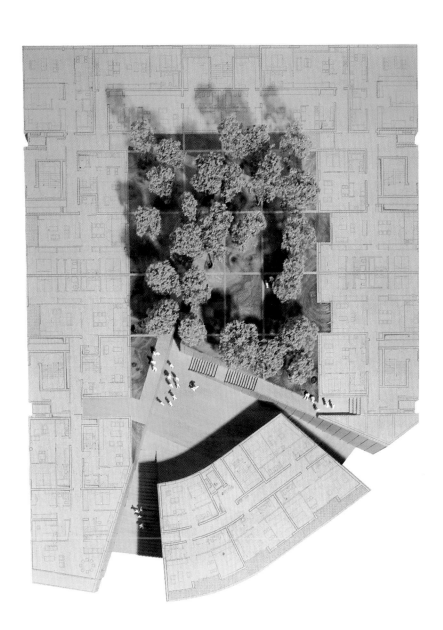

fall, the wall was a wound that had to be closed. We drew on the healing power of the city, with all its functions and all the potency of its daily life, but we also kept in mind that it was a piece of not just any city, but of Berlin. And so it is of a city of voids, a city filled with nature, invaded by water.

The new role of nature is the boldest and at the same time the most fascinating element of the project. Instead of the division created by humanity, we have substituted vegetation and water, as new linking and hinging elements. The woods of the Tiergarten descend from above to invade the area of the project. This dovetailing serves to connect the Kulturforum to the old Berlin park, so that the complex becomes its offshoot.

On the other side, the Landwehrkanal extends to form a lake that invades the scheme from the south, creating a generous expanse of water. The liquid surface, with its transparency and incessant vibration, lightens the volumes and takes away their materiality. At the same time it is a fantastic binder, an element of transition that connects the entire area of the intervention to the rest of Berlin, a city of water and nature.

To the east and north, the project conforms to the disciplined division into blocks required by the urban development plan. This harder, more rigorous urban order interprets another important aspect of Berlin: the city of history.

The size of the territory involved is enormous: six hundred thousand square meters. When the work is finished, it is envisaged that forty thousand people will live and work in the zone. The number will be raised to eighty thousand during the day by the people drawn by the public, commercial, and cultural activities that will be concentrated here. The scale of the project is really that of a small city, and that is how we have treated it, trying to re-create the mix of functions that a city needs to work. Above all, we have sought to satisfy a key requirement of social life by defining a center of aggregation: a square.

The new square envisaged by the project is the hinging element between Alte Potsdamerstrasse and the Kulturforum, and is the fulcrum of the intervention, from the viewpoint of both form and urban function. Berlin is austere, often gray; our project sets out to be a piece of city in a different key, one of joy and sharing. Note that all this is philologically correct. Berlin also knows how to be a lively and cheerful city. We can look back, beyond the tragedies of the war and the postwar period, to the festive atmosphere of the beginning of the century, when it was one of the most dynamic and interesting cities in the world.

In order for the square to become the center of life in this new Berlin, it is necessary to make it lively at all times of day. All the main functions envisaged by the urban development plan will be installed: stores of every kind, residences (various types of accommodations and a hotel), offices, and leisure facilities (restaurants, theater, casino)—sacred and profane, all together. Another strong glue will be the fairly widespread use

The spherical IMAX movie theater inserted into the block that had previously been intended for offices.

The movie theater will look like a moon atop the Potsdamer Platz complex. The addition of a new function is extremely important to the re-creation of an urban character.

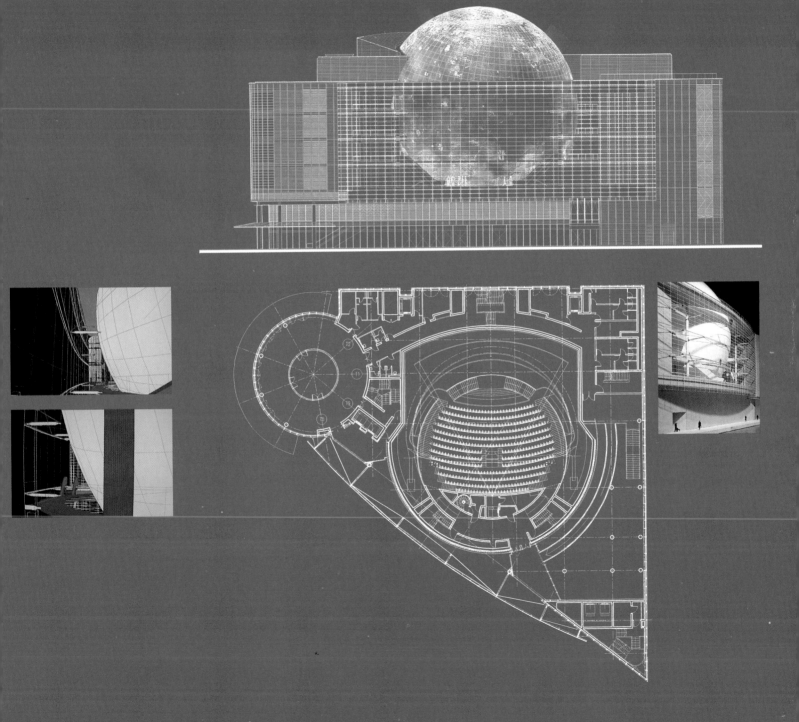

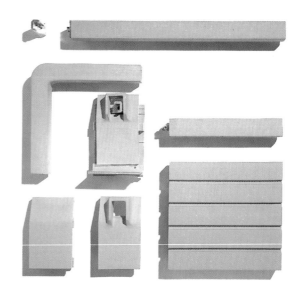

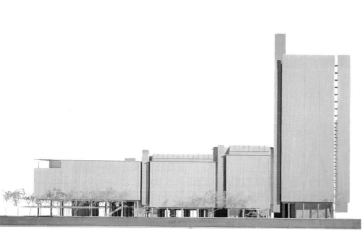

The office tower for Debis, the subsidiary of Daimler-Benz that is managing the intervention. Its facade diminishes the effect of transparency by increasing the terra-cotta elements. This material ensures coherence, and not just among Renzo Piano's buildings. It is the unifying element that he inserted into the master plan and that will be used in different ways by the other architects involved.

of art, in line with a program that has been followed with great care and competence by Hans Jurgen Baumgart: one large work by Tinguely has already been acquired.

A series of new buildings will extend all the way along Alte Potsdamerstrasse, run around the eastern edge of the new square, and curve along the edge of the canal. About halfway along the sequence will be a large movie theater with a panoramic screen. On the outside, the great spherical volume of the theater will assume a totally unaccustomed form: a large moon plopped down in the center of Berlin, an agreeable meteorite that has fallen right there, in an impetus of affection.

The arc of buildings along Alte Potsdamerstrasse will terminate with the tall tower of the Debis offices (the subsidiary of the Daimler-Benz group that is managing the intervention). The Debis tower will fit in with the rest of the constructions, and yet clearly assert its identity: by its height, as well as by its characteristic appearance, the result of a combination of transparent and opaque surfaces. These last, made of terra-cotta, form a double skin of facing, continuing the line of research begun with Rue de Meaux and IRCAM. From the Debis tower onward, the buildings will grow steadily less transparent, resembling more and more the traditional brick houses of Berlin.

In urban interventions modernization must not undermine the character of the city. The terra-cotta facing will provide a unifying element even with areas outside the project. In fact the material has been adopted by the urban development plan, and is one of the key elements of the set of instructions that my office (responsible for the master plan as well as the design of eight of the buildings) has drawn up for all the other architects at work in the zone: Arata Isozaki, Hans Kohloff, Lauber und Wöhr, Rafael Moneo, and Richard Rogers

As in all large-scale urban interventions, the transformation will be at once the cause and the effect of social change. Berlin is, in any case, a city undergoing a process of tumultuous evolution. After the wall was brought down it experienced migration on an epic scale. It used to be a city of old people and very young punks, where it was hard for anyone of an age in between to live: too difficult both for business and for the family. Suddenly it was invaded by big companies and their employees, managers, and consultants. At the same time, Berlin has been accepting more Germans from the east, with their naïveté and expectation, fears and hopes. The large construction sites have attracted a whole population of Russians, Turks, and Poles. As the writer Peter Schneider has pointed out, this immigration represents a powerful injection of energy: of men and women with vitality and freshness in an unfamiliar world. We share Schneider's hope that the immigrants will bring energy and perhaps even gaiety to a very cultured and subtle city, but one that has been rendered sad and weak by fifty years of siege.

The immense construction site in Berlin; divers at work on the laying of the foundations, accomplished without pumping out the water.

I am used to expecting anything to happen on a construction site, but before Berlin I had never used divers on dry land. It happened like this. We had to start digging the foundations for the Debis tower. The site is halfway between the Spree River and the Landwehrkanal, and so there was water just a few meters below the surface. This was where the problem arose. The Greens objected that drainage on such a scale would have lowered the water table, with unpredictable consequences for the ground and for the city's water supply. Another solution had to be found, and so we set to work with the Faulkner engineering office.

If the water could not be drained, we were going to have to work in it: we called in the divers. They came from Russia, chiefly Odessa, and from the Netherlands. There were a hundred and twenty of them, all experts in maritime work. They worked at a depth of fifteen meters, immersed in total darkness. It was winter, and at a certain point the surface of the water froze. Our divers were overjoyed. I found out then that everything was simpler for them under such terrible conditions: their diving suits were heated, and they were easily able to find the point where the previous shift had stopped work. They had only to lower themselves into the same hole in the ice to find themselves right at their destination.

When the construction of the Debis tower was complete, at the end of October 1996, a great public celebration was organized in Berlin. It was attended by all the highest civic authorities and the whole of the Daimler-Benz management. I went with Christoph Kohlbecker, our local partner, and Bernard Plattner, who is the member of my studio in charge of the project. It was a great party: Roger Baumgarten, Giorgio Ducci, Navia Mecattaf, Joost Moolhuijzen, Jean Bernard Mothes, and Muritz van den Staav from the Building Workshop were all there. The only people missing from our work group were Morten Bush Peterson, Antoine Chaaya, Patrick Charles, Misha Kramer, Joachim Ruoff, and Erik Volz. Then there were the friends from Daimler-Benz: Edzard Reuter, whom I hadn't seen for a long time, and Manfred Gentz, our boss right from the start and an indefatigable point of reference for the project, together with Hans-Jürgen Albrecht and Karlheinz Bohn. The show put on for the celebration was a unique, and perhaps unrepeatable event: a ballet of cranes—not the birds, but mechanical cranes. Daniel Barenboim conducted the orchestra from a lifting platform, so that he could be seen by the crane operators. Following the score, twenty cranes (guided by incredible, highly skilled technicians) moved perfectly in time. This spectacle expressed all the energy of the construction site: a great force capable of measured, sure, and gentle movements. A friend of mine used to say that cranes are an essential, irreplaceable part of the urban landscape. He should have seen them dance. I have never seen such big objects move with such agility.

The construction site is always an adventure and there is always something unusual going on. At the Potsdamer Platz we even saw cranes dancing at the direction of Daniel Barenboim.

# 1992 Houston Texas

## Cy Twombly Gallery

Construction: 1993–95

**This small building, located near the Menil Collection, houses a permanent exhibition of the works of Cy Twombly. Here, too, the principal source of light is natural, filtered by four roofs of different materials.**

I always try to make my works living creatures, projects capable of growing and changing with time and use. Every now and then it happens that the creatures come back to look for me.

One day I received a welcome visit from Dominique de Menil and Paul Winkler. They wanted a small museum alongside the Menil Collection: approximately one thousand square meters devoted to a permanent exhibition of the pictures and sculptures of Cy Twombly. The gallery for Twombly was to be designed by the same hand, but at the same time, was to be a distinct entity: not an added wing, and still less a building in competition with the main museum.

Cy Twombly spends his life between Virginia and Rome, and is obviously one of Mme. de Menil's favorite artists. He is a modest person who, when asked to express a preference among the various designs, always opted for the most frugal, and least ostentatious. An outer facing of stone had been proposed, but he preferred raw concrete. For the flooring, he wanted planks of American oak in their natural color, not painted black like the ones in the Menil Collection. I had already worked on projects in close contact with artists from various fields, as well as with many musicians (Boulez, Berio, Nono, Abbado). I have collaborated with Jean Tinguely, who made a series of sculptures for Centre Pompidou, with Emilio Vedova for Nono's *Prometeo*, and with Shingu in Genoa, Amsterdam, and Turin.

Twombly, though very different in character, had equally strong opinions on materials and colors. The same thing had happened to Philip Johnson when he worked on the Rothko Chapel, which stands on a block close to the Menil Collection. Rothko had expressly asked for the chapel to be faintly lit, for that was how he thought his works should be seen.

The new gallery is set amid the bungalows that surround the "museum village." So that it does not look like a mere adjunct of the collection, it has no colonnaded porch, and is not faced with staves of wood, but rather with ocher-toned concrete. In spite of their similar scales, the two buildings produce very different effects. The Cy Twombly Gallery is more peaceful, more sober—an impression that is accentuated by the dimmer lighting inside.

Conceptually, the museum housing the Menil Collection is a single flexible space, which is divided by movable partitions and can be prepared in different ways to house different pieces

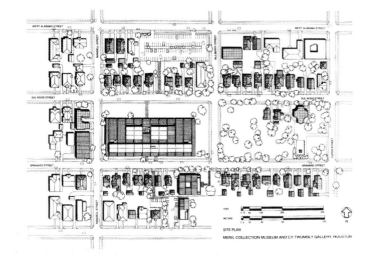

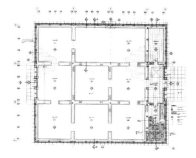

Overall plan of the "museum village" showing the new gallery located immediately to the south of the Menil Collection, not far from the Rothko Chapel (top); external view of the gallery, with the main museum visible at the right (above); plan of the gallery, which is based on a square module (left).

Renzo Piano with Cy
Twombly and Ottavio
Paz.

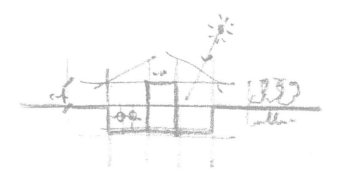

The gallery is built out
of relatively modest
materials, with an
outer facing of raw
concrete and a floor of
natural American oak,
according to the
artist's own
instructions.

from the large collection. The Cy Twombly Gallery, on the other hand, is made to measure for a single artist and his works. The structure is thus more rigorous and better defined.

Unlike the collection, which houses a number of services as well, the new building contains nothing but exhibition spaces. The design of the rooms is based on a structural grid of three by three feet, repeated three times on each side. Each square is an independent gallery. All the galleries, with the exception of the one in the middle, are illuminated by natural light from the ceiling.

The roof takes the form of a series of superimposed layers that filter the light. The highest is a metal grating and the lowest (immediately above the exhibition space) is made of fabric. Between these two layers is a grid of solar deflectors and a layer of glass with fixed skylights. Here too, all the systems for opening, closing, and adjustment of the deflectors are electronically controlled to ensure the optimal level of light. As with the Menil Collection, the work of Shunji Ishida and Mark Carroll, who this time were joined by Michael Palmore, made an invaluable contribution to the project.

In the collection the works are put on show for brief periods in rotation. The Cy Twombly Gallery houses a permanent exhibition, and so the works are much more vulnerable to damage by light. Consequently the level of illumination is lower and constant: 300 lux, as opposed to 1,000 in the museum. In addition, the floor of natural wood reflects more light and contributes to a more diffuse, less direct, and less dramatically overhead illumination.

On the day the gallery opened I had an opportunity for a long talk with Cy Twombly. The poet Octavio Paz was also there and said some very sensitive things about the relationship between Twombly's work and the atmosphere of the small museum. It seemed to them, and to me too, that it helped to make the artist's extremely subtle graffiti even more vibrant and mysterious.

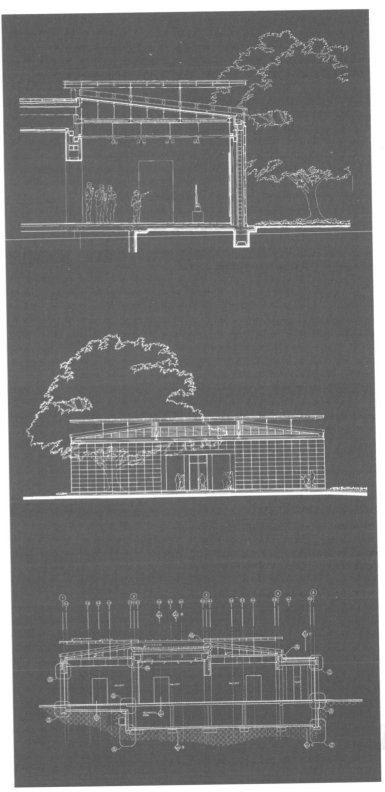

Section of an exhibition hall, showing the various parts of which the roof is composed (top); elevation (above); section (right).

Details of the roofing system.

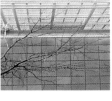

Interior views of some of the exhibition halls.

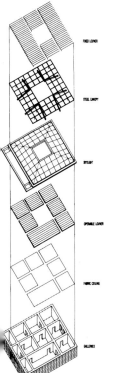

Axonometric of the roofing system with superimposed layers.

# 1992 **Amsterdam** Netherlands

## National Center for Science and Technology

Construction: 1994–97

**This is a new building for the NINT, with its interactive scientific and technological exhibitions. Its roof forms a square overlooking Amsterdam.**

You could say that the National Center for Science and Technology has some nerve: it stands all by itself in the middle of the port of Amsterdam, sticking out into the sea. It is set right on top of the entrance to the underwater tunnel that runs beneath the Oosterdok, heading north.

In a city, indeed in a whole country that has had to wrest its living space from the sea, what better location could there be for a monument to science and technology? The Netherlands is a country where there is no room to spare, and there was nowhere else to put the building; but the site has allowed for the creation of an explicit relationship with the city, free of compromises.

Amsterdam is famous for being a flat city: one of the few in Europe where there are no raised public spaces: squares, ramparts, terraces. You can see the urban landscape from the windows of the houses, it is true, but never from the street. In Paris or Rome, you climb some steps and the expanse of the city is revealed. In Amsterdam, however, there is no way to see it from above. The roof of our building, which is also a square, is probably the only public place in Amsterdam that is open to the light and offers a view of the old city. This is the urban element that characterizes the project.

There is tension with the place here, and this tension is strong. The *topos* is not the nature of the site, but rather a work of engineering constructed by someone else a quarter of a century earlier.

The museum's response to its context is one of extreme clarity. If the city appears as two-dimensional, the construction will accentuate its three-dimensionality, until it unexpectedly assumes a form that is projected upward and outward. If at the base of the museum there are cars that go downward, that descend into the tunnel under the sea, then on one side of the building, asymmetrically, will be set a ramp to induce an opposite movement, taking pedestrians up to the sloping roof, the "square" of the complex.

The square will be a place open to all, a pleasant place to stroll, partly because it is exposed to the sun (when there is sun). On it will be set a number of sculptures by Shingu, works based on interaction with the sun, wind, and water. In front, and surrounding it on three sides, is the sea.

Wharf on which the project was carried out (top); great Dutch works of engineering (above); model of the building, which juts out into the harbor (below); the finished building (right).

Perhaps this project is another postcard from the past, for the structure alludes to the ship: it does not pretend to be a piece of city, but belongs to the harbor; it does not stand, but floats above the entrance to the tunnel, supported by a structure of underwater pilings (obviously the underpass has foundations of its own). The brick walls provide a connection with the city. The rest of the construction is completely clad in copper. Here, once again, we applied a technique with which we are now familiar: covering complex curves with standard metal panels. Exposure to atmospheric agents will soon turn the surface green. The bas-relief is of brick, like the city. But the visible surface, the part that stands out against the skyline of Amsterdam, is made of metal. In this, the tension between object and topography is strong.

As at the Bercy 2 Shopping Center and the Kansai Air Terminal, the structure has a form that responds to the context, and does not reveal the arrangement of the spaces inside. The interior of the science center is organized on different levels that cut diagonally across the building, linked by large holes in the floors, which are illuminated from above. Staircases also pass through these gaps. The wells of light create a sophisticated sequence of spaces, providing a visual connection between the various parts of the construction. As soon as visitors come into the entrance hall they are presented with a view of all the spaces. The apex of the sequence is the room set at the top of the building, enclosed in the curve of the bow. At a fifth level, accessible by means of another staircase, is a panoramic restaurant, with a small terrace.

The ground floor is almost entirely of glass: the copper cladding appears to break off at the height of an imaginary waterline. At the end of this level is the main entrance (also visible to people driving through the tunnel), which opens a square facing onto the old part of the city. At the side are the now obligatory retail store and the workshops of the museum. As in the case of the Menil Collection, the public can see "behind the scenes," getting a momentary glimpse of objects that will be put on view in the future.

The ground floor is paved with tiles, continuing the pattern of the paving outside. This gives the level an extroverted character that sets it apart from the rest of the museum. The other floors, gently illuminated from above and bounded by walls that are not perpendicular, provide introverted spaces, suited to scientific exhibitions. The ten thousand square meters of exhibition space are being prepared to house permanent displays on the subjects of energy, communications, and biotechnology.

It will also be possible to reach the museum by sea, through a long pedestrian tunnel from Amsterdam's central station. Once again, the relationship with the city will be mediated by the harbor.

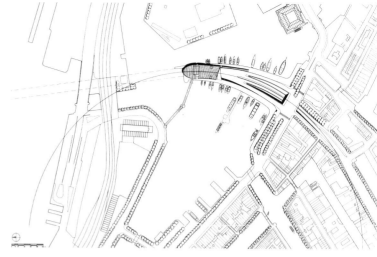

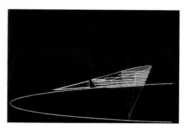

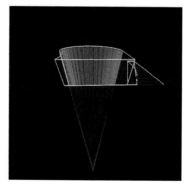

Overall plan (top); model (above); computer studies (left); east elevation (below).

Section showing the route leading from the "square" into the museum.

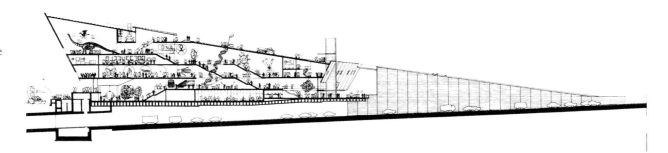

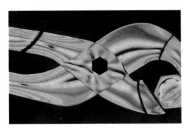

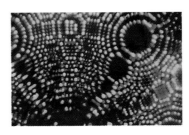
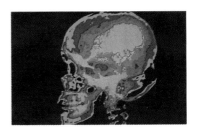

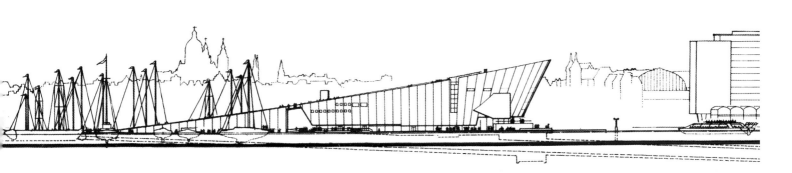

In November 1996 we visited the site with Olaf de Nooyer, the architect of the studio that is supervising the project, and the client, Joost Douma. Joost looked around with an air of absorption. He nodded in response to what I was saying, but it was clear that he was reflecting. Finally, with the typical dryness of the Dutch, he declared: "I really don't know how it could have been done differently." He wanted to pay me a great compliment, and I took it as such.

The installation of laminated-wood panels, which form the walls of the building.

Views of different phases of the construction work. The outer facade is made of preoxidized copper panels, which were installed by the system usually used for the roofs of churches or for zinc roofing.

### Reconstruction of the Atelier Brancusi

Construction: 1993–96

**This project was for the reconstruction of the Atelier Brancusi, demolished at the end of the 1950s, in front of the Centre Pompidou. It is a reconstruction faithful to the spirit of the original studio.**

Constantin Brancusi's studio was his most important work of art; a place filled with a vast number of different objects: pieces of wood, marble, stone, and plaster that were either already sculptures or on the point of becoming them. Brancusi invented machines to make his works rotate, but the rotation was so slow that it took minutes to realize that they were moving. It was an inner landscape, and had to change gently. This was the spirit of Brancusi's studio.

One day, shortly before he died, the decision was made to demolish the whole of the area (Impasse Ronsin, it was called, and many artists worked there, including the young Jean Tinguely). So Brancusi made his will: he left all his work—sculptures, drawings, paintings, photographs—to the French state on the condition that they remained in his studio. Was he hoping to halt the bulldozers? Or did he simply want to save his works from dispersion, ensuring that their context be preserved?

When I was given the task of building the Atelier Brancusi, I talked at great length to everyone who had known and spent time with him: Pontus Hulten first of all. Together we tried to understand what it meant to be faithful to the artist's will. I immediately discarded the idea of creating an exact copy of his studio: just how perfect should it have been—down to the cracks in the wall and the stains on the carpet? Certainly not: the result would have been a pointless waxworks museum, or at best an exercise in the anthropological reconstruction of the artist's life.

What had to be done, and what we did, with Bernard Plattner and Ronnie Self, was to reproduce the sensation of being surrounded by an explosion of art made up of many pieces in different stages. The work consists of the whole, not the parts; of what is a piece of art, and what could become one; of the process and not the (apparent) end result. This is the meaning of the Atelier Brancusi that has been built on the square of the Centre Pompidou. Art is a continuum that indissolubly binds the content to its container.

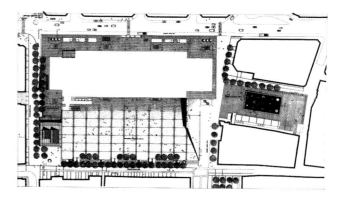

Photographic self-portrait by Constantin Brancusi in his studio on Impasse Ronsin (above); the new studio interior (left); overall plan of the area around Centre Pompidou (below).

Opposite: The new studio entrance. From outside is a view of the private garden; from inside, the ambulatory that surrounds the rebuilt studio.

# 1992 **Riehen** (Basel) Switzerland

## Beyeler Foundation Museum
Construction: 1994–97

**This is yet another museum, immersed in greenery, in the suburbs of Basel. The concept of light from above is further developed and the relationship with the place is entrusted to stone and plants.**

After working with Mme. de Menil, my experience with collectors was enriched by my collaboration with Ernst Beyeler. In some ways they are alike, and they have helped me to understand the spirit that motivates these present-day artistic patrons. The artist creates a work, but the collector creates a collection: it is his or her work of art, his or her way to express sensitivity and love of beauty. By creating museums, collectors provide homes for their creatures, protecting them against the risks of the world forever, and at the same time giving them a second identity. A picture will be remembered not just as a Picasso or a Kandinsky, but also as a piece in the Beyeler collection.

Ernst Beyeler is a very demanding man, it must be said, especially of himself. He is a perfectionist who does not like surprises: before giving me the job, he wanted to see all my previous works. He is a watchful and hands-on client, who wanted to create a close collaboration. I always had to take great care to understand and interpret his desires, as well as to be very forceful, to stop myself from being dragged down the wrong road.

The Beyeler Foundation Museum is being constructed at Riehen, near Basel. It stands amid the venerable trees of what was once the private park of the nineteenth-century Villa Berower, now a historic monument owned by the state.

In plan, the museum is as precise and rigorous as its client. Four main walls of the same length, oriented in a north-south direction, run parallel to the boundary wall. The exhibition galleries extend in straight lines through the resulting spaces. The section is far more dynamic. The walls have different heights. The easternmost one extends into the park and becomes a low wall that guides visitors to the entrance.

The building is covered by a transparent cantilevered roof. Many lighting trials have demonstrated, once again, that overhead light is the best way to give the works softer and more natural colors. This roof is, to some extent, independent of the building. Supported by a very simple metal structure, it extends considerably beyond the perimeter defined by the walls. The supporting structure is not visible from the galleries below, which creates a sense of lightness in clear and deliberate contrast to the rocklike solidity of the outside walls.

All the walls, including the one along the boundary with

The wooden model, set on an aerial photograph, shows the intervention in the park of Villa Berower.

Bernard Plattner, Ernst Beyeler, and Renzo Piano on the construction site.

The area around the site of the museum.

Elevation of the museum, with the park of Villa Berower in the background.

Claude Monet.

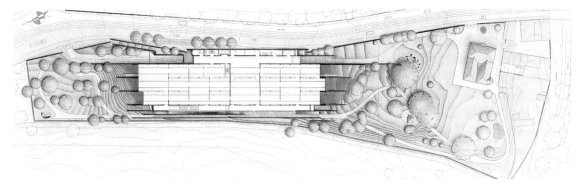

The plan shows how the building is structured around a series of parallel walls.

Piet Mondrian.

Mark Rothko.

Pieces from the Beyeler collection.

Pierre Matisse.

Paul Klee.

African art.

Mirò.

Alberto Giacometti.

Pablo Picasso.

Ernst.

the park, will be faced with a stone that resembles the red sandstone of Basel Cathedral but comes from the other side of the world, where the tenacious Bernard Plattner went to look for it. The use of this material was intended to be our tribute to the place: it was supposed to give the construction the appearance of an outcrop of the local rock. But here we ran into a problem: it is true that sandstone is the typical building material of this part of Switzerland, but it ages badly and flakes easily. In our case it would have posed continual maintenance problems.

Bernard, who is Swiss himself, is a patient craftsperson, and does not give up so easily. He discovered that a similar kind of stone could be found on the slopes of Machu Picchu, in Peru. He went to look at it in person, with Loïc Couton, but was still not satisfied. Eventually he found what he was looking for in Argentina, and also found a way to transport the stone to Europe: a Russian cargo ship. He has also had to face a sailors' strike, but solved that last little problem as well. In any case, he and Jurg Burkhardt, our local engineer, have accustomed us to seeing a whole range of problems solved.

To the west, under the edge of the projecting roof, a glass wall delimits the space of a long and narrow winter garden. This conservatory will be used as a sculpture gallery, as well as a space where visitors, emerging from the intense artistic atmosphere and rarefied light of the museum, can adjust to the greenery of the park and the afternoon sun.

I believe that contemplation, if it is really going to take on a sacred character, has to alternate with the profane spirit of physical and mental repose. The winter garden represents this "complementary" aspect: it allows people to move from the emotion of art to a tranquil enjoyment of nature.

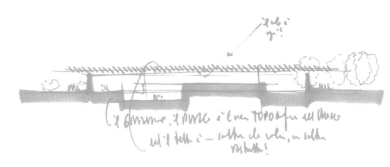

First study model of the system of sheds for the roofing of the museum.

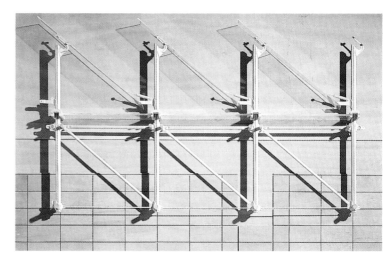

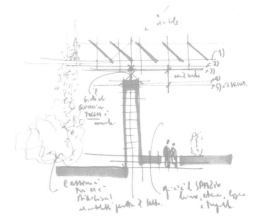

Sketch showing the construction concept of the museum. A transparent roof rests on top of walls faced in stone. The roof is supported by a lightweight metal structure that extends beyond the perimeter of the walls, making the roof independent of them.

The building during the final phase of construction: overall view with the trees of the park in the background; metal supporting structure for the glass sheds; metal supporting structure for the transparent roof.

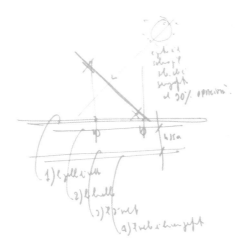

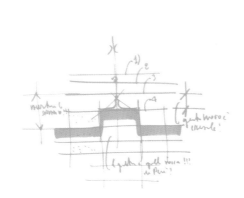

Sketches illustrating the concept of the shed roofing system and the way in which the roof structure rests on the walls.

# 1993 Sindelfingen (Stuttgart) Germany

## Mercedes Benz Design Center

Construction: 1994–

**This is a building of around thirty thousand square meters whose form derives not only from its function, but also from its location on the curved boundary of the Mercedes property. We further developed the research into the use of roofing panels (this time made of aluminum) with a toroidal geometry.**

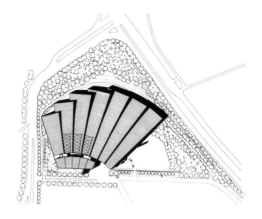

Roof plan.

Construction site with the "fingers," each of which represents a different department and is illuminated by skylights, to ensure privacy.

The new Mercedes Benz Design Center is part of the huge Sindelfingen plant, near Stuttgart. Like all structures of this kind, it needed to meet two basic requirements: provide the designers with the right conditions to concentrate on their creative efforts and conceal the results from prying eyes.

It is difficult for an outsider to imagine the extent to which industrial espionage is feared in the automobile industry. A model under development is surrounded by the kind of security measures you might expect from the military. The logistics of a styling center call for the isolation of the designers not only from the outside world, but also from the rest of the company for which they work. At the same time these precautions should not impede internal communications, which are essential to the circulation of ideas.

One day the head of the Mercedes design department came to our office to explain the two sides of this complex problem. For many years this important post has been held by Bruno Sacco. An Italian from Turin, who has long been an enthusiastic defender of quality, he has found the ideal terrain for his research and his passion at the Stuttgart-based company.

Bruno wandered around the studio, looking at the place with interest and finally (to our great surprise) told us that Sindelfingen wanted to achieve the same kind of result, though on a different scale and in a different context. This was obviously an exaggeration: hundreds, not tens of people work at the Mercedes Design Center. In these cases, quantity makes a difference. You cannot scale up a structure with a pantograph and expect it to maintain the same characteristics. Yet the message was clear. He wanted an open environment that would stimulate participation, or in his own words, where communication between the designers "would not be an obligation but part of the atmosphere."

Despite all this, our first scheme was fairly conventional. Had we allowed ourselves to be conditioned by the rectilinear pattern of the nearby assembly lines? Or had we been intimidated by the client? In this case, it was Bruno Sacco himself

From south to north, each finger is longer than the preceding one and is rotated by an angle of nine degrees.

who got us out of our difficulties. His comment was "Beautiful, but too regular. Too Bauhaus. I want you to be more bold." We obeyed, acknowledging the error.

The building of the Mercedes Design Center now resembles an open hand, whose "fingers" house the various functions: conception, technical drawing, model, prototype, and so on. There are seven fingers, and they radiate from the same central point at a constant angle of nine degrees. From south to north, each is longer than the one before, so that the plan looks a bit like a fan. In reality it is a simple factory made up of sheds (though one where things have been a bit shaken up by a gentle earthquake). All the fingers face onto a common garden to the northwest.

The main walls are cast from concrete and are faced on the outside with special aluminum panels, mounted on a polyethylene support that makes them perfectly flat.

The roofs of the buildings are not perpendicular to the walls, but inclined. The gap that this leaves is filled by large skylights facing northeast and northwest (because the "fingers" turn around). This simultaneously satisfies the needs of illumination and security; in fact, the skylights are windows at the level of the work areas. In section, both the walls and the roofs are curved. The long spans of the roofing are held up by a fairly sophisticated system of supports, joints, and tie beams, which keeps the curve of the roof in tension. The gap between roof and wall increases toward the end of each section, increasing the size of the skylights and the amount of light that enters. The roof proper is made out of a "sandwich" of two layers of steel, with a thick layer of insulating material in between. It is interesting to note that here, as at the Kansai Air Terminal, the roof has a three-dimensional form based on the geometry of toroids. Peter Rice made a contribution to the early part of the project. Subsequently it fell to the patient Musci Baglietto, with the help of Johannes Florin, to coordinate the work of the many and disparate inputs to the design, including that of the local engineer, Christoph Kohlbecker, always keeping the central idea of the project on course.

A hall for the presentation of models is situated to the east of the three shortest fingers. Since this is a relatively public area, it is set apart from the rest of the complex but easily accessible to visitors from the adjacent general service block. The illumination is greater here too: the geometry of the roof is the same, but the steel has been replaced by transparent materials. Inside, several gigantic opalescent screens, with a lenslike section, permit regulation of the natural light. This large space will serve as a studio in which full-scale models can be examined in different settings.

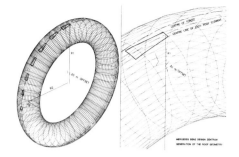

Toroidal geometric scheme that represents the curve of the roof. The view of the construction site shows the rotation of the building and the curve of the roof.

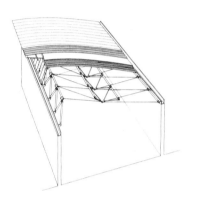

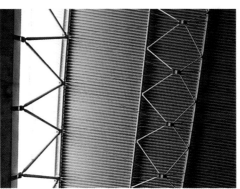

Views during construction. The roof is a sandwich of two layers of corrugated sheet steel, with insulating material in the middle.

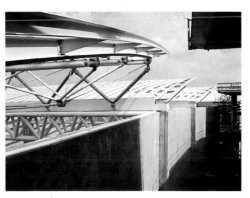

# 1994 **Rome** Italy

## Auditorium

Construction: 1996–

**The project consists of three halls with different capacities (2,700, 1,200, and 500 seats) and characteristics (principally in their flexibility of use) as well as an open-air amphitheater for 3,000 people. The discovery of the remains of an ancient Roman villa has made it possible to strengthen the relationship with the placeform. The greenery that surrounds the buildings is an extension of the park of Villa Glori.**

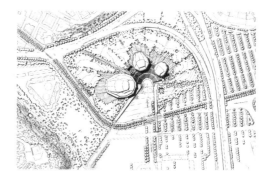

Plan with the three halls and the amphitheater.

My boat is the oasis in which I take refuge when I don't want even my work to reach me. And usually it doesn't. But there have been at least two exceptions. The first got off to an adventurous start. I was sailing off the coast of Corsica in the summer of 1974 when a patrol boat of the French coast guard approached. "Pardon, Monsieur, but the president wishes to see you. At once." Giscard d'Estaing, who had just replaced Pompidou, wanted to remove one storey from the Centre Pompidou. He didn't succeed (the project was too advanced for such a major modification), but he did manage to ruin my vacation.

The second was less dramatic, and indeed quite pleasant. I was in Sardinia with Luciano Berio when a boat drew alongside. They had heard in port that somebody was looking for me urgently, and they had kindly taken the trouble to bring me the message. It was Francesco Rutelli, mayor of Rome: he wanted to inform me personally that I had won the international competition for the new auditorium.

Rome did not have a place devoted to classical music that was on a par with the city's importance and size. The new auditorium, with its halls of different dimensions and possible configurations, will fill the gap by providing a structure of great versatility, with a main hall seating 2,700 people, the largest size that can be built and still retain natural acoustics of high quality. Obviously there was no room for such a huge complex in the historic center of Rome. Even from the urbanistic viewpoint it made sense to locate it somewhat outside the city center, in an area of structures created to handle large flows of people: between the village built to house the athletes for the 1960 Olympics and Pierluigi Nervi's Palazzetto dello Sport and Flaminio Stadium.

To ensure maximum flexibility, while sacrificing nothing in terms of acoustic quality, we decided not to place the three halls in a single building, but to make them three independent constructions. In this way we introduced an element of novelty with respect to the requirements set out in the rules of the com-

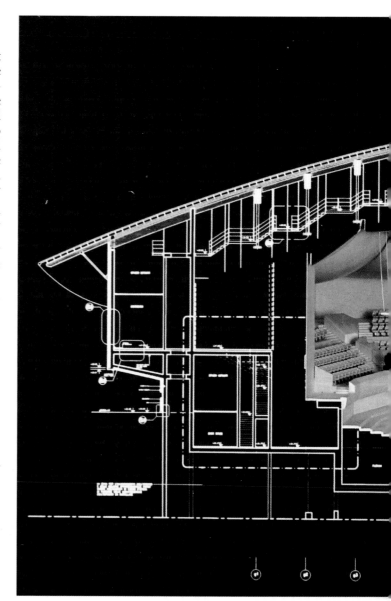

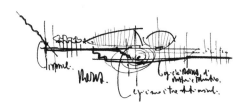

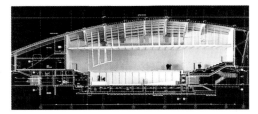

Above: Section through middle-sized hall and small hall.

Below: Section through 2,700-seat hall.

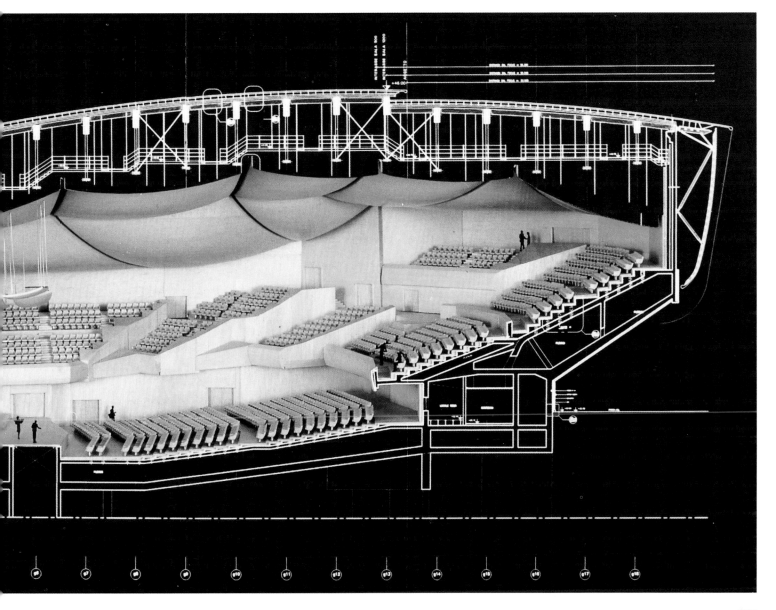

petition. In our project the three halls, each set in a container resembling a giant sound box, were arranged symmetrically around an empty space, which became the fourth auditorium, not included in the initial program: an open-air amphitheater. Amid these constructions, luxuriant vegetation established a connection with the nearby park of Villa Glori.

Working in a city like Rome, dealing with its placeform, is the most difficult thing of all. No one could ignore such a strong identity, even if they wanted to. The various parts of the auditorium bring to mind an analogy, a functional one with musical instruments, inspired by the form and the use of wood. A second analogy derives from the site and the disposition of the buildings. There is something archaeological about these atypical constructions surrounded by greenery: they could be some of Piranesi's ruins, a metaphor for classical antiquity.

But here is a piece of friendly advice: never play around with metaphors. Here, out of the metaphorical ruins came real ones: the foundations of a large Roman villa from the sixth century B.C. It is true that Rome is Rome. Wherever you dig, something turns up. But these were not just a few stones; it was an important find. The *genius loci* was generous and mischievous at one and the same time: on the one hand it made us a gift (for which I am grateful), on the other it held up the work for a year.

The problem became not just one of "preserving" the foundations, but one of making them part of the complex. An essential part in this was played by our collaboration with the head of the archaeological service, as well as with Professor Carandini, who carried out the excavations with his everchanging horde of students. So the position of the buildings was rearranged: in the spaces between them the public will be able to admire some of the objects found in the Roman villa. The foundations themselves will be visible inside the underground foyer, which is the space that provides access to all the halls. As often happens during a project, this revision of the design put the entire team under pressure: Donald Hart, Susanna Scarabicchi, and Maurizio Varratta were able to keep within the very strict time limits imposed by the Commune of Rome, in the persons of Councillor Domenico Cecchini and the project supervisor Maurizio Cagnoni.

Rome was my fourth work in the field of music, and by now I knew where to turn for the best advice. I took care to involve composers like Luciano Berio and Pierre Boulez in the development of the project, as well as, of course, Rome's Accademia Nazionale di Santa Cecilia.

To simulate the properties of the various halls, our acoustics consultant (Helmut Müller, who had worked with us on Lingotto) first built models with reflective surfaces. Using lasers to trace the route followed by reflections, the first diagrams of acoustic response were drawn up. The data obtained from these models was fed into the computer and used to sim-

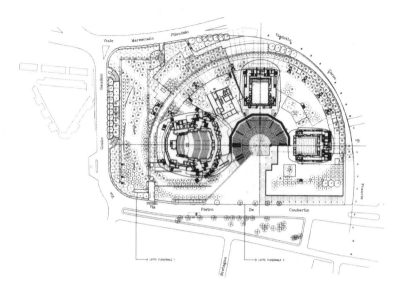

Plan showing the three halls, the auditorium, the archaeological excavation, and the surrounding areas of greenery.

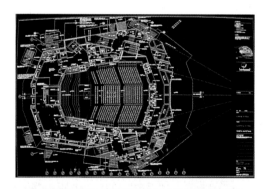

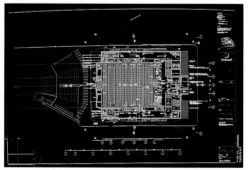

Computer representations of the 1,200- and 500-seat halls (left); the 2,700-seat hall (opposite). The plan shows the subdivision of the space for the audience into "vineyards." This provides everyone with the best listening conditions and also makes possible more direct participation in the concert.

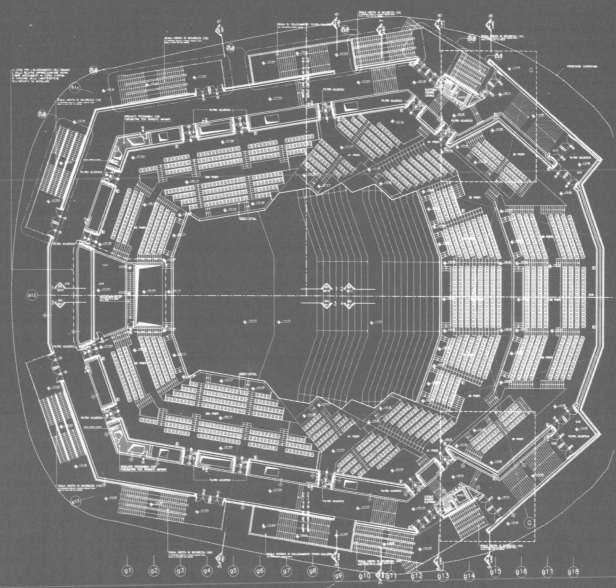
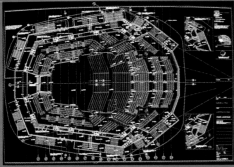

ulate the reflections of the sound waves. The final stage entailed analogical tests, i.e., using real sound, this time on large-scale models (some as big as a room). At this point we knew how the halls themselves would perform.

The three halls have different capacities and characteristics. As might be expected, their versatility is inversely proportional to their size. The smallest, with 500 seats, is a totally flexible space, using some of the solutions adopted in IRCAM in Paris twenty years earlier: movable floor and ceiling, the ability to alter the acoustic properties of the walls. The hall that seats 1,200 people has a number of flexible elements, including a movable stage and an adjustable ceiling; these features recall the auditorium at Lingotto. It will be used for concerts of chamber music and dance performances. The main hall, finally, houses 2,700 people (more would be impossible, because of the acoustics: in the back rows the sound would be overwhelmed by the echo). In many respects this hall is a homage to Hans Scharoun's Philharmonic in Berlin.

As in Berlin, the stage is in an almost central position, surrounded by what Scharoun called vineyards: seats set on plinths at different levels, extending right around the orchestra. This arrangement allows the audience to participate fully in the musical performance. The material factor of physical proximity is reinforced by the feeling of being one with the performers—an immaterial element, but no less effective.

I think it is only right to be frank about your inspirations. In my view the desire to be original at all costs is pointless presumption: it amounts to a refusal to recognize that architecture is founded on a great common heritage, in continual evolution. In this sense I will be proud if I can just add something in terms of quality of sound, visibility, and an increased sense of involvement to Scharoun's extraordinary musical adventure.

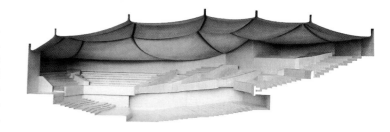

Wooden model of the 2,700-seat hall.

Acoustic model of the hall.

Computer-generated acoustic simulations.

Acoustic measurements made inside the model.

The ancient remains of a Roman villa from the republican era were found during the digging of the foundations. The project was modified to integrate this important element, which further strengthens the relationship with the placeform.

# 1995 **Saitama** (Tokyo) Japan
## Multifunctional Arena

**The prefecture of Saitama required a project for the construction of an immense arena with a capacity of 45,000, to be used for cultural, exhibition, and commercial purposes. The "geographic" character of the project was important.**

Saitama is a Japanese city of small buildings on the extreme periphery of Tokyo, ennobled by the presence of the important Hikawa Shrine. For the creation of Saitama's new urban area, including a square and a multifunctional arena, the civic authorities decided to hold not one, but two international competitions. Kumagai-san asked us to enter the competition for the arena.

Our journey to attend the presentation was an adventurous one: Shunji Ishida and I arrived in Tokyo the day after the nerve-gas attack on the city's subway. Our project did not win; the quest for a misunderstood modernity won the day. I include it here and because I find it beautiful, and the fact that I was unable to realize it is a source of regret.

As it was to be inserted into a disorganized urban fabric, the arena required the creation of a recognizable focus. So we decided to place the building in its context with the force of a geographical feature, giving it the shape and color of a hill. The "hill" would have stood between two railroad lines, like a rise in terrain created by the convergence of natural forces.

The main structure would have been composed of light-weight steel arches (designed with the very likable Kimura, a Japanese engineer who came to see us several times): one for each section of the ceiling, linked together horizontally to ensure their stability. Their copper facing would have oxidized rapidly, taking on its characteristic green color. The contrast between the lightness of the facing and the dynamism of the structure would have given the building a natural elegance.

Certain things become a focus not by virtue of size alone, but also by urban location. The Arena's strong point would have been its link with the Hikawa Temple and Omiya Park that surrounds it. The main connecting road, Hikawa Shrine Sando Avenue, would have had to be extended in a straight line and a bridge constructed in order to create an uninterrupted connection between square, arena, and shrine. This would have created an urban symmetry, and perhaps—who knows?—a bond with the gods of the temple.

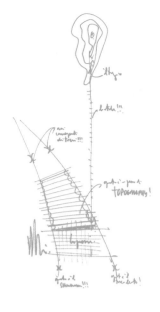

Plan showing the connection of the area of the project with Omiya Park and the Hikawa Shrine Temple. In the model, the "hill" is the result of a compression of the ground between two railroad lines.

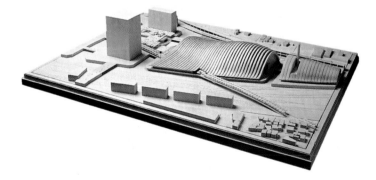

Opposite: Computer images and models of the structure that supports the roof (top); section through the arena (bottom).

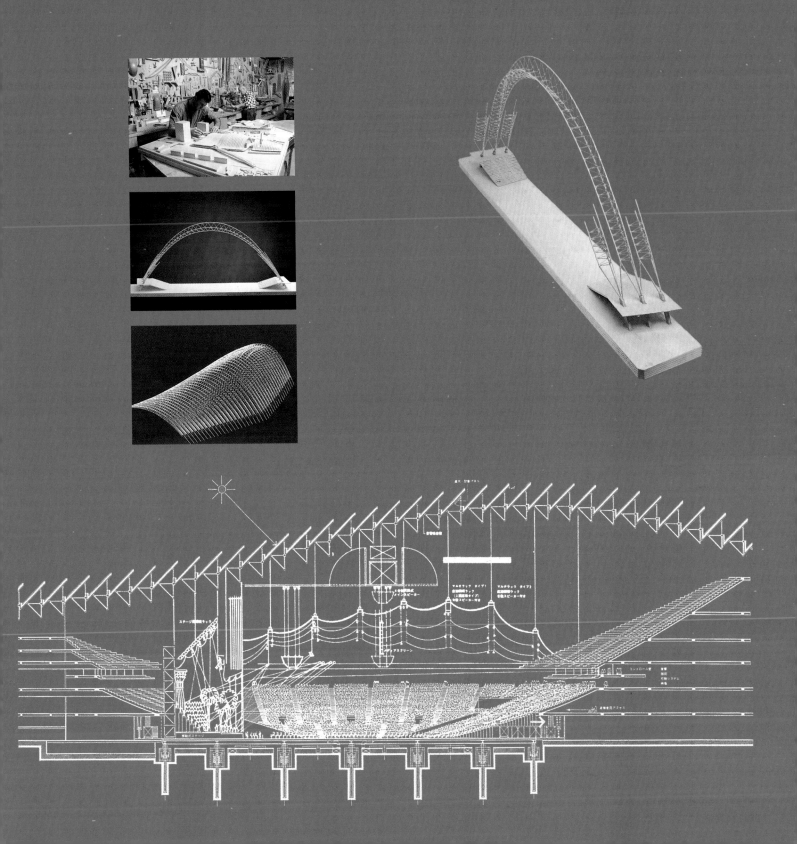

# 1995 Nola (Naples) Italy

## Service Complex

**The project accomodates a series of services to supplement the Interporto of Nola. It addresses the square as a factor in the creation of an urban character and the reference to the "good volcano."**

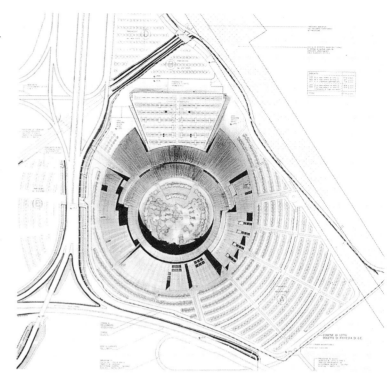

In Campania there is a large and modern center for the collection and sorting of goods. It represents a relocation of many activities that were once carried out at Piazza Mercato in Naples. The Nola complex, situated at a port of exchange not far from the provincial capital, is an example of multifunctionality that has few equivalents in southern Italy. It will comprise not only a large supermarket, but also commercial activities of all kinds and dimensions, including stores, hotels, restaurants, management offices, and leisure facilities.

The complex as a whole, which includes the C.I.S. (International Committee for Exchanges) and the Interporto, is run with great energy and vitality. One of the people involved in its management is Gianni Punzo, a fine example of the spirit of enterprise that represents the true wealth of Naples. Preferring to describe himself as a merchant rather than as a tradesperson, he is able to draw on the considerable insight he has built up over years of continuous experience in Far Eastern markets.

Our project was faced with the problem posed by all multipurpose centers: how to avoid the banal grouping of building volumes and functions, and to give instead a unique and recognizable identity to such a diverse range of service activities. Never before has the form been suggested so strongly by the morphology of the territory, Campania Felix and the nearby Mount Vesuvius. In fact the complex is set inside an artificial hill, which presents itself to visitors from a distance as a movement of the earth's surface, like a peaceful volcano.

The dimensions of the hill have been determined by means of an exercise in radial geometry, with three intersecting solids of rotation. The height of the crater varies from twenty-five to forty-one meters. The functions of the center are arranged on several levels and organized around a central garden. This garden (the "square") is a large open space with a diameter of over 170 meters. Sheltered from the cold winter winds by the building, it is kept cool in summer by the presence of natural elements: trees, vegetation, fountains, and surfaces of moving water.

There are two key elements in this project: the way the volume of the construction appears to belong to the place, when seen from a distance, and the way the square inside shares in that sense of cheerful participation, that urban quality of conviviality, typical of the Italian and in particular the Neapolitan way of life.

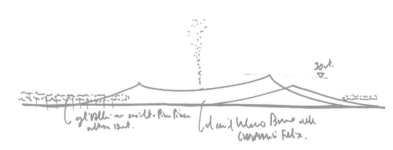

Overall plan and sketch showing the artificial hill in which all the functions are located. Set on three floors, they face onto a square/garden with a diameter of 170 meters.

236

Study model of the insertion of the hill/crater into the area of Nola.

Typical section of the functions located beneath the artificial hill, inside the crater. The height inside ranges from twenty-five to forty-one meters.

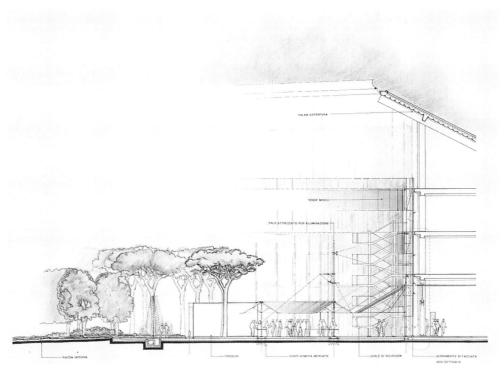

Computer models of the structure of the crater.

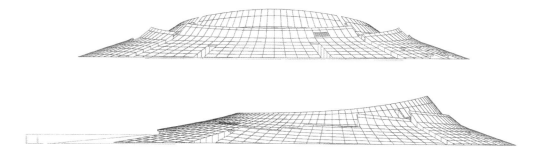

Overall section showing the internal garden onto which all the functions face.

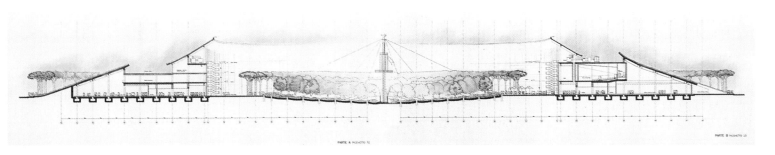

# 1995 Paris France

## Renovation of Centre Georges Pompidou

Construction: 1996–

**After almost twenty years the Centre Pompidou is being renovated to regain the innovative cultural spirit that characterized it at the end of the 1970s. The library and exhibition areas are being expanded, and the public spaces reorganized.**

You remain tied to your works by a sort of umbilical cord. They are your creatures, and in a way you never lose sight of them. Take the Centre Pompidou, for example. Twenty years ago I set up my office a hundred meters away. It's still there, and I feel a bit like Quasimodo, the guardian of the tower.

And the building itself never leaves me alone. First came the IRCAM facilities, then its tower, then Brancusi, and now Grand Beaubourg. Grand Beaubourg represents continuity. It is my return to the scene of the crime, or rather proof that I never left it.

Centre Pompidou had been designed on the basis of a predicted five to six thousand visitors per day. It has been receiving five times as many, and for twenty years now. At the busiest times of year, the number rises to more than fifty thousand per day. In total, it has been visited by almost a hundred and fifty million people. It deserves a bit of a rest, and is in need of a little maintenance.

This will also provide the opportunity for a few improvements. The administrative offices will be moved out of the building, making it possible to expand the areas devoted to exhibitions, enlarge the library, and rearrange the public spaces on the ground floor. Another series of interventions will concern the organization of the entries and surroundings. All of this is possible only because the building had the necessary capacity for adaptation designed into it from the start. When we talked about a "machine for producing culture," a building whose modularity was not just a matter of aesthetics, this is exactly what we meant.

Foreseeing changes in the future does not make us prophets. Every building has a vitality of its own, even those destined for the most conventional and predictable uses. This is all the more true when its purpose is culture, a material that is hard to define and capable of infinite possible developments.

Beaubourg, now run by Jean-Jacques Aillagon, will suspend many of its activities. They will be carried on elsewhere: in New York, Los Angeles, and Tokyo. It will reopen as Grand Beaubourg on the night between December 31, 1999, and January 1, 2000, ready for the third millennium.

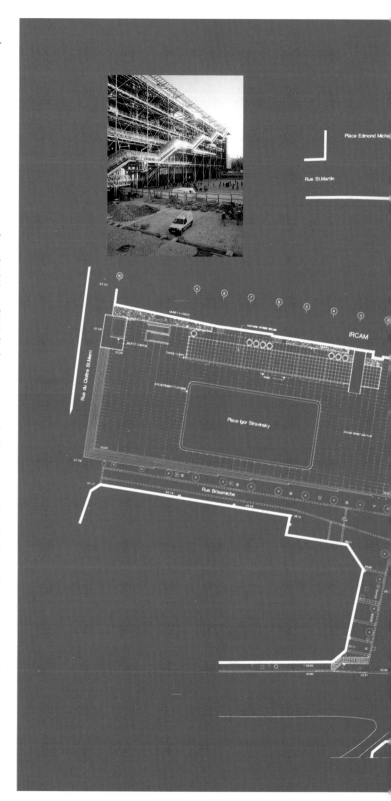

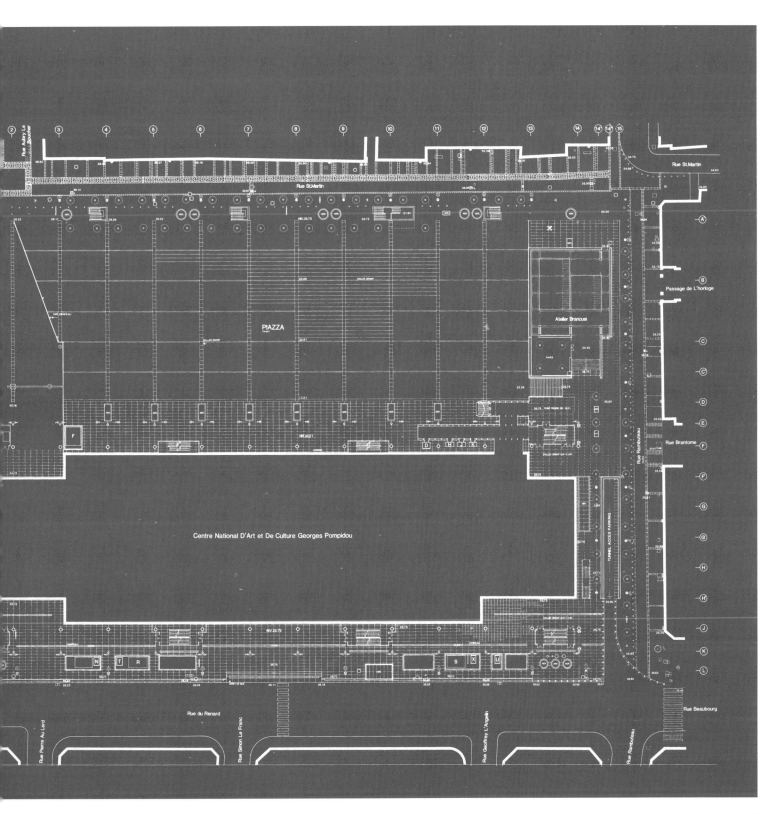

## 1996 **Maranello** (Modena) Italy
### Ferrari Wind Tunnel
Construction: 1996–

**This design openly declares the building's function, even glorifies it. It is an enormous machine measuring eighty by seventy meters.**

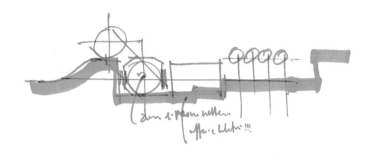

Ferrari wanted us to design a wind tunnel, a machine for, testing the air resistance of racing cars (or any other object, for that matter—we used one to test the huts for Nouméa). But in reality, anything you do for Ferrari must reckon with the legend of the company and the legend of its creator: that genius Enzo Ferrari, a man of great passion, who liked the smell of gasoline, the roar of engines, and driving fast. One day, in a place with no history that could easily have been a field of potatoes, he started to build his cars—his extraordinary cars.

What we are doing (after winning, together with my friend the "builder-philosopher" Gianfranco Dioguardi, a competition held at the behest of Luca di Montezemolo) is to some extent a representation of the same event. We are making a gigantic machine appear out of nowhere in a field of potatoes. And so, after the competition, Maria Salerno, under the attentive guidance of Paul Vincent, began to shuttle between Paris and Maranello to plow the field.

The Ferrari F50 designed by Pininfarina.

There are two ways to build a wind tunnel. One is to shut it up in a box. The other, and this is the one we have tried, is to put the whole mechanism on the outside, flaunting its equipment and its function, so that it looks a bit like the engine of an automobile.

To dramatize the effect we have used a trick as well: the wind tunnel is placed in such a way as to create a slight impression of instability (only an impression, of course; it is extremely stable). It is bent and rests on a small hill. To tell the truth, this is a more functional solution as well, as it permits two entrances to the test chamber.

The wind gallery is eighty meters long and seventy wide; it is a machine, yes, or rather an engine, but completely out of scale. Yet it has a straightforward relationship with its natural surroundings. It is a relationship that, in a way, has always existed between Enzo Ferrari's technological marvels and the rural culture that serves as their backdrop.

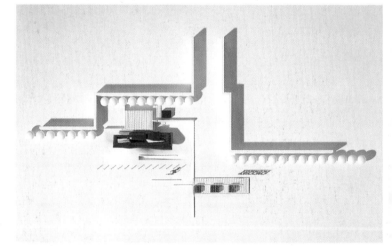

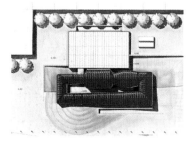

The study model and the plan draw attention to the relationship between the wind tunnel, the production plant, and the landscape.

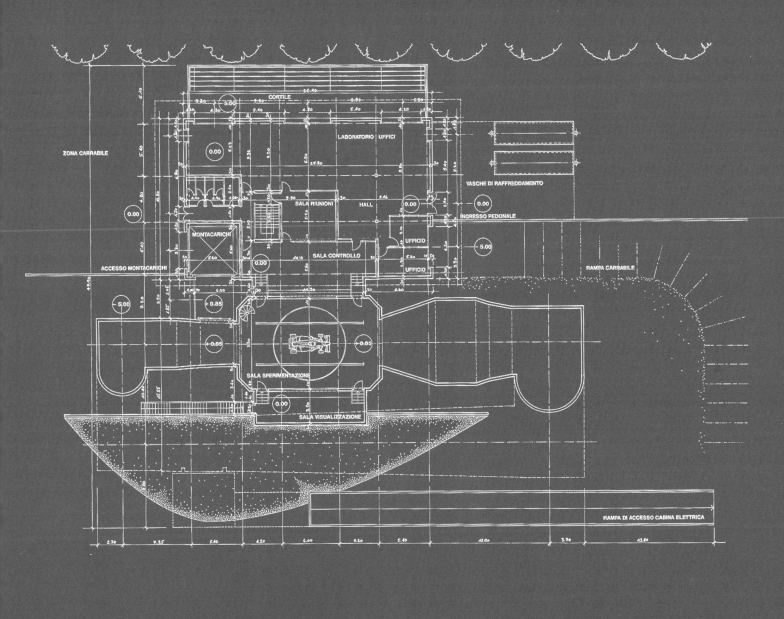

ZONA CARRABILE

CORTILE

LABORATORIO UFFICI

VASCHE DI RAFFREDDAMENTO

SALA RIUNIONI    HALL

INGRESSO PEDONALE

MONTACARICHI

UFFICIO

SALA CONTROLLO

ACCESSO MONTACARICHI

UFFICIO

RAMPA CARRABILE

SALA SPERIMENTAZIONE

SALA VISUALIZZAZIONE

RAMPA DI ACCESSO CABINA ELETTRICA

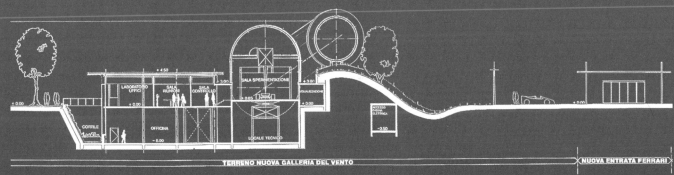

LABORATORIO UFFICIO

SALA RIUNIONI

SALA CONTROLLO

SALA SPERIMENTAZIONE

VISUALIZZAZIONE

CORTILE

OFFICINA

LOCALE TECNICO

ACCESSO CABINA ELETTRICA

TERRENO NUOVA GALLERIA DEL VENTO

NUOVA ENTRATA FERRARI

# 1996 **Sydney** Australia

## Mixed-Use Tower Complex

Construction: 1997–

**As this book was going to press, we had just received the commission: a tower for offices and a building for residences. The challenge is to blend functionality and sociality, to build a tower that catches the breeze and that holds a dialogue with the nearby park and the Opera House.**

I close with Sydney even though nothing exists as of yet, except a commission. It seems appropriate to finish with the adventure that is just beginning. It is the magic moment. All possibilities are there, and you look through them for clues, for the signs that will lead you down the right road.

The client is Lend Lease, the largest construction company in Australia and one of the biggest in the world. The project is for a tower to be built for 2000, the year of the Sydney Olympics. It is being commissioned by a private company, but the tower will be a homage to the city, so I expect that the local authorities and public opinion will be involved in some way. On my first visit to the site, I met the mayor, the minister of public works, and the premier of New South Wales, which indicates the degree of interest in this project. It is inevitable, necessary, and even natural that the public authorities be involved in a major project like this. It's nothing to be frightened of; it's all part of the job.

The tower will be two hundred meters tall and consist of a main block connected to a lower one, an imposing monument. The ambition is clearly to produce something more memorable than one of Sydney's many skyscrapers (including several that are of excellent quality). We have four or five trails to follow.

One is historical. The site is on Macquarie Street, a historic avenue. Perhaps the adjective should be put in quotation marks. Obviously Australia has no old cities in the European sense of the word. We are talking about constructions dating from between the middle of the last century and our own day. However, in some of the nearby buildings there is an architectural quality that should not be neglected.

There are urbanistic points of reference, both existing and to be created. Sydney is a young city but a great one, dynamic and important. The fact that it is young may even be an advantage. New projects really should seek a very powerful role; they should complete and solidify an urban fabric that is not yet completely settled.

Then there is the social trail. It is important that we don't turn this tower into a Tower of Babel: a series of floors set one on top of the other without any connections, without any functional logic, without any common language. In Manhattan you see these enormous enigmatic volumes: a huge entrance, the

Sydney Bay.

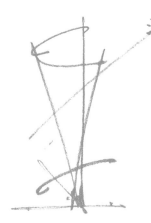

"On-the-spot" inspection, aboard a sailboat.

First sketch of the office tower.

Opposite: Drawings and models of the office tower, which was designed to catch the breeze and maintain a dialogue with the park beneath and with the Opera House.

elevator operator says "Good morning," and then—whoosh!—shoots you upward. We intend to introduce a different concept of sociability. Our first idea is to create a sort of elevated plaza every two or three floors, a place where people can meet. It's clear that this will have to have an equivalent at street level: a sort of forum, or a square, or perhaps a covered foyer. Something must make the building look like a place for meeting, a center of urban life, from the outside.

There is the question of form and language. The nearest reference, and one that cannot be ignored, is Jørn Utzon's Sydney Opera House, which is one of the city's symbols. Above all, it is only eight hundred meters away. A dialogue between the two objects will be inevitable. There is also a whole culture of detail that is typical of the architecture of this city.

Finally, there is the very important trail linked to the environment, to the climate. Australia is particularly sensitive to these aspects. In a way, it is the culture of the Pacific, something that even has a connection with the sense of nature developed for the Kanak project on New Caledonia. A small example of this sensitivity is provided by the request not to make shade, not to overshadow the trees in the botanical park located close to the site, which would suffer from a lack of light. Of course, it is difficult to build a tower that casts no shadow, but we can carry out studies of orientation, so as not to block the sun at the best times of day. We want to respect not only the letter but also the substance of this restriction, and try to make the project the bearer and promoter of a message that is deeply rooted in this land.

Architecture is a human science, and in a way it is non-ecological by definition, because it is the exercise of a right to self-defense on the part of human beings. Humanity uses architecture to create protection against the environment. Yet architecture can be sustainable. Progress can be turned into something else. A muscular assertion of power can become the search for a subtle balance.

In September 1996, I went to visit the site with Mark Carroll and Shunji Ishida. We explored it in every possible way, flying over it in a helicopter, walking up and down Macquarie Street, sailing across Sydney Bay. We took photographs and tried to imagine the profile of our tower on the city skyline. Upon our return to the studio, at the Punta Nave, Tom Barker and the Ove Arup team arrived. They came to hear what the wind was like and how to make the best use of it. We want to capture the breezes off the sea, to improve the efficiency of the air-conditioning with a system of natural convection.

I have learned (and it may seem like a tautology, but it is not) that when you work well, the work turns out well. Always. But you have to take the trouble to collect elements firsthand, you mustn't take anything for granted, and you have to distrust prepackaged ideas. This is my way of beginning the adventure. The opening is important: it decides the game.

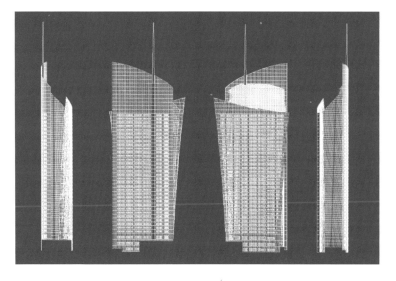

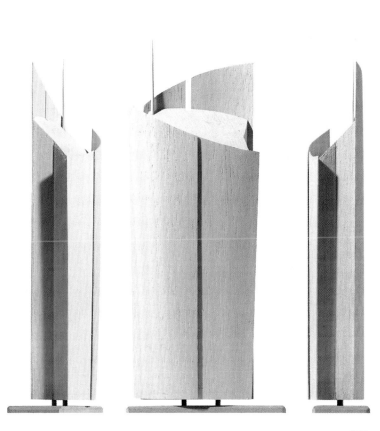

**From Builder's Son to Architect**

## Thirty Years of Work

The more than fifty projects in this book are arranged in chronological order. Without meaning to, without any particular intention, they have traced the lines of a history. There is a thread running through them, a natural process of growth that has gradually turned the son of a builder into an architect.

You can see a progressive broadening of vision: from the individual casting, from the structures of the early works, to the complete architectural organism; from the building by itself to the building in its context, in relation to its surroundings; from the individual building to the city, as a complex organism.

In the Middle Ages there was the figure of the "master craftsman," who was granted an entry into the sacred world of art. A supreme example of this is Leonardo da Vinci in the Renaissance. The idea that technique and art belong to separate and parallel universes is as harmful as it is recent.

If the spirit of adventure is one of the driving forces in my work, another is certainly obstinacy. Obstinacy and tenacity are very important qualities, whether on the professional plane or the cultural one. This is not an arrogant attitude, I see it more as a matter of intellectual honesty. I am not a do-gooder; yet I believe there is a morality in architecture, based on being true to your own ideas, to your own commitment, to your own method. The problem is this: how to be moral without turning into a moralist; how to be consistent without becoming dogmatic? I think that, just as there is a light way of using intelligence, there is also a light way of using method.


## Apparent Contradictions

Architecture is an art filled with contradictions. The more learned among us translate these contradictions into antitheses: between discipline and freedom, between technology and environment, between modernity and tradition. Those with a taste for perversity put the problem as a blunt alternative: are you for art or for science? for nature or for nurture? for the Mets or the Yankees? A way of papering over the contradictions can always be found, but this is exactly what I mean by a heavy use of method. In so doing, you eliminate the complexity, the richness, and the positive values of our profession.

I have an instinctive distrust of all these commonplaces. For instance, freedom and discipline are apparently in contradiction. But is it really so? Discipline sets limits to freedom, yet it is also its container: the thing that gives it form. These two elements coexist and interact.

In architecture it is the blank sheet that paralyzes, not the constraints imposed by the context. The context is a resource; it is material to draw on, a score to be interpreted. A similar relationship can be found between originality and memory. Art is a continual reference to what has already been done. Sometimes this amounts to outright pillage, for it cites, interprets, and manipulates the past. Architectural invention cannot ignore history, tradition, or the context of construction. It may decide to break with all that, but even then it has to take these influences into account, though in terms of opposition, of overturning.

It is something else to feign the absence of memory. There is nothing more ridiculous than the obsession with being original at any cost. The desire to astonish is a classic sign of insecurity, of those who have to prove just how clever they are. Personally I find that my desire to go down unexplored paths is perfectly in keeping with my sense of tradition. Perhaps this is a European trait, even a specifically Italian one. Certainly it is the legacy of a humanist culture that permits the most reckless innovations: there is always the safety net of our past to protect us.

In the early part of the twentieth century, rationalism, in the name of modernity, did away with decoration in architecture. It was a position based on legitimate and respectable grounds. Yet it served as a justification (or alibi, if you will) for the poverty of the whole of postwar construction. One way of reacting to this excess, to this excessive denuding of architecture, is to take a plunge into tradition, so rich in ornamentation. This is very easy to do, especially when the tradition is the kind that we find in cities like Venice, Florence, or Rome. But this is imitation and it paralyzes creative intelligence, which has to operate in freedom. It is an aesthetic fence sitting, that imitates the wrapping and does not respect the spirit. The people we see as classics were great innovators in their time. Looking back to their work should mean rediscovering its values, not its results: otherwise you are just applying a formal code, while betraying the real intention. As has always been the case, the attempt to avoid complexity leads to impoverishment: for every person who wants to forget the past, there is someone who wants nothing to change.

The theme of creativity, which to some extent runs through all these antitheses, comes up again in the contrast between instinct and reason. Over many years of work I have come to the conclusion that so-called instinct, which is supposed to guide art and creativity, is nothing but a rapid process of synthesis, a turbocharged form of rational thinking. Once it used to bother me to talk about intuition. I was a bit ashamed of it, as it seemed to be just a cover for concepts like the gift of the artist, the inspiration of the muse—in short, things I have always detested.

Now I am no longer ashamed to use the word, for I have come to understand that intuition is no more than my metabolized experience. If I look at a plan I am much quicker on the uptake than someone else. I see what is important right away. But this has nothing to do with genius—it is experience. It is exactly the same as the skill of the expert fisher, or mushroom picker, or jazz musicians when they improvise. Recently I heard Keith Jarrett playing live at La Scala. He

247

has such a grasp of music, all kinds of music, that when he is improvising he cites with great naturalness from classical music, bebop, rock, folk. His hands move by themselves, they know exactly where to go.

## Sustainable Architecture

Architecture is a second nature that is laid on top of the real one. When people who practice our profession speak of the environment they ought to remember this. We live in sheltered places, known as houses, because for the majority of people on this planet it is either too cold or too hot most of the year. From this point of view, for instance, nature is hostile: it is the architect's adversary. Architects modify the territory to make it comfortable and pleasing to human beings. If "respect for the environment" means putting on slippers to walk on the grass, then I'm not interested.

On the other hand it is perfectly right to talk about the sustainability of architecture, which is quite another thing: it means understanding nature, respecting animals and plants, siting buildings and factories correctly, making use of sunlight and wind. This is what we are trying to do today in two projects in the Pacific region, the Tjibaou Cultural Center in New Caledonia and the Mixed-Use Tower in Sydney: establishing an intelligent relationship with the environment that (like all intelligent relationships) allows for a certain amount of tension between the artificial and the natural.

I find the distrust of advanced technology still more ludicrous, especially when it culminates in the fiercely academic tones used in the condemnation or acclaim of high-tech. Architects work with the tools that their time offers them. Even Brunelleschi in the fifteenth century designed and built Santa Maria del Fiore in Florence using the most modern techniques available to him. Refusing to deal with contemporary material culture is totally futile, perhaps even a bit masochistic. Let's put it this way: technology is like a bus. If it helps you to get where you want to go, you take it. If it's going in another direction, you don't. Listening to the same piece of music on a CD player or on a hand-cranked gramophone makes absolutely no difference to its poetic quality.

Indeed one of the refinements of technology is that it offers the possibility of using traditional materials in a new way. In the church of Padre Pio we are using stone for an extremely difficult structural exercise, and we are able to do so thanks to modern techniques of calculation and the computer. The result is an understatement: technology is used, is exploited to the hilt, but it is not flaunted. It becomes part of the place without taking it over. This is the exact opposite of a certain muscular kind of high-tech. Moreover, sticking to my own experience, the Menil Collection uses building and service techniques that are far more sophisticated than those of the Centre Pompidou, so sophisticated that they are invisible.

248

## Regionalism and Universalism

Architecture is local by definition: local in the etymological sense, i.e., linked to the place, the topography, the terrain. But it incorporates aesthetic values and develops models of housing that go beyond the place, that are supranational and shared by different countries. Architecture's aspiration to be universal is an ancient one. Paradoxically, though, the universality of the message lies in the ability of the language to adapt. Architecture is born of its own time, and has to be capable of expressing this. To do this it has to bring into play all the instruments available to it, gratitude toward the past as well as curiosity about a future in which we will live.

The universality of language does not depend on the speed of communication, but it is certainly influenced by it. New technologies are bringing peoples and cultures into contact with an ease that is unprecedented in human history. I believe in the positive value of this possibility.

The Kansai Air Terminal in Japan emerged out of the needs expressed by a Japanese client. But the CAD designs for the project have traveled halfway around the world by modem, pictures of the work have been broadcast by the television channels of many countries, and some of the parts were made in Britain, France, and Italy and taken to Japan by air or sea. If I am working in Kobe and a special technique of welding is available in America, then why shouldn't I use it?

Conversely, there are people who must construct a building on the other side of the world, in New Caledonia or Sydney, and it just so happens that they find their architect on the heights of Genoa, at the Punta Nave. No problem: telephone, fax, modem, internet, a few hours on a plane when it's necessary to meet in person. This is what we called "technological ubiquity" earlier, and it represents a great improvement in the quality of contemporary life.

## Contradiction and Complexity

In short, we should not let ourselves be intimidated by all the apparent contradictions of our profession. There is a degree of complexity that cannot be avoided. Excessive simplification is ridiculous. In thirty years of work as an architect I have become convinced that there is not, that there cannot be, an irremediable conflict between the past and the present, between the individual and society, between memory and originality. It simply doesn't work that way. These antinomies are not contradictions; they are the salt of life, the essence of architecture. The architect works by bringing materials together, not separating them.

## My Architecture

If what I'm talking about is a method—however deliberately light in its approach—then it can be applied to the contents of the architecture. And so, the question is where is Renzo Piano's architecture going?

One thing that is coming to fruition through my projects is the way of entering into a relationship with the environment. Communications has changed the way we perceive distance, so that in real terms Genoa is not the same distance from New York as it was a century ago. Space has been folded back on itself, and wrapped around things in a different way. This is what I was saying earlier, and I want to stress it again: I am seeking a contemporary way, not a nostalgic one, of relating to space.

At the same time, the problem of the relationship between local and universal is not just a matter of logistics: it is also cultural, aesthetic, symbolic. Kenneth Frampton has recently come up with an interesting way of looking at this, and he repeats it in the introduction to this book: he says that the *placeform* and the *produktform* are the two terms between which the tension of architecture is created. I find this a good way of conveying the tension between the ground and the structure, the setting and the building, the local and the universal.

The problem is all there, in the relationship, in the connection, in the tension. What interests me is shaping form and product together: forcefully sculpting the land, leaving a deep mark on the preexisting nature or urban structure; but at the same time making the architecture an accomplice, a partner, imbued with the characteristics of its surroundings.

As the descriptions of the projects will make clear, my most recent works demonstrate a particularly strong and tight relationship between the primary structure and the building proper. The structure on which the building stands is normally made out of materials from the place itself: it is like a bas-relief carved into the site. This means that every project has a topographical component: this is true of the stadium in Bari and of the buildings in New Caledonia, and it will also be the case in Sydney.

To interpret the "placeform," every project requires a specific study, a deep understanding of its history, geography, geology, and climate. Sometimes this tribute to the context is reciprocated. During the excavations for the auditorium in Rome we even found the foundations of a villa dating from the sixth century B.C. There, the *topos* was not just metaphorical; it was real. The bed of the building, like the bed of a river, expresses a rocklike sense of belonging to the place—it is mass, opacity, permanence. It has something eternal about it, in the Roman sense of the word (*topos* derives from the Latin for an "age"). The construction, on the contrary, is light, transparent, and temporary—not because it is going to be

250

dismantled, but because it belongs to another level, has a different value.

## Space

My insistence on transparency is often misunderstood and interpreted as insensitivity to the "space" of architecture. In the jargon of our profession, to say that you have no sense of space is the vilest of insults.

I see an ancestral reason for this. Lightness, when all is said and done, conflicts with our deepest perception of architecture: in our unconscious there is a natural association of "house-shelter-protection-solidity." We instinctively seek enclosure, a fixing of limits, in what is built. Space does not exist except insofar as it is precisely—and solidly—circumscribed.

This is a concept of space that disturbs me. It feels like the filling in a sandwich of bricks, a layer of air squeezed between the walls that surround it. I have a less suffocating idea of space: the space of architecture is a microcosm, an inner landscape. There is nothing new about this.

Look at Brancusi's studio (I'm talking about the original one on the Impasse Ronsin in Paris). He saw his studio as a metaphorical forest in Romania. The space was of a piece with the objects that it contained: sculptures, blocks of stone, tree trunks. Some pieces were already art; others were about to become it. For Brancusi, there was no difference.

## The Immaterial Elements of Space

Of course space is made up of volumes, high and low volumes, compressions and expansions, calm and tension, horizontal planes and inclined planes. They are all elements intended to stir the emotions, but they are not the only ones. I believe that it is very important to work with the immaterial elements of space, and I am fascinated by this research. I think that it is one of the main currents in my architecture.

The Gothic cathedral moves us with its spaces soaring into the sky, which draw the sinner's soul upward. It also stirs our feelings with elongated windows that shoot blades of light into the dark church, and by the colors that filter through the stained glass. We have to give our profession back its capacity to arouse the emotions by creating dramatic spaces, serene spaces, participatory spaces, secluded spaces. The choice is linked to the function and use of the setting.
If you are designing a museum, you offer contemplation. It is not enough for the light to be perfect. You also need calm, serenity, and even a voluptuous quality linked to contemplation of the work of art.

251

This is what Ernst Beyeler asked from me one day, paraphrasing the words of Matisse.

If you are building a concert hall, it is not enough to provide perfect acoustics: you must encourage participation in the music. Why is it that, at a concert, you can enjoy a symphony that, played on a perfect sound system at home, might leave you cold? Because you are involved: with the conductor on the podium, with the hundred and twenty members of the orchestra who are playing, with the other hundred, five hundred, two thousand people who are experiencing the same emotion at the same moment.

If you build a house, on the other hand, what you are aiming for is a sense of protection, of comfort. You have to create a feeling of intimacy and privacy for its occupants—but without excluding the world outside, nature, the city, and people.

The objectives change each time, but they always turn around the need to stir the emotions. Thirty years ago Reyner Banham wrote *The Architecture of the Well-Tempered Environment*. It was a significant contribution to the opening of a debate on this important concept: that the idea of space, emotionally speaking, is like that of music—it is immaterial.

## Lightness and Transparency

I have spoken of immaterial elements. These are such things as light, transparency, vibration, texture, and color: elements that interact with the form of the space (in some cases they are a consequence of it) but are not just a function of it. To make the most of immaterial elements I started out in an ingenuous, even rather primitive way, from lightness.

Anyone can build using a lot of material. If you make a wall a meter thick, then it is going to stand up. Taking weight away from things, however, teaches you to make the shape of structures do the work, to understand the limits of the strength of components, and to replace rigidity with flexibility.

Once I went to the Ecole des Arts et Métiers in Paris to watch Jean Prouvé teaching. He gave his students a sheet of paper, a small piece of card, and a pair of scissors. He said: "Use this piece of paper to make a bridge from here to here." From here to here was longer than the sheet, and so, whichever way you looked at it, something had to be invented. Some of the students cut the paper up, some folded it, some twisted it. And Jean, as he went by, placed his pencil on the bridge to see if it would stay up. It was a beautiful way of explaining structures. Theory is not enough; drawing has nothing to do with it. You have to use your hands to grasp the principle, as people have always done.

Reducing structures to their essentials means working by elimination, and there is something iconoclastic about that. Taking away is a challenge, a game. When you have finished removing things, you know what is really necessary. Then the emperor has no clothes, for you know that everything else was really superfluous. Perhaps this is why people have taken up the same challenge in painting, in writing, in music.

When you're looking for lightness, you automatically find something else that is precious, and that is very important on the plane of poetic language: transparency. By taking things away, you also remove the opacity from material. In my early days, I liked to work with transparent plastic and glass. Somewhere in this there was a confused, almost unconscious quest for elegance. Lightness is an instrument, and transparency is a poetic quality: this is a very important difference.


## Light

When you are working with light, in the quest for lightness and transparency, there is a logical and poetic continuity. Natural light (often diffused from above) is a constant feature of my work. Ever since the time of my first studio in Genoa and right up to the present one at the Punta Nave, in such projects as the IBM Traveling Pavilion and the museums, I have always paid a great deal of attention to the effects of light on the surroundings, both in terms of perception of the volumes and in those of emotional response. In the de Menil Collection light was consciously used to dematerialize the space, creating the necessary concentration on the works of art. In the church of Padre Pio, on the other hand, we are trying to give light a different role: we are trying to produce a diffuse and indirect illumination in the whole of the church, dramatized by beams of direct light directed at the altar.

To exploit the potential of light we have often created spaces with multiple and successive vertical planes. The museum that houses the de Menil Collection is not an enormous building, but it produces a sense of infinity. The reason lies in the spaces that are superimposed one after the other, in successive planes, lending depth to the visual field. Something similar happens in the great gallery leading to the airplanes in the Kansai Air Terminal. You can't see the end—partly because the dimensions really are incredible, but also because the perspective is distorted: this great space is twenty meters high in the middle, but only six at the end.

Light has not just an intensity, but also a vibration, which is capable of roughening a smooth material, of giving a three-dimensional quality to a flat surface. Light, color, and texture are part of a patient *work in progress* in my studio.

## Ornament

I am using these elements to reintroduce the theme of ornament—not decoration, but ornament. In the baroque era, in the nineteenth century, and in much of the twentieth-century, ornament was handled in an extraordinarily expressive manner (although the snares of academicism were always lying in wait). I believe that architecture has to be given back its richness. It should show the mark of the person who made it, what Peter Rice used to call the "trace of the hand." The quality of the building is also expressed through the quality of the detail.

There is an interesting analogy with the mathematics of fractals. I can indefinitely increase the complexity of a segment. In the same way I can multiply the hierarchies of detail. In Japanese architecture this is an extremely important aspect. There is a ritual way of building houses, with a precise hierarchy of details: from the *tatami* to the partition. But the walls themselves are made up of details: the frame, the rice paper that fills it. Naturally, the rice paper has its own grain, and there is a whole discipline dealing with this. And so on. Quality is based on perfect harmony among all the components, something that is most apparent from very close-up, but that contributes to the pleasure of living in the house. In my work, this attention to the quality of detail has often been combined with research into materials.

Building Workshop has taken another look at terra-cotta, wood, and stone—elements that are found in the most ancient works of architecture—and has tried in some way to "reinvent" their use. Sometimes these materials have been given structural tasks, as in the case of the stone arch in the church of Padre Pio. At others they have served as facings and ornamentation, as with the extruded terra-cotta used for the IRCAM Extension. In both cases the rediscovery of the functional properties of the materials has coincided with a reclamation of their expressive qualities in close relation to the context.

## Nature

My use of natural materials and forms has often given rise to a misunderstanding: the very widespread belief that I am emulating nature in my works. This is not something I even try to do. Nature does things well, and careful observation of it can teach us many things, but imitation is naive and ridiculous. At the most, it is possible to recognize common elements that derive from the application of the laws of physics and mechanics.

The roof of a building may look like a shell, for the shell is an amazing structure, the fruit of millions of years of evolution. That roof, however, is not a metaphor. A church is a church, a shell a shell. If the similarity remains, I would call it allusion rather than imitation.

You recognize something, as often happens in music. You're conscious of having recognized something, but you don't know what it is. And here, once again, it is the relationship between structure, space, and feeling that lies at the center of my work.

## Style

Someone has said that the designs that come out of my studio can be recognized. In reality there is not what might be called a unity of form; there is no constant way of composing volumes. There is no, thank heaven, "Piano sense of space." There is the spatiality of the church, the spatiality of the museum, the spatiality of the auditorium. When style is forced to become a trademark, a signature, a personal characteristic, then it also becomes a cage. The effort to be recognizable at any cost, to put your hallmark on things, kills the architect and his or her freedom to develop. The mark of recognition lies in the acceptance of the challenge. And then, yes, it does become identifiable: but by a method, not by a trademark.

Perhaps my style lies in the way I interpret architecture: the sort of challenge represented by responding in a straightforward and different way to needs and expectations that are themselves always different. Heraclitus said that you never step in the same river twice. Everything flows through our fingers, and changes as it flows. Profiting from experience and memory does not mean coming up with the same old solutions. On the Rue de Meaux Housing, on the IRCAM Extension, on the bank in Lodi, and on the Potsdamer Platz project in Berlin, I used ceramics, but never in the same way twice.

Perhaps the secret is not to keep your dreams in the drawer. They have to be used. They have to be risked. I don't like to hear people say: I had a beautiful idea, but the client didn't want to know about it, so it stayed a dream. If you're really convinced of the value of a design, then you will put it into practice, sooner or later, because you will have the tenacity to propose it again, to develop it, to improve it. And when you have done it, then you will go ahead, and come up with another one, for the adventure continues.

## Language

Rejecting the logic of the trademark does not eliminate the problem of adopting a language. Students and teachers, scientists and technicians, artists and craftspeople, we are all engaged in a search for the language of our time, a time that is born out of the most rapid change that humanity has ever undergone: a revolution in customs, habits, society, technology, and political geography.

You cannot ignore change, and work as if nothing had happened: what I want from my house is different from what my father wanted, or my grandfather. The language of architecture changes as its means and ends evolve. I feel obliged to take part in this quest. It is a journey into the unknown territory of experimentation.

What form will this language take? I can only express my hopes what I would like it to be, and what I would like it not to be. In part, it has to derive from problems that are new or perceived in a new way, such as those relating to the environment. The vocabulary of architecture translates all this into the use of plants, the choice of materials, the application of solutions that save energy.

In part, it has to stem from the language of technology and science: the search for contemporary forms of expression cannot be divorced from technical innovation, perhaps the most characteristic trait of our civilization and the one that has the most influence on the material culture of design. Architecture also speaks the language of electronics, of data processing and telecommunications, of systems for control of the microclimate (but also that of innovations in process: methods of calculation, adhesives, transport systems).

Above all, the new language has to respond to changing needs with a greater attention to the quality of life and work, and an awareness that the inadequacy of housing is the source of much of the malaise in contemporary society.

And what, on the other hand, does the language of architecture need to free itself from? In the first place, I believe, the rhetoric of modernity. What does modern really mean? We often make the mistake of thinking in terms of up-to-dateness: it's in fashion this year, so it must be modern. This is a misunderstanding. Chronology is an inadequate criterion.

The streetcar does not pollute; it is cheap, rational, and reliable: it is a more modern means of transport than the bus, even though it is a hundred years old. Prefabricated concrete panels create rigid spaces that cannot be modified: the walls are held up by a metal framework, and so nothing in the house, no door, window, or partition, can be moved. The house is no longer flexible in its function. So why should reinforced concrete be considered more modern than wood or brick? We have to be on our guard against this deception. True modernity can lie in the oldest of materials, construction techniques, and ideas.

## The Modernity of the Old City

When I'm asked what the city of the future will be like, I answer: like that of the past, I hope. Our century has done terrible damage to that great human invention, the city. Its positive values—social life, the mix of functions, the quality of the buildings—are all leftovers from the past, and barely survive in the urban centers of the present day. And yet they are indisputably modern values.

Today, we speak of multifunctionality, and try to bring it into our designs. Yet until just a few decades ago, cities were multifunctional

256

by definition. The specialization of areas (financial district industrial zone dormitory) is a recent development. There is a microhistory of the contemporary metropolis that I always use to explain these phenomena. After the last war and up until the sixties, cities exploded in size, stealing space from the countryside and nearby towns. The many decaying suburbs that surround us are the offspring of the atrocious city planning of that period. In the seventies the cities ground to a halt: they had to some extent reached the physiological limits of their growth. In the eighties they began to implode and to reabsorb the urban voids created by deindustrialization.

Does this mean that the city is regenerating, healing its wounds? Perhaps. But it is a long process, and one that needs to be assisted if we are going to avoid repeating many of our mistakes. We will have to learn the lesson of the old cities, whose model of urban planning has proved itself open to modification and updating, allowing it to survive for centuries.

## A Humanistic Approach to Architecture

Living on the frontier means avoiding confines. I have chosen to muddy the waters and mix up the disciplines in my work. I'm not interested in the differences between the arts and the sciences; I'm interested in the similarities: the same worries, the same expectations, the same search for rules to learn and then break.

It is the endless prospect of research, which is the same for all disciplines. As Norberto Bobbio says: I have often reached the threshold of the temple, but I have never gone in, such is the inadequacy of our hands in comparison with the force of our ideas. You cannot enter the temple, no one can. And it is no good seeking an unattainable perfection: perfection kills research, and kills architecture. Pierre Boulez once said that research is like hunger: it torments you until you satisfy it, and then it starts all over again.

In the sixteenth century, doctors in Padua used to steal corpses to study human anatomy. In the same years Galileo was studying the motions of the stars. The telescope had been invented to keep an eye on ships, but he decided to use it to look at the stars. These images mean a great deal to me: a way of understanding humanism, a powerful lesson in independence of thought, in the courage to explore the unknown.

Architects, too, are explorers: they live on the frontier, and every so often they cross it, to see what's on the other side. They, too, use the telescope to look for what is not written in the sacred texts.

Living on the frontier means being stateless in a way, because you never feel that you belong completely to one of the two opposing sides. This always prompts the accusation of ambiguity. But if refusing to cut the knot of complexity means being ambiguous, then so be it. Indeed, I wear the label proudly. For duplicity in this sense has a great dignity.

I believe that the architect must lead a double life. On one hand is a taste for exploration, for being on the edge, an unwillingness to accept things for what they appear to be: a disobedient, transgressive, even rather insolent approach. On the other is a genuine, and not formal, gratitude to history and nature: the two contexts in which architecture has its roots. Perhaps this double life is the essence of the only humanistic approach that is possible today.

# The "Workshop" of Architecture

Giulio Macchi

This book does not bring the adventure of the architect Renzo Piano to a close. On the contrary, it marks the beginning of another adventure into less explored territory: that of teaching architecture, something that is persistently requested of those who, like Renzo Piano, have been "constructors" and have never held formal teaching posts.

Piano's "workshop" is already an academy where his young collaborators are involved every day in the actual work of architecture. Renzo's two laboratory-studios, one at Vesima near Genoa, and the other in Paris, just a few meters from the Beaubourg, really do make you think of Renaissance workshops: places where the architect is still considered the master craftsman, the person who, unlike the apprentice, knows how to associate practice with theory, handwork, with the speculation of the intellect.

It seems that what is happening here is a breakdown of the ancient and rigid division between the liberal arts, which make use of words and reflection, and the mechanical arts, regarded as inferior because they are dependent on the use of the hands and tools, a mechanics that even in its Greek root was classified as ignoble and servile.

In Piano's two workshops, on the contrary, everyone participates in each phase of the work, working with their hands as well as their heads. Even those who answer the telephone, make a drawing, operate the computer, or carve a model out of wood are able in the end to recognize their roles, their contributions to the completed work, however great or small.

The work is not organized into rigid schemes, and yet if you look closely you can discern a subtle ritual of initiation: a ritual that certainly escapes the notice of beginners but not that of an attentive observer. The pace of production is rapid and the "initiated" individuals do not realize the extent to which they have adjusted to subtle rules obeyed by all. What should we call those dozens of people who work on the final details of a project before it passes on to the acid test of the construction site, "the scene of the crime"? And how shall we define the people who gather around a new client with blank sheets of paper?

Clearly each of them is an architect, but in a special way. Looking back in time, I could give them the learned title of *doctor lathomarum* ("docteur espiorres," as Pierre de Montreuil described himself in the thirteenth century), or *master mason*, *architectarius*, *artifex*, *ingeniator*, *carpentarius*, *geometricus*. In the end I must fall back on the more elementary designation of

*operarius*, the one best suited to those who operate in Piano's workshops, where things are built up stone by stone, idea by idea, drawing by drawing, calculation by calculation.

They are humanists who work in stone, as well as steel, wood, concrete, ceramics. Here experimentation is continuous. The elements are fused, just as they should be for the true architect, the one who, etymologically speaking, is αρχὴ (*archi*, chief) and τέκτων (*tekton*, builder), i.e. chief builder. To Piano's two studios I would like to add a third: the airplane, where as in a decompression chamber, the "theory" is refined and summarized so that these architects arrive fully prepared at the building site, the real university of architectural communication.

This book sets out to illustrate this ancient and modern methodology, to which one more project is being added: a project that is not a building but a new attempt at communicating the activity of architecture. Other means will be used in addition to the printed page: CD-ROMs, film, and traditional educational materials ranging from models to tapestries, all used to create traveling exhibitions linked in real time with the studio-workshops and the construction sites. These are advanced technologies, but always used with the spirit of the master craftsman who prefers comprehensibility to abstraction. By actually watching the construction, it will be possible to understand its processes, and in the end to appreciate the architecture, for once not presented in the traditional elegant gloss of specialized magazines where everything is spick–and–span but devoid of human beings, deserted like the squares in de Chirico's paintings, even though in these at least the black shadows are strong signs of life.

The architecture that communicates is the kind marked by the presence of its users, who "make it dirty" in a sense but also show it for what it is and allow us to judge it on its merits and defects. The work of architecture is a living body that is nourished by human beings and has to adapt to them and not the other way around. It has to demonstrate its dynamic possibilities.

Sometimes the use to which the construction is put surprises its creator, and sometimes the creator is able to incorporate this into future projects. In practice as well as theory, the process of construction is always in movement, "never finished."

Tracing these stages will allow us to draw attention to the values that are of greatest concern to the best architects of today, who want to free themselves from cumbersome architecture and move toward transparency, as a dialogue between artifice and nature, toward lightness as a way of revealing structure and eliminating the superfluous, lightness that, taken to an extreme, turns out to be linked to transparency. It is building with delicacy and love in the same way our ancestors did when they emerged from their caves and used their skillful hands to "weave" the first huts to receive the hunters home.

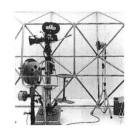

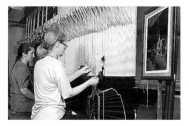

# Biography

A construction site.

Carlo Piano.

Carlo Piano Jr.

Matteo Piano.

Lia Piano.

Giulio Macchi,
Mario Fazio,
and Giovanni
Berengo Gardin.

Louis I. Kahn.

Ermanno Piano.

Giulio Macchi.

Jean Prouvé.

Pierluigi Nervi.

Up to now I have been telling the story of my professional career; now I will try to take the same approach to the story of my life, though I have to admit I find it a little difficult to talk about myself.

I was born in Genoa in 1937, to a family of builders. I have already talked at length about my father: it is to him that I owe my passion for construction. My father's company was taken over by my brother Ermanno, only to close down when he came to a premature death in 1993. It is clear that there has always been a rather special tie with these two, my father and my brother, which derived from our common passion for building. But there have always been very strong emotional ties with the women of my family as well: my mother, Rosa, the tireless defender of a foolish and undisciplined child; my sister, Anna, innocent victim of my first experiments with mechanics. The support of my father and brother allowed me, immediately after graduation, to go down the road of experimentation with materials and technologies: experiences that left a fairly deep mark on the rest of my adventure.

A name that appears among the credits of *Habitat* (the television broadcast that we made with Giulio Macchi) is that of Magda Arduino, my first wife and companion in the long process of my growth. Carlo, Matteo, and Lia are the children born of that marriage. Carlo, now thirty-one, is a journalist, whose reporting is tinged with a great flair for irony. Matteo, twenty-eight, part inventor and part Pythagorean Archimedes, works independently as an industrial designer. Lia, twenty-four, is stubbornly attached to the idea of architecture: I hope that she follows some of the indirect advice in this book.

I have already spoken at some length about the people I consider my "teachers" in the rest of the book, but perhaps this is the place for a heartfelt tribute to Jean Prouvé, to whom I am bound not just by ties of affection but also by a certain affinity in our attitude toward the profession.

Another person who certainly deserves a mention is Franco Albini. He was my teacher in a more literal sense, for I worked in his studio during the years I was studying in Milan.

I also owe a great deal to Ernesto Rogers, who was my professor at the Milan Polytechnic and to Giancarlo De Carlo, who set an indispensable example to students of my age. Two much more distant teachers, whom I hardly met, but to whom I feel very close, were Buckminster Fuller and Pierluigi Nervi.

The two years I spent as Marco Zanuso's assistant, just after graduation, instilled in me a strong interest in industrial design. Bruno Zevi has often given me imperious advice at crucial moments of my career.

I learned a lot from Gino Valle, often met Richard Rogers in London and Herman Hertzberger in Amsterdam, and enjoy discussions about the logic of design with Cesare De Seta. And I like to venture beyond the confines of architecture, to the company of writers, musicians, artists, poets, and anyone who takes a different approach to their work.

I'd like to be able to talk about my best friends, both those known to the public and those who are not. There are not very many whom I can really consider such.

I think it would be better, however, to refer to them in general, for that's how it is in reality: each of them is part of me, just as, I hope, I am for them.

I will make an exception for one person who is no longer with us: Peter Rice. You will have come across him frequently in this book, as we worked together on many projects. He was a great friend, a person from whom I think I learned not to give up, to keep on questioning everything until the best solution was reached.

If you are keen and patient readers of the credits, then you will have noticed another name that crops up often in the projects of the last six or seven years: that of E. Rossato. This is Milly, my wife since 1992. It is difficult for me to find the words here to convey the importance of her role in my life.

A few significant dates. In 1964 I graduated from the Milan Polytechnic, after studying at Florence University for two years. Between 1964 and 1970 I worked chiefly in Milan, with frequent trips to London. In 1970 I began my partnership with Richard Rogers, which led to our participation in the competition for the Centre Pompidou. These were also the years in which I commenced my fruitful collaboration with Peter Rice. After 1980 my studio was transformed into the Building Workshop, with offices in Paris and Genoa. This name was deliberately chosen to express the sense of collaboration and teamwork that permeates our work.

I would like to take this opportunity to thank the people who have been my companions on this adventure from the outset. You will have already encountered their names in the individual projects. But you will have seen many other names there too, just as there are very many more whom I have not been able to mention. You will find them all at the end of the book, in the list that we call the "thousand"—so many are the people who have spent time at the Building Workshop. All of them, to some degree or other, have left a mark. I hope that something has remained in them as well.

Genoa.

Richard Rogers and Milly Piano.

Talia and Luciano Berio.

Flavio Marano.

Robert Bordaz and Richard Rogers.

Peter Rice.

Reyner Banham and Peter Rice.

Shunji Ishida.

Bernard Plattner.

# Register of Works

**1964–65**
**Reinforced Polyester Space Frames**
Genoa, Italy
Studio Piano

**1965**
**Woodworking Shop**
Genoa, Italy
Studio Piano
With: R. Foni, M. Filocca, L. Tirelli
Contractor: Impresa E. Piano

**1966**
**Mobile Sulfur Extraction Factory**
Pomezia (Rome), Italy
Studio Piano
Contractor: Impresa E. Piano

**1966**
**Space Frame in Small Inflatable Units**
Genoa, Italy
Studio Piano

**1966**
**Prestressed Steel and Reinforced
Polyester Structure**
Genoa, Italy
Client: IPE, Genoa
Studio Piano
Design team: F. Marano
Contractor: Impresa E. Piano

**1967**
**Pavilion for the 14th Triennale**
Milan, Italy
Client: Milan Triennale
Studio Piano
Design team: F. Marano, O. Celadon,
G. Fascioli

**1967**
**Reinforced-Concrete Construction
System**
Bologna, Italy
Client: Vibrocemento, Bologna
Studio Piano
Design team: F. Marano, G. Fascioli
With: R. Iascone

**1968**
**Industrialized Construction System for
a Residential District**
Genoa, Italy
Client: IPE, Genoa

Studio Piano
Design team: F. Marano, O. Celadon,
G. Fascioli
Consultant: Sertec (structural engeener)
Contractor: Impresa E. Piano

**1968**
**Roofing for Olivetti Factories**
Scarmagno (Ivrea), Italy
Client: Olivetti S.p.A.
Studio Piano
Design team: F. Marano, O. Celadon,
G. Fascioli, M. Zanuso, E. Vittoria

**1968**
**Roofing Components for the Olivetti-
Underwood Factory**
Harrisburg, Pennsylvania
Client: Olivetti Ltd., Harrisburg
Studio Piano
Design team: F. Marano, L. J. Kahn
Consultant: Sertec (structures)

**1968–69**
**Vertical Building Extension**
London, England
Client: DRU (Design Research Unit) and
Piano & Rogers
Studio Piano & Rogers
Design team: M. Goldschmied,
P. Botschi, Y. Kaplicky

**1968–71**
**Shopping Center on Fitzroy Street**
Cambridge, England
Client: Cambridge City Council
Studio Piano & Rogers
Design team: J. Young,
M. Goldschmied, J. Morris

**1969**
**Studio Piano**
Genoa, Italy
Client: R. Piano
Studio Piano
Design team: F. Marano, O. Celadon,
T. Ferrari
Builder: Impresa E. Piano

**1969**
**Olivetti Factory Roofing**
Crema (Cremona), Italy
Client: Olivetti S.p.A.
Studio Piano
Design team: F. Marano, G. Fascioli,
M. Zanuso, E. Vittoria
Builder: Impresa E. Piano

**1969**
**Free-Plan House**
Garonne (Alessandria), Italy
Client: Olivetti S.p.A.

Studio Piano
Design team: F. Marano, G. Fascioli,
T. Ferrari
Builder: Impresa E. Piano

**1969**
**Italian Pavilion, Osaka Expo**
Osaka, Japan
Client: Italpublic, Rome
Studio Piano
Design team: F. Marano, G. Fascioli,
G. Queirolo, T. Ferrari
Consultant: Sertec (structures)
Builder: Impresa E. Piano

**1970**
**ARAM Module**
Client: ARAM (Association for Rural
Aids in Medicine), Washington, D.C.
Studio Piano & Rogers
Design team: M. Goldschmied, J. Young

**1970–74**
**Free-Plan Houses**
Cusago (Milan), Italy
Client: Luci, Giannotti, Simi, Pepe
Studio Piano & Rogers
Design team: C. Brullmann,
R. Luccardini, G. Fascioli
With: R. and S. Lucci
Consultant: F. Marano

**1971–73**
**B & B Italia Offices**
Novedrate (Como), Italy
Client: B & B Italy, Como
Studio Piano
Design team: C. Brullmann, S. Cereda,
G. Fascioli

**1971–78**
**Centre Georges Pompidou**
Paris, France
Client: Ministry of Cultural Affairs,
Ministry of National Education
Studio Piano & Rogers
Design team: R. Piano, R. Rogers,
G. F. Franchini (competition, program,
interiors)
Substructure and mechanical services:
W. Zbinden, H. Bysaeth, J. Lohse,
P. Merz, P. Dupont
Superstructure and mechanical services:
L. Abbott, S. Ishida, H. Naruse,
H. Takahashi
Facade and galleries: E. Holt
Internal/external interfaces, audiovisual
systems: A. Staton, M. Dowd, R. Verbizh
Coordination and site supervision:
C. Brullmann, B. Plattner
IRCAM: M. Davies, N. Okabe,
K. Rupard, J. Sircus, W. Zbinden

Interiors: J. Young, F. Barat, H. Diebold,
J. Fendard, J. Huc, H. Sohlegel
Secretaries: F. Gousinguenet,
C. Spielmann, C. Valensi
Consultants: Ove Arup & Partners
(P. Rice, L. Grut, R. Pierce, T. Barker)
(structures and M.E. services);
M. Espinoza (cost control)
Contractors: GTM (Jean Thaury, site
engineer) (main contractor); Krupp,
Mont-a-Mousson, Pohlig (structure);
Voyer (secondary structures); Otis
(elevators and escalator); Industrielle de
Chauffage, Saunier Duval (heating and
ventilation); CFEM (glazing)

**1972**
**Reinforced-Concrete Pleasure Boat**
Genoa, Italy
Client: ATIBIS S.r.l.
Studio Piano
Design team: R. Gaggero, F. Marano,
C. Brullmann, G. Fascioli, T. Ferrari

**1972**
**Conversion of a Canal Boat**
Paris, France
Client: Piano & Rogers
Studio Piano & Rogers
Design team: C. Brullmann, F. Marano

**1973**
**Chemical Laboratory for Perfume
Production**
Ashford, England
Client: UOP Fragrances Ltd., London
Studio Piano & Rogers
Design team: M. Goldschmied,
J. Young, R. Bormioli, P. Flack,
N. Winder, P. Ullathorne
Consultant: Antony Hunt Associated
(structures)

**1973**
**Factory Building**
Ovada (Alessandria), Italy
Client: ATIB S.r.l.
Studio Piano & Rogers
Design team: G. Fascioli
Consultant: F. Marano (structures)

**1973**
**Paris Atelier**
Paris, France
Client: Atelier Piano
Studio Piano

**1976**
**Electromechanical Laboratory**
Cambridge, England
Client: Pat Division, Cambridge
Studio Piano & Rogers

Design team: J. Young,
M. Goldschmied, M. Burckhardt,
D. Gray, D. Thom, P. Ullathorne
Consultant: Felix J. Samuely (structures)

**1976**
**Telephone Exchanges**
Client: F.lli Dioguardi S.p.A.
Studio Piano & Rice
Design team: S. Ishida, N. Okabe

**1977**
**Office Blocks**
Milan, Italy
Studio Piano & Rice
Design team: S. Ishida, N. Okabe

**1977**
**Studio and Workshop**
Genoa, Italy
Client: Studio Piano
Studio Piano

**1977–80**
**Lodgings and Laboratories**
Marne la Vallée (Paris), France
Client: Etablissement Public de la Ville
Nouvelle de Marne la Vallée
Studio Piano & Rice
Design team: B. Plattner, W. Zbinden,
J. Lohse

**1978**
**Kronenbourg Company Factory**
Selestat (Strasbourg), France
Client: Kronenbourg e Ingetec eng.
Studio Piano & Rice
Design team: M. Down, B. Plattner,
R. Verbizh, W. Zbinden
With: N. Okabe, J. Lohse, C. Ostrej
Consultants: GETTEC, Inex, NNN
(structures)

**1978**
**Wall System**
Client: F.lli Dioguardi S.p.A.
Studio Piano & Rice
Design team: S. Ishida, N. Okabe

**1978**
**Housing District Competition**
Cergy (Pontoise), France
Client: Studio Piano & Rice
Design team: M. Dowd, B. Plattner,
R. Verbizh, W. Zbinden

**1978**
**Flying Carpet**
Client: IDEA S.p.A.
Studio Piano & Rice
Design team: S. Ishida, N. Okabe, IDEA
Institute (F. Mantegazza, W. De Silva)

**1978**
**Mobile Construction Unit**
Dakar, Senegal
Client: UNESCO, Dakar Regional
Office, M. Senghor, Breda of Dakar
Studio Piano & Rice
Design team: R. Verbizh, O. Dellicour,
S. Ishida

**1978**
**Monopiano Competition**
Studio Piano & Rice
Design team: S. Ishida, N. Okabe,
G. Picardi, F.lli Dioguardi S.p.A.
With: S. Pietrogrande, D. M. Fontana

**1978–80**
**VSS**
Client: Fiat Auto S.p.A., Turin: IDEA
Institute
Studio Piano & Rice
Design team: S. Ishida, N. Okabe,
L. Abbott, B. Plattner, A. Stanton,
R. Verbizh
With: IDEA Institute, S. Boggio,
F. Conti, O. Di Blasi, W. De Silva,
M. Sibona
Consultants: Ove Arup & Partners
(T. Barker) (structures); S. Brown
Assoc. (acoustics)

**1978–82**
**Il Rigo Evolutive Housing**
Corciano (Perugia), Italy
Client: Vibrocemento Perugia S.p.A.,
Perugia
Studio Piano & Rice
Design team: S. Ishida, N. Okabe
With: E. Donato, G. Picardi
Consultants: P. Rice, F. Marano,
H. Bardsley in collaboration with
Vibrocemento Perugia (structures)

**1978–82**
**Rigo Quartier**
Corciano (Perugia), Italy
Client: Municipality of Corciano
Studio Piano & Rice
Design team: S. Ishida, N. Okabe,
L. Custer
With: E. Donato, G. Picardi,
O. Di Blasi, F. Marano
Consultants: P. Rice assisted by
H. Bardsley, F. Marano in collaboration
with Edilcooper, R.P.A. Associati,
Vibrocemento Perugia (structures);
L. Custer, F. Marano (directors of works)

**1978–82**
**Vacation Houses**
S. Luca di Molare (Alessandria), Italy
Client: Immobiliare S. Luca

Studio Piano
Design team: S. Ishida, G. Picardi,
E. Donato, O. Di Blasi, F. Marano,
G. Fascioli
Consultant: O. Di Blasi (director of
works)

**1979**
**UNESCO Urban Reconstruction**
**Workshop**
Otranto, Italy
Client: UNESCO (S. Busutill,
W. Tochtermann)
Studio Piano & Rice
Design team: E. Donato, G. Fascioli,
R. Gaggero, S. Ishida (associate in charge),
R. Melai, N. Okabe (associate architect),
R. Piano, G. Picardi, P. Rice, R. Verbizh
With: M. Arduino Piano, M. Fazio,
G. Macchi, F. Marano, F. Marconi
Consultants: Ove Arup & Partners,
IDEA Institute, G. P. Cuppini,
G. Gasbarri, Editech; G. F. Dioguardi
(coordination and administration)

**1979**
**Habitat Television Program**
Client: RAI (Radiotelevisione Italiana)
Studio Piano & Rice
Design team: S. Ishida, N. Okabe,
G. Picardi, S. Yamada, M. Bonino,
R. Biondo, G. Fascioli, R. Gaggero
Consultants: G. Macchi (broadcast);
V. Lusvardi (director); M. Arduino
Piano (text and screenplan)

**1979**
**ANACT Office-Factory**
Client: Piano & Rice
Studio Piano & Rice
Design team: M. Dowd

**1979–81**
**Emergency Dwelling Prototype**
Macolin, Switzerland
Client: Département Affaires Etrangères
de la Confédération Helvetique
Studio Piano & Rice
Design team: Studio Piano & Rice
(competition); B. Plattner, P. Rice
(design development)

**1980**
**Burano Island Restructuring**
Burano (Venice), Italy
Client: Municipality of Venice
Studio Piano & Rice
Design team: S. Ishida
With: P. H. Chombard De Lauwe,
University of Venice, Coordination
Foundation 3 Oci, G. Macchi and
A. Macchi assisted by H. Bardsley,

M. Calvi, L. Custer, C. Teoldi
Curator: M. Arduino Piano

**1980**
**CAGE Multifunctional Food Provision**
**Center**
Genoa, Italy
Client: Municipality of Genoa
Studio Piano/Building Workshop
Design team: S. Ishida, F. Marano,
E. Donato, F. Doria, G. Fascioli
Consultants: F. Torrieri (services);
Ansaldo S.p.A., Elsag S.p.A., Molinari
Appalti S.r.l., Aerimpianti S.p.A.,
Termomecanica S.p.A. (mechanical
services)

**1980**
**Cultural and Exhibition Center**
Passaggio di Bettona (Perugia), Italy
Client: Sig.ri Lipsi
Studio Piano & Rice/Building
Workshop
Design team: S. Ishida, L. Custer,
F. Marano
With: F. Icardi, R. Ruocco

**1980**
**PEX Exhibition Complex**
Milan, Italy
Client: Nidosa, Gruppo Cabassi
Studio Piano/Building Workshop
Design team: S. Ishida, F. Doria,
E. Frigerio, A. Traldi, F. Marano, G. Trebbi
With: M. Carroll, O. Di Blasi, R. Melai,
E. Miola, G. Fascioli, R. Gaggero
Consultants: M. Arduino Piano,
M. Bonino, S. Battini (documentary
film-makers);: C. Giambelli, D. Zucchi,
Ove Arup & Partners (engineers); Italian
Promoservice (trade fair consultant);
B. Richards (transport consultant);
G. Lund (trade fair technical consultant;
APT (fire and safety)

**1980**
**Beach and Port Detail Plan**
Loano (Savona), Italy
Client: Municipality of Loano
Studio Piano/Building Workshop
Design team: S. Ishida, A. Traldi,
F. Doria, M. Carroll, G. Picardi
Consultants: Brizzolara (engineer)

**1980**
**Loano Civic Center**
Loano (Savona), Italy
Client: Municipality of Loano
Studio Piano/Building Workshop
Design team: S. Ishida, A. Traldi,
F. Doria, M. Carroll, G. Picardi
Consultants: Brizzolara (engineer)

**1980–81**

**Bearing Structure for the Milanofiori
Conference Center**
Milan, Italy
Client: WTC Milan
Studio Piano/Building Workshop
Design team: S. Ishida, F. Marano

**1980–81**

**Arvedi Tubular Structural System**
Cremona, Italy
Client: Arvedi S.p.A.
Studio Piano & Rice/Building
Workshop
Design team: S. Ishida, O. Di Blasi
Consultants: P. Rice, H. Bardsley,
Arvedi, Gosio, Galli (structures)

**1980–82**

**District Laboratory for Local
Maintenance Services**
Bari, Italy
Client: Impresa F.lli Dioguardi, Bari
Studio Piano/Building Workshop
Design team: N. Costantino,
S. Pietrogrande, G. Ferracuti, S. Ishida,
F. Marano, E. Frigero, E. Donato,
G. Fascioli, C. Teoldi
Consultants: Impresa Dioguardi, SES
Engineering, L. Malgieri assisted by
A. Alto, G. Amendola (structures);
M. Arduino Piano (curator)

**1981**

**Restoration Plan for the Old Pier
District and Services Center**
Genoa, Italy
Client: Municipality of Genoa
Studio Piano/Building Workshop
Design team: S. Ishida, A. Traldi,
F. Marano, A. Bianchi, E. Frigerio
With: R. Ruocco, F. Icardi, R. Melai,
E. Miola
Consultants: V. Podestà, G. Amedeo di
Tekne Planning (technical consultant for
urban planning); F. Pagano (lawyer);
M. Arduino Piano (curator)

**1981**

**Restructuring of a Block in the Old
Town Center**
Turin, Italy
Client: Municipality of Turin
Studio Piano/Building Workshop
Design team: S. Ishida, F. Marano,
R. Ruocco, F. Icardi, E. Frigerio
Curator: M. Arduino Piano

**1981**

**Extension of the Nationalgalerie and
Residence**
Berlin, Germany

Client: IBA, Berlin
Studio Piano/Building Workshop
Design team: S. Ishida , C. Susstrunk
With: F. Doria, N. Okabe, A. Traldi

**1981–83**

**Building for Banca Agricola
Commerciale, Automobile Club
Italiano, and Public Services**
Reggio Emilia, Italy
Client: Banca Agricola Commerciale
Studio Piano/Building Workshop
Design team: E. Donato, F. Doria,
S. Ishida, F. Marano, C. Susstrunk
Consultants: A. Rossi (engineer);
S. Ferretti (coordinator)

**1981–84**

**Schlumberger Facilities Restructuring**
Montrouge (Paris), France
Client: Compteurs Montrouge
(Schlumberger Ltd.)
Atelier Piano
Design team: T. Hartman, S. Ishida,
J. Lohse, R. Piano, B. Plattner (associate
in charge), N. Okabe (associate in
charge), D. Rat, G. Saintjean,
J. F. Schmit, P. Vincent
With: M. Alluyn, A. Gillet, F. Laville,
G. Petit, C. Susstrunk
Consultants: GEC (R. Duperrier,
F. Petit), Paris (cost control); P. Rice
(engineer for tension structure);
A. Chemetoff, M. Massot, C. Pierdet
(landscaping); M. Dowd, J. Huc (interiors)

**1982**

**OPEC Headquarters Competition**
Kuwait
Client: Organization of Petroleum
Exporting Countries
Studio Piano/Building Workshop
Design team: S. Ishida, A. Traldi,
F. Doria, B. Mehren, M. Carroll,
E. Frigerio, Tekne V.C.R.
With: C. Bottigelli, Parodi, Seratto

**1982**

**Alexander Calder Retrospective
Exhibition**
Turin, Italy
Client: Municipality of Turin (curator:
G. Carandente)
Studio Piano/Building Workshop
Design team: O. Di Blasi, S. Ishida
(associate architect)
With: G. Fascioli, F. Marano,
P. Terbuchte, A. Traldi
Consultants: Ove Arup & Partners
(plans); Tensoteci (tensile structures);
P. Castiglioni (lighting); P. L. Cerri
(graphic design)

**1982**

**Centocelle Management Center**
Rome, Italy
Client: Brioschi Finanziaria, Gruppo
Cabassi
Studio Piano/Building Workshop
Design team: S. Ishida, F. Marano,
A. Traldi, B. Merhen, M. Carroll,
E. Frigerio, A. Bianchi, F. Doria
Consultant: Clerici (engineer)

**1982**

**Universal Exposition 1989**
Paris, France
Client: French Ministry of Culture
Atelier Piano
Design team: N. Okabe, J. F. Schmidt,
G. Petit, C. Clarisse
Consultants: P. Rice, H. Bardsley
(engineers); C. Hodeir (historical
research)

**1982**

**Pietra Area Detail Plan**
Omegna (Novara), Italy
Client: Municipality of Omegna
Renzo Piano Building Workshop
Design team: S. Ishida, E. Frigerio,
D. L. Hart, F. Marano, A. Bianchi
With: M. Calosso, R. Ripamonti,
F. Santolini
Consultant: Studio Ambiente S.r.l.,
Milan (urban planning)

**1982**

**Banca Agricola Commerciale Agency**
Modena, Italy
Client: Banca Agricola Commerciale
Renzo Piano/Building Workshop
Design team: S. Ishida, E. Frigerio
Consultants: Ceccoli (engineer); Jascone
(associate engineer)

**1982–86**

**Menil Collection**
Houston, Texas
Client: Menil Foundation (President:
D. De Menil; Director: W. Hopps; Vice
Director: P. Winkler)
Piano & Fitzgerald
Design team: S. Ishida (associate in
charge), M. Carroll, F. Doria,
M. Downs, C. Patel, B. Plattern,
C. Susstrunk
Consultants: Ove Arup & Partners
(P. Rice, N Nobel, J. Thornton)
(structures); Hayne & Whaley
Associates, Houston (services);
Galewsky & Johnston, Beaumont
(local services): R. Jensen, Houston
(fire prevention)
Contractor: E. G. Lowry, Houston

**1983**

**Restructuring and Extension of Centre
Georges Pompidou**
Paris, France
Client: Centre Georges Pompidou
Renzo Piano/Atelier Paris
Design team: N. Okabe, J. Lohse,
B. Vaudeville, P. Vincent
Consultants: Albion, Paris, Etenien
Lenglume (structures); GEC (Robert
Duperrier, Francis Petit), Paris (cost
estimation); Inex, Paris (services);
P. Castiglioni (lighting)

**1983**

**Extension and Site Planning of the
Valpolcevera Purification Plant**
Genoa, Italy
Client: Municipality of Genoa
Renzo Piano Building Workshop
Design team: S. Ishida, M. Carroll,
D. L. Hart, F. Marano
With: P. Beccio, F. Icardi, L. Ruocco
Consultant: Italimpianti

**1983–84**

*Prometeo* **Musical Space Design**
Venice and Milan, Italy
Client: Ente Autonomo, Teatro alla
Scala, Milan
Renzo Piano Building Workshop
Design team: C. Abagliano, D. L. Hart,
S. Ishida (associate in charge), A. Traldi,
M. Visconti
Consultants: M. Milan, S. Favero
(structures); L. Nono (music);
M. Cacciari (text); C. Abbado (director)
With: R. Cecconi
Contractor: G. F. Dioguardi S.p.A

**1983–86**

**IBM Traveling Pavilion**
Client: IBM Europe
Renzo Piano/Building Workshop
Design team: O. Di Blasi, F. Doria,
G. Fascioli, S. Ishida (associate in
charge), A. Traldi
Consultants: Ove Arup & Partners
(P. Rice, T. Barker) (structures and
mechanical engineering); Renzo Piano
Atelier de Paris (N. Okabe, P. Vincent,
J. B. Lacaudre) (site coordination)
Contractor: Calabrese engineering
S.p.a., Bari

**1983–91**

**Subway Stations**
Genoa, Italy
Client: Municipality of Genoa
Renzo Piano Building Workshop
Design team: D. H. Hart (Dinegro,
Caricamento, Darsena, De Ferrari,

Principe, Sarzano stations, 1983–94), S. Ishida (associate architect), C. Manfreddo (Caricamento, Darsena stations, 1983), F. Marano (associate engineer), V. Tolu (Canepari, Principe stations, 1983–94), M. Varratta (Brin station, 1983–90), M. Carroll, O. Di Blasi, E. Frigerio
With: A. Alborghetti, E. Baglietto, K. Cussoneau, G. Fascioli, N. Freedman, P. Maggiora, M. Mallamaci, M. Mattei, B. Merello, D. Peluffo, D. Cavagna, E. Miola (models)
Consultants: MAGECO S.r.l. (L. Mascia, D. Mascia), Genoa (station structure); INCO S.p.A., Milan, REICO S.p.A., Milan (route structure); Aerimpianti S.p.A., Milan (plans); M. Desvigne (landscaping)
Contractors: Ansaldo trasporti S.p.A., Genoa, Imprese Riunite, Genoa

### 1983–95
### Lingotto Factory Conversion
Turin, Italy
Client: Fiat S.p.A.
Renzo Piano Building Workshop
Design team: S. Ishida (associate in charge), C. Di Bartolo, O. Di Blasi, M. Carroll, F. Doria, G. Fascioli, E. Frigerio, R. Gaggero, D. L. Hart, P. Terbuchte, R. V. Truffelli
*Feasibility Study, 1985*
Client: Municipality of Turin
Renzo Piano Building Workshop
Design team: S. Ishida (associate in charge), E. Frigerio (associate architect), O. Di Blasi, K. Dreissigacker, M. Mattei
With: G. G. Bianchi, G. Fascioli, M. Visconti
Consultants: G. De Rita (economics); R. Guiducci (sociology)
*Final Project, 1991*
Client: Lingotto S.r.l.
Renzo Piano Building Workshop
Design team: S. Ishida (associate in charge), P. Ackermann, E. Baglietto, A. Calafati, M. Carroll (test track, landscaping, south tower, 1994), M. Cattaneo (interiors, 1994), A. Carisetto, G. Cohen, F. Colle, I. Corte (CAD), P. Costa, M. Cucinella (pavilion five, 1987), S. De Leo, A. De Luca, S. Durr, K. Frasen, A. Giovannoni, D. Guerrisi (CAD), C. Hays, G. Hernandez, C. Herrin, W. Kestel, G. Langasco (CAD), P. Maggiora, D. Magnano, M. Mariani, K. A. Naderi, T. O'Sullivan, D. Piano (completion), G. Robotti (CAD), M. Rossato Piano, A. Sacchi, S. Scarabicchi (public floor, hotel, offices, 1994), P. Sanso,

L. Siracusa (CAD), A. Stadlmayer, R. V. Truffelli (completion), M. Varratta (fair center, 1992; concert hall, 1994), N. Van Oosten, H. Yamaguchi
With: S. Arecco, F. Bartolomeo, N. Camerada, M. Carletti, R. Croce Bermondi, I. Cuppone, A. Giovannoni, M. Nouvion, P. Pedrini, M. Piano, D. Cavagna, E. Miola, P. Varratta (models)
Consultants: Ove Arup & Partners (concept design), A. I. Engineering, Fiat Engineering (final design) (structures and mechanical engineering); Arup Acoustic, Müller Bbm (acoustics); Davis Langdon Everest (cost control); Techplan (theater); ECL (exhibition area management); CSST (commercial); P. Castiglioni (lighting); P. L. Cerri, ECO S.p.A. (graphic design); F. Santolini (compliance); Studio Vitone e Associati (fair center, 1992), F. Levi, G. Mottino (second phase, 1994) (site supervision); Studio Program (I. Castore) (fair center, 1992) R. Montauti, B. Roventini, G. Vespignani, S. Rum, E. Bindi (second phase, 1994) (building inspectors)
Contractor: Fiat Engineering, Turin (pavilion five)
Temporary association of contractors: Recchi, Pizzarotti, Guerrini, Rosso, Borini e Prono (fair center, 1992)

### 1984
### Leisure Center Study
Cremona, Italy
Client: Acciaieria tubificio Arvedi
Renzo Piano Building Workshop
Design team: S. Ishida (associate), O. Di Blasi
With: G. Fascioli, F. Santolini
Consultant: A. Stanton, London

### 1984
### S.p.A. Exhibition Area
Genoa, Italy
Client: Spazio espositivo S.p.A.
Renzo Piano Building Workshop
Design team: S. Ishida (associate), M. Carroll

### 1984
### Tourist Center Restructuring Study
Sestriere (Turin), Italy
Client: SAES S.p.A., Turin
Renzo Piano Building Workshop/Atelier de Paris
Design team: S. Ishida, E. Frigerio (associate architect), F. Marano, A. Vincent, N. Okabe, T. Hartman
With: M. Mattei, R. V. Truffelli, M. Visconti, M. Varratta, J. B. Lacoudre, B. Plattner, N. Prouvé, P. Vincent

Consultants: AI Engineering S.r.l., Turin (structures); AI Studio S.r.l., Turin (urban planning)

### 1984
### Olivetti Office Block
Naples, Italy
Client: Coginvest S.p.A., Naples
Renzo Piano Building Workshop
Design team: S. Ishida (associate), M. Carroll, F. Marano
With: G. Fascioli, F. Santolini, M. Varratta
Consultants: S. Cirillo, Naples (structures); R. Cecconi, Naples (director of works)
Contractor: Cogeco S.p.A., Naples

### 1984
### Gulf Exhibition and Business Center
Lissone (Milan), Italy
Client: Ahmed Idris Nasreddin, Milan
Renzo Piano Building Workshop
Design team: S. Ishida (associate), F. Marano, F. Santolini, A. Traldi

### 1984
### Kenya Energy Laboratories Project
Nairobi, Kenya
Client: Ministry of Energy, Kenya
Renzo Piano Building Workshop/Cesen
Design team: S. Ishida (associate), G. Fascioli, F. Santolini, E. Miola (models)
Consultants: Studio Phoebus, Catania (structures and mechanical engineering)

### 1984–85
### Indesit Electrical Appliances
Client: Indesit elettrodomestici S.p.A., Turin
Renzo Piano Building Workshop
Design team: N. Okabe, J. P. Lacoudre
With: N. Prouvé, D. Laville (models)
Consultants: Peutz et Associés, The Hague (H. Straatsma, Y. De Querel), Paris (acoustics); S. Boggio, Turin (industrialization)

### 1984–85
### Lowara Company Offices
Montecchio Maggiore (Vicenza), Italy
Client: Renzo Ghiotto (Lowara)
Renzo Piano Building Workshop
Design team: S. Ishida (associate), O. Di Blasi (associate architect)
With: G. Fascioli, D. L. Hart, M. Mattei, M. Varratta
Consultants: M. Milan, S. Favero, Venice (structures); Studio Sire, Venice (landscaping)
Contractor: Trevisan Tachera

### 1985
### Competition for Airport Hangars Restructuring
Le Bourget (Paris), France
Client: UTA (Union Transport Aériens), Paris
Renzo Piano Building Workshop
Design team: A. Vincent, N. Okabe, J. B. Lacoudre
With: F. Laville, N. Prouvé
Consultants: GEC, Paris (technical studies); F. Petit (cost control)

### 1985
### Fruit and Vegetable Market Competition
Genoa, Italy
Client: Municipality of Genoa
Renzo Piano Building Workshop
Design team: S. Ishida, D. L. Hart, F. Marano
With: G. G. Bianchi, C. Manfreddo
Consultant: Ansaldo S.p.A., Genoa

### 1985
### Regional Conference Center
Genoa, Italy
Client: Centro congressi S.p.A., Genoa
Renzo Piano Building Workshop
Design team: S. Ishida, D. L. Hart, F. Marano, R. V. Truffelli
With: G. G. Bianchi
Consultants: Ansaldo S.p.A., Genoa, Italimpianti, Genoa, Elsag S.p.A., Genoa (structures and mechanical engineering)

### 1985
### Calabrese Business Center
Bari, Italy
Client: Calabrese veicoli industriali S.p.A., Bari
Renzo Piano Building Workshop
Design team: S. Ishida (associate), E. Frigerio, F. Marano
With: M. Mattei
Consultants: Calabrese Engineering S.p.A., Bari (structures and mechanical engineering)

### 1985
### Vallone Bank Agency Building
Bari, Italy
Client: Le Valli Immobiliari S.r.l., Lecce
Renzo Piano Building Workshop
Design team: S. Ishida (associate), E. Frigerio, M. Mattei
With: G. Fascioli, F. Marano, M. Visconti
Consultants: Calabrese Engineering S.p.A., Bari (structures, mechanical engineering, director of works)
Contractor: B. Montinari, Lecce

**1985**
**Fiat Prototype Display Space**
Turin, Italy
Client: Centro stile Fiat S.p.A., Turin
Renzo Piano/Atelier de Paris
Design team: N. Okabe, B. Vaudeville
Consultant: Ove Arup & Partners
(P. Rice, T. Barker), London

**1985**
**Treasury Training and Professional
Development Center**
Marne-la-Vallée (Paris), France
Client: French Economic and Finance
Ministry
Renzo Piano/Atelier de Paris
Design team: A. Vincent, N. Okabe,
J. F. Schmit, G. B. Lacoudre
With: C. Clarisse, F. Laville, N. Prouvé
Consultants: A. Benzeno, GEC, Paris
(cost control); C. Simon
(documentation); D. Collin,
Paris (landscaping); Sodeteg, Paris
(structures and mechanical engineering)

**1985**
**Office Tower**
Naples, Italy
Client: Coginvest S.p.A., Naples
Renzo Piano Building Workshop
Design team: S. Ishida, M. Carroll,
D. L. Hart, F. Marano
With: C. Manfreddo, F. Santolini
Consultants: G. Di Meglio, M. Mattei
(general coordination)

**1985**
**Urban Planning and Town Hall
Extension**
Cagliari, Italy
Client: Municipality of Cagliari
Renzo Piano Building Workshop
Design team: S. Ishida, M. Carroll,
O. Di Blasi, F. Marano
With: F. Santolini, M. Varratta

**1985**
**Monticello Area Redevelopment**
Savona, Italy
Client: Municipality of Savona
Renzo Piano Building Workshop
Design team: S. Ishida, D. L. Hart,
F. Marano
With: G. G. Bianchi
Consultants: Studio Ambiente S.r.l.,
Milan (urban planning)

**1985**
**Industrial Area Restructuring Study**
Genoa, Italy
Client: Azienda municipalizzata gas e
acqua

Renzo Piano Building Workshop
Design team: S. Ishida, M. Carroll,
F. Marano
With: F. Santolini, M. Varratta

**1985**
**Reuse of Venetian Dockyards
in Khania**
Khania, Crete, Greece
Client: UNESCO
Renzo Piano Building Workshop
Design team: G. G. Bianchi,
T. Hartman, S. Ishida, E. Karitakis,
N. Prouvé

**1985**
**Study for the Conversion of an
Industrial Area into a Glass Exhibition
and Demonstration Center**
Murano (Venice), Italy
Client: Società veneziana conterie S.p.A.,
Murano, Samim S.p.A., Rome
Renzo Piano Building Workshop
Design team: B. Plattner, A. Vincent
With: P. Vincent
Consultant: C. Simon

**1985**
**Service-Supporting Mobile Office Wall
System**
Client: Unifor, Milan
Renzo Piano Building Workshop
Design team: J. B. Lacoudre, N. Okabe,
A. Vincent
With: N. Prouvé, J. Y. Richard
(models)
Consultants: Albion (E: Lenglume),
Paris (structures); Peutz et Associés,
Paris (acoustics)

**1985**
**Magic Box (Operating Mobile Unit)**
Genoa, Italy
Client: Ansaldo S.p.A., Genoa
Renzo Piano Building Workshop
Design team: O. Di Blasi, S. Ishida
With: Cesen
Consultants: Calabrese Engineering
S.p.A., Bari (structures)

**1985**
**Study for the Conversion of an
Industrial Area into an Office Park**
Genoa, Italy
Client: Ansaldo S.p.A., Genoa
Renzo Piano Building Workshop
Design team: M. Carroll, S. Ishida,
R. V. Truffelli
With: F. Santolini, M. Varratta,
Cesen
Consultants: Calabrese
Engineering S.p.A., Bari (structures)

**1985**
**Technical and Scientific Documentation
Center Competition**
Nancy, France
Client: CNRS (Centre National de la
Recherche Scientifique), France
Renzo Piano Building Workshop
Design team: N. Okabe, J. F. Schmit,
A. Vincent
With: I. Da Costa, N. Prouvé
Consultants: Sodeteg, Paris
(structures and mechanical
engineering)

**1985**
**Auvergne Regional Headquarters**
Clermont-Ferrand (Auvergne), France
Client: Region of Auvergne
Renzo Piano Building Workshop
Design team: N. Okabe, A. Vincent,
P. Vincent
With: P. Chatelain, C. Clarisse,
T. Hartmann, J. Lelay, J. Lohse,
N. Prouvé, D. Rat
Consultants: Seer, Clermont-Ferrand
(technical services); Douat, Forheaud,
Harland, Clermont-Ferrand (local
architects); Corajoud, Dalnoky,
Desvigne, Paris (landscaping);
G. Noel, Clermont-Ferrand (acoustics);
GEC, Paris (cost control);
Immo Maquette, Paris (models);
Glitec, Lyons (building inspectors)
Contractor: Socae, Clermont-Ferrand

**1985**
**Quark Television Program Set**
Rome, Italy
Client: RAI (Radiotelevisione Italiana),
Rome
Renzo Piano Building Workshop
Design team: O. Di Blasi, S. Ishida
With: G. Fascioli
Consultants: P. Angela (editing)

**1985**
**Competition for Pirelli Bicocca Area
Restructuring**
Milan, Italy
Client: Industrie Pirelli S.p.A.,
Milan
Renzo Piano Building Workshop
Design team: O. Di Blasi, E. Frigerio,
D. L. Hart, S. Ishida
With: G. G. Bianchi, K. Dreissigacker,
M. Mattei, M. Visconti
Consultants: A. Secchi, Milan
(urban planning); Ove Arup
& Partners, London (structures
and mechanical engineering),
E. Miola (models);
A. Vincent (cost control)

**1985–86**
**Office Building Restructuring**
Fegino (Genoa), Italy
Client: Ansaldo S.p.A. (Genoa)
Renzo Piano Building Workshop
Design team: G. G. Grandi, S. Ishida,
V. Truffelli
With: G. Fascioli, C. Manfreddo,
M. Visconti
Consultants: Ansaldo, Genoa (structures
and direction of works); Aerimpianti
S.p.A., Milan (mechanical plans)
Contractor: Coopsette S.r.l., Reggio
Emilia

**1985–87**
**Municipal Laboratories**
Paris, France
Client: Municipality of Paris
Renzo Piano Building Workshop
Design team: B. Plattner, J. F. Schmit,
A. Vincent
With: J. L. Chassais, C. Clarisse,
J. B. Lacoudre
Consultants: GEC (F. Petit), Paris
(technical studies); A. Benzeno (cost
control)
Contractor: Dumez (Paris)

**1985–87**
**Institute for Research into Light Metals**
Novara, Italy
Client: Aluminia S.p.A., Italy
Renzo Piano/Atelier de Paris
Design team: B. Plattner (associate in
charge), R. Self, R. J. Van Santen,
J. Lelay, B. Vaudeville, L. Pennisson,
A. Benzeno, A. Vincent
With: J. Y. Richard (models)
Consultants: M. Mimram, Paris
(structures); Sodeteg, Paris (services);
Italstudio (facade); Omega, Turin (local
engineers); M. Desvigne, Immo
Maquette (landscaping)
Contractors: Cattaneo, Bergamo
(building); Alucassa, Rho, Italy (facade)

**1985–92**
**Credito Industriale Sardo**
Cagliari, Italy
Client: Credito Industriale Sardo
*Competition, 1985*
Renzo Piano Building Workshop
Design team: G. G. Bianchi, M. Carroll
(associate architect), O. Di Blasi,
S. Ishida (associate in charge),
F. Marano, F. Santolini
With: M. Calosso, M. Cuccinella,
D. L. Hart, P. Mantero, A. Ponte,
M. Varratta, S. Vignale (models)
Consultants: Aster S.p.A. (structures and
mechanical engineering)

*Construction, 1985–92*
Renzo Piano Building Workshop
Design team: E. Baglietto (associate architect), R. V. Truffelli (associate architect), G. G. Bianchi, M. Carroll, O. Di Blasi, D. L. Hart, S. Ishida (associate architect), C. Manfreddo, F. Marano (associate engineer), F. Santolini, M. Varratta
With: M. Calosso, D. Campo, R. Costa, M. Cucinella, S. Vignale, G. Sacchi, D. Cavagna (models)
Consultants: Mageco S.r.l. (L. Mascia, D. Mascia), Genoa, Manens Intertecnica S.r.l., Verona (structures and mechanical engineering); Pecorini, Cagliari, G. Gatti, Milan (geological studies)
Contractors: R. Tireddu, I.R.C., SO.G.DI.CO., Vibrocemento Sarda

**1985–92**
**Columbus International Exposition**
Genoa, Italy
Client: Municipality of Genoa, Ente Colombo '92
Renzo Piano Building Workshop
Design team: S. Ishida (associate in charge), E. Baglietto (Italian pavilion), G. G. Bianchi (Cotton Warehouses, scenography, italian pavilion), P. Bodega, M. Carroll (aquarium, Italian pavilion), O. De Nooyer (Bigo), G. Grandi (bonded warehouses, service spine), D. L. Hart (conference center), C. Manfreddo (Mandraccio services, printing center, Molo Vecchio), V. Tolu, R. V. Truffelli (bonded warehouses)
With: A. Arancio, M. Cucinella, S. D'Atri (CAD), S. De Leo (CAD), G. Fascioli, E. L. Hegerl, G. Langasco (CAD), M. Mallamaci, G. Mc Mahon, M. Michelotti, P. Persia (CAD), A. Pierandrei, F. Pierandrei, S. Smith, R. Venelli, L. Vercelli, S. Shingu (sculptures)
Consultants: Ove Arup & Partners (P. Rice), London, L. Mascia, D. Mascia, P. Costa, L. Lembo, V. Nascimbene, B. Ballerini, G. Malcangi, Sidercard, M. Testone, G. F. Visconti (structures); Manens Intertecnica, Verona (mechanical engineering); M. Semino (supervisor for urban area and historic buildings); Cambridge Seven Associates (P. Chermayeff), Boston (aquarium); F. Doria, M. Giacomelli, S. Lanzon, B. Merello, M. Nouvion, G. Robotti, A. Savioli (technical consultants); STED (S. Baldelli, A. Grasso), Genoa (cost control); D. Commings, Paris (acoustics); P. Castiglioni (lighting); E. Piras, Genoa (director of works for special aquarium equipment); L. Moni (site supervision); Scène, Paris (scenography); Cetena (naval engineer); G. Macchi (Italian Pavilion exhition curator); Origoni/Steiner (graphic design)
Contractor and management: Italimpianti, Genoa

**1986**
**Jules Verne Amusement Park Competition**
Amiens, France
Client: City of Amiens
Renzo Piano Building Workshop
Design team: N. Okabe, B. Vaudeville, A. Vincent
With: B. Hubert, D. Laville (models), R. J. Van Santen, M. Veith
Consultants: M. Mimram (structures); M. Corajoud, C. Dalnoki, M. Desvigne (landscaping)
Contractor: Dumez, Paris

**1986**
**Study for IBM Traveling Exhibition and "Lady Bird" Traveling Pavilion**
Client: IBM Europa
Renzo Piano Building Workshop
Design team: K. Dreissigacker, S. Ishida, M. Visconti
Consultants: Ove Arup & Partners (P. Rice, T. Barker) (structures and mechanical engineering)

**1986**
**Building Method for Crystal Tables**
Milan, Italy
Client: Fontanarte
Renzo Piano Building Workshop
Design team: S. Ishida, O. Di Blasi
Contractor: Fontanarte

**1986**
**Sports Center**
Ravenna, Italy
Client: Municipality of Ravenna
Renzo Piano Building Workshop
Design team: S. Ishida, F. Marano, M. Cucinella, O. Di Blasi, E. Fitzgerald, D. Magnano, C. Manfreddo, S. Montaldo, F. Moussavi, F. Pirandrei, S. Smith, M. Visconti, Y. Yamaguchi
With: E. Baglietto, G. Fascioli, N. Freedman, M. Mallamaci, M. Mattei, B. Merello, D. Peluffo, M. Bassignani, D. Cavagna (models)
Consultants: Ove Arup & Partners (P. Rice, R. Hough), London, M. Milan, S. Favero Engineers, Venice (structures and mechanical engineering)
Contractor: Di Penta, Rome

**1986**
**Palladian Basilica Nave and Town Hall Reuse Project**
Vicenza, Italy
Client: Municipality of Vicenza
Renzo Piano Building Workshop
Design team: G. G. Bianchi, P. Bodega, G. Grandi, S. Ishida, M. Michelotti, G. Sacchi (models)
Consultants: Ove Arup & Partners, M. Milan, S. Favero (structures and mechanical engineering); Sivi (lighting; S. Baldelli, A. Grasso (cost control)
Contractor: Fontanarte

**1986**
**Ancient Moat Rehabilitation**
Rhodes, Greece
Client: UNESCO
Renzo Piano Building Workshop
Design team: G. G. Bianchi, S. Ishida
Consultants: Municipality of Rhodes (S. Sotirakis, architect) (local coordination); D. De Lucia, architect (historical documentation); E. Sailler (photographic documentation)

**1986**
**City Gate**
Valletta, Malta
Client: Government of Malta
Renzo Piano Building Workshop
Design team: A. Chaaya, B. Plattner
With: P. Callegia, D. Felice, K. Zammit Endrich
Consultants: M. Mimram

**1986**
**Management Training Center**
Rome, Italy
Client: Italscal S.p.A. (Rome)
Renzo Piano Building Workshop
Design team: S. Ishida, R. V. Truffelli
With: G. G. Bianchi, G. Grandi

**1986–95**
**Cité Internationale**
Lyons, France
*Competition*
Client: City of Lyons
Renzo Piano Building Workshop
Design team: N. Okabe (associate architect), A. Vincent (associate engineer), T. Hartman, B. Vaudeville
*Feasibility Studies, 1986*
Client: City of Lyons
Renzo Piano Building Workshop
Design team: P. Vincent (associate in charge), A. Vincent (associate engineer), R. Plottier (partnership), T. Hartman, J. B. Lacoudre, J. L. Chassais, J. Lelay, A. Benzeno, S. Planchez
Consultant: M. Corajoud (landscaping)
*Preliminary Design, 1988*
Client: City of Lyon
Renzo Piano Building Workshop
Design team: P. Vincent (associate in charge), A. Vincent (associate engineer), F. Canal, G. Fourel, A. O'Carroll, E. Tisseur, A. O'Carroll, E. Tisseur, A. H. Téménidès, C. Ardiley, B. Kurtz
Consultants: M. Corajoud (landscaping); O. Doizy, C. d'Ovidio, A. Schultz (models)
*Design Development, 1990*
Client: Sari Régions, City of Lyon
Renzo Piano Building Workshop
Design team: P. Vincent (associate in charge), J. P. Ricard (sociology), B. Tonfoni, M. Wollensak, A. El Jerari, J. B. Mothes, J. Moolhuijzen, P. Charles, G. Mormina, A. H. Téménidès, D. Nock
Consultants: P. Darmer (models); A. Vincent (administration); Sari Ingénírie, Ove Arup & Partners (concept); P. Castiglioni (lighting); Peutz (acoustics); M. Corajoud (landscaping)
*Construction, 1992*
Client: SPAICI1 (development), Cecil (conference center), City of Lyon (museum), UGC (cinema)
Renzo Piano Building Workshop
Design team: P. Vincent (associate in charge), Curtelin-Ricard-Bergeret (associated architect), A. Catani (associated architect), M. Henry, J. B. Mothes, A. Gallisian, A. Chaaya, B. Tonfoni, A. El Jerari, D. Rat, C. Valentinuzzi, A. H. Téménidès, C. Jackman, M. Howard, W. Yassal, M. Salerno
With: E. Novel, E. Vestrepen, G. Modolo, Y. Surti, M. Boudry, S. Eisemberg, K. Mc Lone, M. Pimmel, T. Rolland, H. Cocagne
Consultants: A. Vincent Syllabus (administration); S. Gunera Syllabus (engineer); GEC Ingénérie (synthesis, cost control); Peutz (acoustics); Végétude (landscaping); Joel (lighting); CSTB (facades); P. Bernard (signage); Barbanel (conference room systems); ESB (conference room structure); Labeyrie (conference room scenography); Merlin (equipment); Agibat (museum structures); Courtois (museum ventilation); HGM (museum systems); B. E. Belzunce (cinema structures); Inex (cinema ventilation); C. Fusée (cinema systems); Jerdil (fountain); J. P. Allain, O. Doizy, M. Fau, M. Goudin (models); M. Corajoud (landscaping)

**1987**
**European Synchrotron**
Grenoble, France
Client: ESRF
Renzo Piano Building Workshop
Design team: N. Okabe, J. L. Chassais,
C. Clarisse, J. B. Lacoudre, J. Lelay,
P. Merz, C. Morandi, A. O'Carroll,
S. Planchez, R. J. Van Santen, P. Vincent
(associate architect)
Consultants: Ove Arup & Partners
(P. Rice, T. Barker) (structures,
environmental controls);
Ansaldo (lighting); Initic (fire
prevention); M. Corajoud (landscaping);
Seri Renault, Novatome, France,
Interatome, Germania, USSI, France
(planning)

**1987**
**Sistiana Bay Restoration Project**
Trieste, Italy
Client: Finsepol S.p.A., Trieste
Renzo Piano Building Workshop
Design team: B. Plattner, L. Couton,
A. Chaaya, P. Copat, R. Self, M. Salerno
With: E. Agazzi, F. Joubert, R. Keiser,
B. Leboudec, O. Lidon, J. Lohse,
R. J. Van Santen, G. Torre, O. Touraine,
O. Doizy, A. Schultz (models)
Consultants: Ove Arup & Partners
(P. Rice, A. Day), London, M. Milan,
Studio Boghetto, Manens Intertecnica
(structures and mechanical engineering);
CMS (environmental study); Studio
architetti associati (G. Pauletto,
G. Furlan, G. Galli), Venice (local
architect); M. Desvigne, C. Dalnoky
(landscaping); Studio Ambiente, Milan,
Sodeteg, Paris (urban planning)

**1987**
**Petriccio Multipurpose Complex**
Urbino, Italy
Client: Costruzioni Edili Bertozzini S.p.A.
Renzo Piano Building Workshop
Design team: G. G. Bianchi, S. Ishida,
F. Marano

**1987**
**Sports Center**
Trani, Italy
Client: City of Trani
Renzo Piano Building Workshop
Design team: D. Campo, R. Costa,
E. Frigerio, C. Manfreddo, F. Marano
Consultants: S. Baldelli, A. Grasso,
M. Montanari, S. Vignale (models)

**1987**
**Kandahar Center**
Sestriere (Turin), Italy

Client: Kandahar Center
Renzo Piano Building Workshop
Design team: E. Frigerio, S. Ishida,
P. Maggiora, F. Marano
Consultant: Raineri (structures)
Contractor: Impresa Macciotta

**1987**
**Amiu Training Center Project**
Genoa, Italy
Client: Amiu, Genoa
Renzo Piano Building Workshop
Design team: E. Baglietto, S. Ishida,
G. Grandi, F. Marano
Consultants: S. Baldelli (cost control);
Mageco S.r.l. (L. Mascia, D. Mascia),
Genoa (structures)
Contractor: Tradeco S.r.l. (G. Chiesa),
Milan

**1987**
**Infrastructure Network Study**
Urbino, Italy
Client: Municipality of Urbino
Renzo Piano Building Workshop
Design team: G. G. Bianchi, S. Ishida,
F. Marano
With: S. Smith

**1987**
**Museum of American Contemporary
Art**
Newport Beach, California
Client: Newport Harbor Art Museum
Renzo Piano Building Workshop
Design team: A. Arancio, M. Carroll,
M. Desvigne, N. Freedman, S. Ishida,
F. Pierandrei
Consultants: Blurock Partnership
(local architect); Ove Arup & Partners
(P. Rice, T. Barker), London/Los
Angeles (structures and mechanical
engineering)

**1987**
**Intervention in the Excavated City**
Pompeii (Naples), Italy
Client: IBM
Renzo Piano Building Workshop
Design team: G. G. Bianchi,
N. Freedman, G. Grandi, S. Ishida,
F. Marano, E. Piazza, A. Pierandrei,
S. Smith

**1987**
**Restoration of the Sassi**
Matera, Italy
Client: Camera di commercio
Renzo Piano Building Workshop
Design team: G. G. Bianchi,
D. Campo, M. Cattaneo, S. Ishida,
F. Marano

Consultants: Ove Arup & Partners
(P. Rice, T. Barker) (structures and
mechanical engineering)

**1987–90**
**San Nicola Stadium**
Bari, Italy
Client: Municipality of Bari
Renzo Piano Building Workshop
Design team: O. Di Blasi, S. Ishida,
F. Marano, L. Pellini, D. Cavagna
(models), G. Sacchi (models)
Consultants: M. Desvigne (landscaping);
Ove Arup & Partners (P. Rice, T. Cafrae,
A. Lenczer), M. Milan, Venice
(structures and mechanical engineering);
Studio Vitone, V. Gianuzzi, L. Maggi,
N. Cardascia, F. Bonaduce (reinforced
concrete); N. Andidero (supervision of
prefabricated components); J. Zucker,
M. Belviso (site supervision)
Contractor: Bari 90 S.r.l.

**1987–90**
**Bercy 2 Shopping Center**
Charenton le Pont (Paris), France
Client: GRC
Renzo Piano Building Workshop
Design team: J. F. Blassel, S. Dunne,
M. Henry, K. McBryde, A. O'Carroll,
N. Okabe, B. Plattner, R. Rolland,
M. Salerno, N. Westphal
With: M. Bojovic, D. Illoul, P. Senne,
Y. Chapelain, O. Doizy, J. Y. Richard
(models)
Consultants: Ove Arup & Partners
(P. Rice, A. Lenczer), Otra (J. P. Rigail),
J. L. Sarf (reinforced concrete), OTH
S.I. (J. Herman) (structures and
mechanical engineering); Veritas
(security); Copibat (inspection);
M. Desvigne, C. Dalnoky (landscaping);
Crighton Design management (interiors)
Contractors: Tondela N.F., Cosylva, E.I.,
S.P.P.R.

**1987–91**
**Crown Princess**
Monfalcone (Gorizia), Italy
Client: P&O, Fincantieri
Renzo Piano Building Workshop
Design team: S. Ishida, N. Okabe,
K. McBryde, M. Carroll, R. Costa,
M. Cucinella, R. J. Van Santen,
F. Santolini, R. Self, S. Smith, O. Touraine
With: G. G. Bianchi, D. Cavagna
(models), N. Freedman, G. Grandi,
D. L. Hart, F. R. Ludewig, P. Maggiora,
C. Manfreddo
Consultants: Studio Architetti Associati,
Venice; Danish Maritime Institute,
Lyngby-DK (wind-tunnel text)

Contractor: Fincantieri Monfalcone,
Trieste

**1987–91**
**Rue de Meaux Housing**
Paris, France
Client: RIVP, le Mutuelles du Mans
Renzo Piano Building Workshop
Design team: F. Canal, C. Clarisse,
T. Hartman, U. Hautch, J. Lhose,
B. Plattner (associate architect),
R. J. Van Santen, J. F. Schmit
Consultants: GEC (structures and
mechanical engineering); M. Desvigne,
C. Dalnoky, P. Conversey (landscaping)
Contractor: Dumez

**1988**
**Venice Expo 2000 Project**
Venice, Italy
Client: Venice Expo 2000
Renzo Piano Building Workshop
Design team: G. G. Bianchi, S. Ishida,
R. V. Truffelli
With: A. Pierandrei, F. Pierandrei

**1988**
**Meridiana Shopping Center and Offices**
Lecco (Como), Italy
Client: Camera di commercio
Renzo Piano Building Workshop
Design team: P. Bodega, I. Corte (CAD),
S. D'Atri (CAD), V. Di Turi, G. Grandi,
S. Ishida, C. Manfreddo, F. Marano,
F. Santolini, S. Schafer
With: A. Bordoni

**1988**
**La Nave**
Trieste, Italy
Client: Fincantieri Trieste
Renzo Piano Building Workshop
Design team: N. Okabe,
R. J. Van Santen, O. Touraine

**1988–90**
**Thomson Optronics Factory**
Saint Quentin-en-Yvelines (Paris),
France
Client: Thomson CSF
Renzo Piano Building Workshop
Design team: A. Gallissian (Thomson 1),
M. Henry (tower), A. El Jerari,
L. Le Voyer, A. O' Carroll, D. Rat
(Thomson 2), A. H. Téménidès,
P. Vincent (associate in charge),
A. Vincent (associate in charge)
With: C. Ardilley, C. Bartz, M. Bojovic,
F. Canal, O. Doizy, C. d'Ovidio
(models), G. Fourel, A. Guez, B. Kurtz
Consultants: GEC (F. Petit,
F. Thouvenin, C. Baché) (synthesis,

systems, ventilation, cost control); Ove Arup & Partners (P. Rice, R. Hough) (structures); Ouvrage snc (administration); M. Desvigne, C. Dalnoky in collaboration with P. Convercey (landscaping); Copitec (C. Knezovic), Planitec (M. Lopez) (inspection); Peutz (acoustics) Contractors: Durand, Danto Rogeat, Svoie, Villequin

## 1988–90
### IRCAM Extension
Paris, France
Client: Ministry of Culture, Centre Georges Pompidou, IRCAM
Renzo Piano Building Workshop
Design team: P. Vincent (associate architect), N. Okabe (competition design), J. Lelay
With: F. Canal, A. O'Carroll, J. L. Chassais, N. Prouvé, O. Doizy, J. Y. Richard (models)
Consultants: AXE IB (structures and services); GEC (cost control); GEMO (direction) (project management)
Contractors: SICMEG (foundation and steel structure); DURAND (facade); CG2A (elevators)

## 1988–94
### Kansai Air Terminal
Osaka, Japan
Client: Kansai International Airport Co. Ltd.
*Competition*
Renzo Piano Building Workshop/Ove Arup & Partners
Basic design and design development: Renzo Piano Building Workshop in collaboration with Ove Arup & Partners, Nikken Sekkei Ltd.
Basic concept, functional aspects, and design of the moving elements: Aéroports de Paris
Negotiations with CIQ + CAB, design of the CIQ facilities, and airplane planning: Japan Airport Consultants, Inc.
Competition team: Renzo Piano Building Workshop
Design team: N. Okabe (associate in charge), J. F. Blassel, R. Brennan, A. Chaaya, L. Couton, R. Keiser, L. Koenig, K. McBryde, S. Planchez, R. Rolland, G. Torre, O. Touraine
With: G. le Breton, M. Henry, J. Lelay, A. O' Carroll, M. Salerno, A. H. Téménidès, N. Westphal
Consultants: Ove Arup & Partners (P. Rice, T. Barker) (structures and mechanical engineering); M. Devigne (landscaping)

*Basic Design and Design Development*
Renzo Piano Building Workshop
Design team: N. Okabe (associate in charge), J. F. Blassel, A. Chavela, I. Corte, K. Fraser, R. S. Garlipp, M. Goerd, G. Hall, K. Hirano, A. Ikegami, S. Ishida, A. Johnson, C. Kelly, T. Kimura, S. Larsen, J. Lelay, K. McBryde, T. Miyazaki, S. Nakaya, N. Takata, T. Tomuro, O. Touraine, M. Turpin, M. Yamada, H. Yamaguchi, T. Yamaguchi
With: A. Autin, G. Cohen, A. Golzari, B. Gunning, G. Hastrich, M. Horie, I. Kubo, S. Medio, K. Miyake, S. Montaldo, S. Mukai, K. A. Naderi, K. Nyunt (landscaping), S. Oehler, T. O'Sullivan, P. Persia, F. Pierandrei, M. Rossato, R. Shields, T. Takagawa, T. Ueno, K. Uezono, J. M. Weill, T. Yamakoshi
Consultants: Ove Arup & Partners (P. Rice, T. Barker) (structures and mechanical engineering); Peutz (Y. Dekeyrel) (acoustics); R. J. Van Santen (facades); David Langson & Everest, Futaba Quantity Surveying Co. Ltd. (cost control); Koung Nyunt (landscaping)
*Site Supervision*
Design team: Renzo Piano Building Workshop
Design team: N. Okabe (associate in charge), A. Ikegami, T. Kimura, T. Tomuro, Y. Ueno
With: S. Kano, A. Shimizu
Consultants: RFR (J. F. Blassel) (facades); Toshi Keikan Sekkei Inc. (S. Okumura) (canyon)

## 1989
### "Russian and Soviet Art 1870–1930" Exhibition in Lingotto Display Area
Turin, Italy
Client: Fiat Lingotto
Renzo Piano Building Workshop
Design team: M. Cattaneo, S. Ishida, M. Rossato, M. Varratta (associate in charge)
Consultants: P. Castiglioni (lighting); P. Cerri (graphic design); G. Carandente (curator)
Catalog: Gruppo Editoriale Fabbri
Installation: Gruppo Bodino

## 1989
### "Toward the New Lingotto" Exhibition
Turin, Italy
Client: Fiat
Renzo Piano Building Workshop
Design team: P. Bodega, M. Cucinella, J. Desscombe, S. Durr, E. Frigerio,

S. Ishida, P. Maggiora, F. Marano, A. Piancastelli, M. Rossato, M. Varratta (associate in charge), S. Vignale
With: I. Corte (CAD), M. Desvigne, C. Dalnoky (landscaping), E. Miola (models)
Consultants: CINE.MA S.r.l. (M. Arduino Piano) (video); Grosz (graphic design)
Catalog: Gruppo Editoriale Fabbri
Installation: Gruppo Bodino

## 1989–91
### UNESCO Laboratory and Workshop
Scoglio Nave, Genoa
Client: Renzo Piano Building Workshop
Renzo Piano Building Workshop
Design team: M. Cattaneo (associate in charge), S. Ishida (associate), M. Lusetti, F. Marano (associate), M. Nouvion
With: M. Carroll, M. Desvigne (landscaping), O. Di Blasi, R. V. Truffelli, M. Varratta, D. Cavagna (models)
Consultants: A. Bellini, L. Gattoronchieri (soil engineers); P. Costa (structures); C. Di Bartolo (bionic research)
Contractors: Edilindustria S.p.A., Andidero, Nuovo Verde, Ratti Serra (landscaping), Fiocchi, SIV (roofing and glazing), Gruppo Bodino (interior furniture and fittings), Habitat Legno (wood stucture and interior floors), Maspero Elevatori (elevators), Model System Italy (solar-controlled louvers and sunscreens), Pati, Montefluos (roofing)

## 1989–95
### Ushibuka Bridge
Kumamoto, Japan
Client: Prefecture of Kumamoto, Department for the Environment and Fishing
Renzo Piano Building Workshop
Design team: S. Ishida, N. Okabe (associate in charge), M. Yamada
With: J. Lelay, T. Ueno, D. Cavagna (models)
Consultants: Ove Arup & Partners (P. Rice, J. Nissen, P. Brooke, J. Batchelor), Maeda Engineering Co. (T. Matsumoto, S. Tsuchiya, S. Kawasaki) (structures and mechanical engineering)

## 1990
### Roofing for Private Gardens
Villejuif, France
Client: Département du Val de Marne, Direction des Espaces Verts Départementaux (B. Dauvergne, J. Dauvergne)

Renzo Piano Building Workshop
Design team: P. Vincent (associate in charge), N. Prouvé, R. J. Van Santen, C. Ardilley, A. H. Téménidès, E. Tisseur; O. Doizy (models)
Consultants: GEC, F. Petit, M. Thouvenin, Société Ouvrage, A. Vincent
Contractor: Banneel

## 1990
### "Car Production and Design 1879–1949" Exhibition
Milan, Italy
Client: Municipality of Milan, Alfa Romeo
Renzo Piano Building Workshop
Design team: M. Carroll, O. Di Blasi, S. Ishida, M. Varratta
With: M. Nouvion, R. Trapani
Consultants: L. Mascia (structures); P. Castiglioni (lighting); F. Origoni and A. Steiner (graphic design)
Installation: Gruppo Bodino

## 1990
### "American Art 1930–1970" Exhibition
Turin, Italy
Client: Lingotto S.r.l.
Renzo Piano Building Workshop
Design team: M. Cattaneo (associate in charge), S. Ishida (associate), M. Varatta
Consultants: A. Codognato, N. Bevilacqua (curators); P. Castiglioni (lighting); P. Cerri (graphic design)
Catalog: Gruppo Editoriale Fabbri
Installation: Gruppo Bodino

## 1990
### "Andy Warhol's First Successes in New York" Exhibition
Turin, Italy
Client: Lingotto S.r.l.
Renzo Piano Building Workshop
Design team: M. Varratta (associate in charge), S. Ishida
Consultants: A. Codognato, D. Desalvo (curators); P. Castiglioni (lighting); Grosz (graphic design)
Catalog: Gruppo Editoriale Fabbri
Installation: Gruppo Bodino

## 1990
### "The Culture of Cars: Music and Cars" Exhibition
Turin, Italy
Client: Lingotto S.r.l.
Renzo Piano Building Workshop
Design team: M. Cucinella, S. Ishida, P. Maggiora, A. Piancastelli, M. Rossato, M. Varratta (associate in charge), S. Vignale

Consultants: A. Bassignana, A. Marchis, A. Signetto (curators); Grosz (graphic design); E. Miola (models)
Catalog: U. Allemandi & Co
Installation: Gruppo Bodino

### 1990–91
**"Jean Prouvé" Exhibition**
Paris, Centre National d'Art et de Culture, France
Client: Centre National d'Art et de Culture
Renzo Piano Building Workshop
Design team: B. Plattner, M. Henry, R. Rolland
With: Prouvé family; A. Ghilleux, R. Guidot (curators); Ateliers du CCI
With the support of: Pont-à-Mousson S.A.
Contractors: Malet et Clements (paintings), Perret (lighting), Miroiterier du Temple (framing and glazing)

### 1991
**"Padua and Galileo" Exhibition**
Padua, Italy
Client: Municipality of Padua
Renzo Piano Building Workshop
Design team: S. Ishida, N. Okabe, P. Ackermann, M. Cattaneo
With: C. Garbato (documentation), D. Cavagna (models)
Consultants; G. Macchi; P. Castiglioni (lighting)
Scientific consulting committee of the University of Padua: E. Bellone, M. Bonsembiante, R. Hipschman

### 1991–
**Tjibaou Cultural Center**
Nouméa, Nuova Caledonia
Client: Agency for the Development of Kanak Culture, Marie Claude Tjibaou (president)
*Competition, 1991*
Architects: Renzo Piano Building Workshop
Design team: A. Chaaya, P. Vincent (associate in charge)
With: F. Pagliani, J. Moolhuijzen, W. Vassal, O. Doizy (models), A. Schultz (models)
Consultants: A. Bensa (ethnologist); Desvigne and Dalnoky (landscaping); Ove Arup & Partners (P. Rice) (structures and ventilation); GEC (cost control), Peutz (acoustics), Scène (scenography)
*Conceptual Design, 1992*
Architects: Renzo Piano Building Workshop
Design team: A. Chaaya (coordination,

zoning concept), D. Rat (structures, CAD), J. B. Mothes (CAD), A. H. Téménidès (feasibility), P. Vincent (associate in charge)
With: R. Phelan, C. Catino, A. Gallissian, R. Baumgarten, P. Darmer (models)
Consultants: A. Bensa (M. A. Joredie, L. Poigoune) (ethnologist); GEC (F. Petit, C. Baché in collaboration with T. Plantagenest) (technical coordination, cost control); GEMO (planning studies); Ove Arup & Partners (P. Rice, M. Banfi) (structures, climate control); CSTB (climate-control feasibility); Agibat (structures); Scène (scenography); Peutz (acoustics); Qualiconsult (security); Végétude (landscaping)
*Design Development, 1993*
Architects: Renzo Piano Building Workshop
Design team: A. Chaaya (concept, zoning, village 1), D. Rat (structures, systems), W. Vassal (structures, details), J. B. Mothes (zoning, village 2), M. Henry (landscaping, village 3), A. El Jerari (low volumes, lodgings), A. H. Téménidès (room 400), A. Galissian (facades), F. Pagliani (facades), D. Mirallie (landscaping), P. Vincent (associate in charge)
Consultants: A. Bensa (M. A. Joredie, L. Poigoune) (ethnologist); GEC (F. Petit, C. Baché in collaboration with P. Vivier, T. Plantagenest) (general coordination); Ove Arup & Partners (T. Barker, J. Wernick, A. Guthrie, M. Chawn, M. Banfi, A. Allsop) (structures, climate control); CSTB (J. Grandemer) (climate control); Agibat (D. Quost, J. M. Marion) (structures); Scène (J. H. Manoury) (scenography); Peutz (Y. Dekeyrel, S. Mercier) (acoustics); Qualiconsult (J. L. Rolland) (security); Végétude (C. Guinaudeau) (landscaping)
*Executive Phase, 1994*
Architects: Renzo Piano Building Workshop
Design team: A. Chaaya, M. Henry, J. B. Mothes, G. Modolo, W. Vassal, P. Vincent (associate in charge)
With: A. El Jerari, A. Gallissian, A. H. Téménidès, D. Mirallie, F. Pagliani, O. Doizy (models)
Consultants: A. Bensa (ethnologist); GEC (F. Petit, C. Baché); Ove Arup & Partners (A. Guthrie, M. Banfi); CSTB (J. Grandemer); Agibat (D. Quost); Scène (J. H. Manoury); Peutz (Y. Dekeyrel); Qualiconsult (J. L. Rolland); Végétude (C. Guinaudeau)

### 1991–
**Padre Pio Pilgrimage Church**
S. Giovanni Rotondo (Foggia), Italy
Client: Frati Minori Cappuccini (Province of Foggia)
*Preliminary Phase, 1991–94*
Renzo Piano Building Workshop
Design team: P. Bodega, I. Corte (CAD), S. D'Atri (CAD), V. Di Turi, E. Fitzgerald, K. Fraser (associate architect), G. Grandi (associate in charge), L. Lin, E. Magnano, C. Manfreddo, M. Palmore
With: H. Hirsch, A. Saheba, G. Stirk, M. Bassignani, D. Cavagna (models)
Consultants: Ove Arup & Partners (P. Rice, T. Barker) (structures and mechanical engineering); Müller Bbm (acoustics); G. Muciaccia, Foggia (site supervision and local support); Mons. C. Valenziano, Rome (liturgical advisor); G. Grasso o.p., Genoa (teological advisor); STED (A. Grasso, S. Baldelli) (cost estimation); Studio Ambiente (G. Amadeo), Milan (planning)
*Construction, 1995–*
Renzo Piano Building Workshop
Design team: G. Grandi (associate in charge), M. Byrne, M. Bassignani, D. Cavagna (models), I. Corte (CAD), S. D'Atri (CAD), B. Ditchbum, E. Magnano, C. Manfreddo, M. Palmore, M. Rossato Piano
Consultants: Ove Arup & Partners, G. Del Mese, A. Lenczer (structures); Manens Intertecnica, Verona; CO.RE. Ingegneria, Rome (R. Calzona) (mechanical engineering); Müller Bbm (acoustics); G. Muciaccia, Foggia (site supervision and local support); Mons. C. Valenziano, Rome (liturgical advisor); Austin Italy, Milan (cost control); G. Amadeo (planning)
Contractors: F.lli Dioguardi, Bari, Andidero, Bari, Ciuffeda, Foggia, Fabbrica della Chiesa sacrl

### 1991–
**Banca Popolare di Lodi**
Lodi, Italy
Client: Banca Popolare di Lodi
*Preliminary Phase, 1991–92*
Renzo Piano Building Workshop
Design team: A. Alborghetti, V. Di Turi, S. D'Atri (CAD), G. Fascioli, E. Fitzgerald, G. Grandi (associate in charge), C. Hayes, G. Langasco (CAD), P. Maggiora, C. Manfreddo, V. Tolu
With: A. Shaffer, A. Sacchi
*Construction Phase, 1992–*
Renzo Piano Building Workshop
Design team: A. Alborghetti, V. Di Turi,

S. D'Atri (CAD), G. Grandi (associate in charge), M. Howard, G. Langasco (CAD), F. Santolini
Consultants: M.S.C., Milan (structures); Manaens Intertecnica, Verona (services and mechanical engineering); Müller Bbm (acoustics); P. Castiglioni (lighting); P. Cerri (graphic design)
Contractors: Co.Fin. S.p.A., Lecco (general contractor); Eiffel, Paris (special steel structures); Gruppo Bodino, Turin, Il Palagio, Florence (exterior cladding); Focchi S.p.A., Rimini (glazing); Sunglass, Padua (special glass); Sadi, Vicenza (dropped ceiling and computer flooring)

### 1992
**Manifeste Exhibit**
Paris, France
Client: Centre Georges Pompidou
Renzo Piano Building Workshop
Design team: B. Plattner (associate in charge), R. Self (associate in charge)
Consultants: F. Bertolere (documentation); GEC (cost control)
Contractors: Villequin, AMB, Zachary, Spie Trindel, Cegelec in collaboration with SIV, I Guzzini, Abet Print-France

### 1992–95
**Cy Twombly Gallery**
Houston, Texas
Client: Menil Foundation
Renzo Piano Building Workshop
Design team: M. Carroll (associate in charge), S. Ishida (associate in charge), M. Palmore
With: S. Comer, A. Ewing, S. Lopez, M. Bassignani (models)
Consultants: R. Fitzgerald & Associates (R. Fitzgerald, G. Krezinski) (local architect); Ove Arup & Partners (T. Barker, J. Hewitt, K. Holden, S. Meldrum, M. Parker, J. Peel Cross, A. Sedwich) (structures and mechanical engineering); Haynes Whaley Associates Inc., Houston (structures); Lockwood Andrews & Newman, Houston (civil engineering)
Contractor: Miner Dederick

### 1992–96
**Reconstruction of the Atelier Brancusi**
Paris, France
Client: Centre Georges Pompidou
Renzo Piano Building Workshop
Design team: B. Plattner (associate in charge), R. Self (associate in charge), R. Phelan (site supervisor), A. Galissian, J. L. Dupanloup
With: C. Aasgaard, Z. Berrio, C. Catino

P. Chappell, J. Darling, P. Satchell
Consultants: GEC (cost control, structures, and electric plan), INEX (mechanical), Isis (parking)

**1992–97**
### National Center for Science and Technology
Amsterdam, Netherlands
Client: NINT
*Preliminary Phase, 1992*
Renzo Piano Building Workshop
Design team: S. Ishida (associate in charge), O. de Nooyer (associate in charge), H. Yamaguchi, J. Fujita, A. Gallo, M. Alvisi
With: I. Corte (CAD), D. Guerrisi (CAD), Y. Yamaoka, E. Piazze, A. Recagno, K. Shannon, F. Wenz, M. Bassignani, D. Cavagna (models)
Consultants: Ove Arup & Partners (P. Rice, T. Barker, J. Wernick) (structures and mechanical engineering); Brink Groep (project management); Bureau Bouwkunde (D. Hoogstad) (local support); D3BN (J. Kraus) (structures); Hiusman en Van Muijen B. V. (R. Borrett) (services); Peutz (scientific consultant)
*Design Development, 1994–97*
Renzo Piano Building Workshop
Design team: O. De Nooyer (associate in charge), J. Backus, A. Hayes, H. Pénaranda, H. Van Der Meys, J. Woltjer
Consultants: Brink Groep (H. Meijer) (project management); Bureau Bouwkunde (D. Hoogstad) (local support); D3BN (J. Kraus) (structures); Hiusman en Van Muijen B. V. (R. Borrett) (services); Peutz (scientific consultant)

**1992–**
### Potsdamer Platz Reconstruction
Berlin, Germany
Client: Daimler Benz Ag
*Competition, 1992*
Renzo Piano Building Workshop/C. Kohlbecker
Design team: B. Plattner (associate in charge), R. Baumgarten, J. Bergen, E. Balik, A. Chaaya, P. Charles, J. Moolhuijzen
With: A. Schmid, U. Knapp, M. Kohlbecker, P. Helppi, P. Darmer (models), M. Goudin (models)
Consultants: Schlegel Gmbh (Dr. Ing. Spiekermann) (logistics)
*Master Plan, 1993*
Renzo Piano Building Workshop/C. Kohlbecker
Design team: B. Plattner (associate in

charge), R. Baumgarten, P. Charles, J. Ruoff, G. G. Bianchi, J. Moolhuijzen, F. Pagliani, L. Penisson, A. Schmid, C. Hight
With: E. Belik, J. Berger, A. Chaaya, W. Grasmug, N. Miegeville, G. Carreira, E. del Moral, H. Nagel, R. Phelan, B. Tonfoni, K. Franke, O. Skjerve, M. Werth, P. Darmer (models)
Consultants: Drees & Sommer, Stuttgart (project management)
*Design Development, 1993–94*
Renzo Piano Building Workshop/C. Kohlbecker
Design team: B. Plattner (associate in charge) R. Baumgarten, P. Charles, J. Ruoff, J. Moolhuijzen, F. Pagliani, S. Baggs, N. Mecattaf, L. Penisson, C. Hight, M. Kramer, D. Putz, G. Oug (Paris); A. Giordano (coordinator), S. Ishida, G. G. Bianchi, E. Musci, I. Corte, O. De Nooyer, E. Piano, E. Baglietto, J. Fujita, D. Guerrisi, G. Langasco, R. Sala, S. Schaefer, K. Shannon, R. V. Truffelli, F. Wenz, H. Yamaguchi, J. P. Allain (models), M. Goudin (models), D. Cavagna (models) (Genoa)
Consultants: Drees & Sommer, Stuttgart (project management)
*Construction, 1996–*
Renzo Piano Building Workshop/C. Kohlbecker
Design team: B. Plattner (associate in charge) R. Baumgarten, A. Chaaya, P. Charles, G. Ducci, M. Kramer, N. Mecattaf, J. Moolhuijzen, J. B. Mothes, M. B. Petersen, J. Ruoff, M. van der Staay, E. Volz
With: E. Audoye, G. Borden, C. Brammen, D. Drouin, B. Eistert, M. Hartmann, O. Hempel, M. Howard, W. Matthews, G. M. Maurizio, D. Miccolis, M. Pimmel, S. Stacher, M. Veltcheva, P. Furnemont (models), C. Colson (models)
Kohlbecker collaborators: J. Barnbrook, H. Falk, A. Hocher, R. Jatzke, M. Kohlbecker, M. Lindner, N. Nocke, A. Schmid, W. Spreng
Consultants: Ingenieurgemeinschaft IGH/Ove Arup & Partners, Schmidr Reuter Partner (technical consultants); Ingenieurgemeinschaft Boll & Partners GmbH, Stuttgart, Ove Arup & Partners, Ingenieurgemeinschaft IBF (Dr. Falkner)/Weiske & Partner (statics); Müller BBM (physics); Hundt & Partner (extraction); IBB Burrer Ludwigsburg, Berlin, Ove Arup & Partners (electrical engineering); ITF Intertraffic, Berlin (trafficking); Attelier Dreiseitl,

Überlingen (hydraulic system); Möhrle und Kruger, Stuttgart, Berlin (landscaping)

**1993**
### Margherita Theater Restoration Project
Bari, Italy
Client: F.lli Dioguardi S.p.A.
Renzo Piano Building Workshop
Design team: E. Baglietto, M. Cattaneo, R. Fernandez Prado, S. Ishida, S. Nobis, F. Pierandrei
Consultants: G. Amendola; Beacon Construction Company; Studio Gorjux Architetti Associati; Studio Tecnico Lab; Sovrintendenza beni AA.AA.AA.SS.; Studio Vitone & Associati

**1993**
### University Hospital Extension Competition
Strasbourg, France
Client: University Hospital
Renzo Piano Building Workshop
Design team: I. Corte (CAD), K. Fraser, S. Ishida, G. Langasco (CAD), M. Palmore, R. V. Truffelli
Consultants: BEEM Engineering ( M. A. Laurenceau), Guyancourt (hospital organization); M. C. Bucher, Schiltigheim (urban planning); Setec, Paris (structures and mechanical engineering); GEC (M. F. Petit), Marly-le-Roi (cost control)

**1993**
### Basic Design for Railway Stations of Turin, Venice, Mestre, and Bari
Turin, Venice, Mestre, Bari, Italy
Client: Italfer Sis T.A.V. (Ferrovie dello Stato)
Urban Area Committee: Susanna Agnelli, Giuseppe De Rita, Carlo Maria Guerci, Renzo Piano
Renzo Piano Building Workshop
Design team: R. V. Truffelli (associate in charge), E. Baglietto, M. Cattaneo, J. Cohen, K. Fraser, D. Hart, S. Ishida (associate in charge), C. Manfreddo, O. de Nooyer, D. Piano, F. Pierandrei, S. Scarabicchi
With: N. Baldassini, M. Belviso (CAD), I. Corte (CAD), A. Ewing, M. Fawcett, J. Fujita, D. Guerrisi, A. Hopkins, N. Malby, G. Pauletto (CAD), M. Penna, T. Reynolds, G. Robotti, K. Shannon, F. Wenz, H. Yamaguchi, M. Bassignani (models), D. Cavagna (models), P. Varratta (models)
Consultants: P. Costa (structures); Sted (cost control); G. Scorza (compatibility)

**1993**
### Old Town Center and Pier Design
Genoa, Italy
Client: UNESCO
Renzo Piano Building Workshop
Design team: S. Ishida, D. L. Hart
With: M. Menzio, C. Leoncini

**1993–97**
### Beyeler Foundation Museum
Riehen (Basel), Switzerland
Client: Beyeler Foundation, Ernst Beyeler; F. Vischer, U. Albrecht (consultants)
*Preliminary Phase, 1993*
Renzo Piano Building Workshop/J. Bürckhardt + Partner AG Basel
Design team: B. Plattner (associate in charge), L. Couton
With: J. Berger, E. Belik, W. Wassal, A. Schultz (models), P. Darmer (models)
Consultants: Ove Arup & Partners (T. Barker, J. Wernick, A. Sedgwick)
*Executive Phase, 1994*
Renzo Piano Building Workshop/J. Bürckhardt + Partner AG Basel
Design team: B. Plattner (associate in charge), L. Couton
With: P. Hendier, W. Mathews, L. Epprecht, J. P. Allain (models)
Consultants: Ove Arup & Partners (T. Barker, J. Wernik, A. Sedgwick)
Collaborators: C. Burger + Partner AG, Bogenschütz AG, J. Forrer AG, Eledtrizitäts AG Basel

**1993–**
### Mercedes Benz Design Center
Sindelfingen (Stuttgart), Germany
Client: Mercedes-Benz AG
Renzo Piano Building Workshop/C. Kohlbecker
Design team: E. Baglietto (associate in charge), G. Cohen, J. Florin, A. Hahne, S. Ishida , F. Santolini
With: D. Guerrisi, C. Leoncini, S. Nobis, M. Ottonello, C. Sapper, L. Viti, M. Bassignani (models)
Consultants: Ove Arup & Partners (T. Barker) (structures and mechanical engineering, preliminary project); IFB Dr. Braschel & Partner GmbH (structures); FWT Project und Bauleitung Mercedes-Benz AG (mechanical engineering)
Contractors: Züblin-Baresel-Hochtief (reinforced concrete); Greschbach (metal structures); Friess (glazing)

**1994**
### Grande Stade Planning
S. Denis, France
Renzo Piano Building Workshop/Jourda

& Perraudin
Design team: B. Plattner (associate in charge), S. Ishida (associate in charge), L. Penisson, M. Salerno (associate in charge), B. Tonfoni, F. Jourda, G. Perraudin
With: G. G. Bianchi, P. Charles, P. L. Coppat, S. Drouin, G. Ducci, J. L. Dupanloup, B. Galtier, M. Garrasi, W. Mathews, J. Moolhuijze, P. Murphy

## 1994
### Auditorium-Competition
Rome, Italy
Client: City of Rome
Renzo Piano Building Workshop
Design team: S. Ishida (associate in charge), K. Fraser (architect in charge), C. Hussey, J. Fujita
With: G.G. Bianchi, S. Canta, G. Cohen, G. Langasco, L. Lin, M. Palmore, E. Piazze, A. Recagno, R. Sala, C. Sapper, R.V. Truffelli, L. Viti; M. Bassignani and Elio Doria (models)
Consultants: Ove Arup & Partners (structures); Ove Arup & Partners (mechanical engineering); Müller-Bbm Gmbh (acoustics); Davis Langdon & Everest (cost control); Franco Zagari, Emilio Trabella (landscaping); Tecnocamere (security)

## 1994
### Auditorium
### (project development)
Rome, Italy
Client: City of Rome (special auditorium office, Maurizio Cagnoni, technical director)
Renzo Piano Building Workshop
Design team: S. Ishida, M. Carroll, D. Hart (associate in charge), S. Scarabicchi (associate in charge), M. Varratta (associate in charge)
With: M. Alvisi, W. Boley, S. D'Atri, M. Ottonello, D. Cavagna (models), S. Rossi (models)
Consultants: Studio Vitone e Associati (structures); Manens Intertecnica (mechanical engineering); Müller Bbm (acoustics); Austin (cost control); Franco Zagari, Emilio Trabella (landscaping); Tecnocamere (security)

## 1995
### Ile Seguin
Paris, France
Client: Renault
Renzo Piano Building Workshop
Design team: P. Vincent (associate in charge), A. Chaaya
With: C. Calafelle, M. Cella, G. Modolo,

E. Novel, S. Purnama, T. Roland, M. Salerno, W. Vassal, J. P. Allain (models), M. Goudin (models)
Consultants: Desvigne and Dalnoky (landscaping); Syllabus (A. Vincent) (project management); GEC (ecominics); Qualiconsult (security, geography, geotechnics)

## 1995
### Multifunctional
### Arena Competition
Saitama (Tokyo), Japan
Renzo Piano Building Workshop
Design team: S. Ishida (associate in charge), C. Sapper, L. Viti, A. Zoppini
With: M. Carroll, M. Palmore, R. V. Truffelli, M. Carletti, L. Imberti, S. Rossi (models)
Consultants: Toshihiko Kimura, Mutsuro Sasaki (structures); Manens Intertecnica (electrical engineer); Müller Bbm (acoustics); P. Castiglioni (lighting); Hitachi Zosen Ltd. (event space and movable mechanisms); Dentsu Ltd. + Isaia Communications (cultural events and entertainment)
Contractors: Kumagai Gumi, Shimamura Kogyo, Turner Construction

## 1995
### Tate Gallery of Modern Art
London, England
Renzo Piano Building Workshop
Design team: S. Ishida (associate in charge), G.G. Bianchi (associate in charge), L. Couton, M. Palmore, C. Sapper
With: M. Carroll, A. Chaaya, G. Ducci, A. Gallo, F. Pagliani, M. B. Petersen, A. Pierandrei, E. Stotts, L. Viti, J. P. Allain (models), C. Colson (models)
Consultants: Ove Arup & Partners (structures, services, and lighting); Davis Langdon & Everest (cost control)

## 1995
### Service Complex
Nola (Naples), Italy
Client: Interporto Campano S.p.A.
Renzo Piano Building Workshop
Design team: M. Carroll, I. Corte (CAD), G. Grandi, E. Magnano, M. Palmore
With: M. Byrne, J. Breshears, L. Massone, H. Pénaranda
Consultants: T.P.E. (M. Milan), Venice (structures); Manens Intertecnica, Verona (mechanical engineering); Austin Italy, Milan (cost control); Amitaf, Turin (fire prevention and security)

## 1995–96
### Genoa Old Port Restoration
### Competition
Genoa, Italy
Client: Porto Antico S.p.A.
Renzo Piano Building Workshop
Design team: D. Piano, V. Tolu, R. V. Truffelli (associate in charge)
With: A. Giovannoni, G. Langasco (CAD), M. Nouvion, C. Pigionanti
Consultants: B. Ballerini (structures); E. Lora (mechanical engineering); Sted (cost control); M. Gronda (naval engineering)
Contractors: Coopsette, Reggio Emilia, Ecoline, Genoa, Officine Mariotti, Genoa, Nadalini, Ferrara

## 1995–
### Renovation of Centre Georges
### Pompidou
Paris, France
Client: Centre Georges Pompidou
Renzo Piano Building Workshop

## 1996
### Fila U.S.A. Headquarters
Baltimore, Maryland
Client: Fila
Renzo Piano Building Workshop
Design team: P. Vincent, A. Chaaya, R. Self
With: G. Borden, G. Modolo, P. Furnemont (models)
Consultant: Zieger and Snead (local architects)

## 1996
### Fila U.S.A. Headquarters
Seoul, Korea
Client: Fila
Renzo Piano Building Workshop
Design team: P. Vincent, J. Moolhuijzen, D. Rat, O. Doizy (models)

## 1996–
### Ferrari Wind Tunnel
Maranello (Modena), Italy
Client: Ferrari/Dioguardi
Renzo Piano Building Workshop
Design team: J. B. Mothes, N. Pacini, M. Pimmel, D. Rat, M. Rossato Piano, M. Salerno (associate in charge), P. Vincent (associate in charge)
With: J. P. Allain (models), S. Abbado, T. Damisch, O. Doizy (models), J. C. M'Fouara
Consultants: CSTB (M. Gandemer); Agibat MTI (D. Quost); Végétude (C. L. Guinaudeau, E. Nardomme)
Contractors: Tangerini, Delle Fratte, Lipari

## 1996–
### Mixed-Use Tower Complex
Sydney, Australia
Client: Lend Lease Development
Renzo Piano Building Workshop
Design team: S. Ishida (associate in charge), M. Carrol (associate in charge), J. Mc Neal, M. Amosso
With: E. Magnano, H. Penarando, S. Rossi (models), I. Corte (CAD), M. Palmore, C. Tiberti, M. Frezz, G. Alvisi
Consultants: Ove Arup & Partners (T. Barker, J. Hancock, A. O'Sullivan, T. Carfrae, J. Perry) (services and facades); Lend Lease Design Group (structures)

## Renzo Piano Building Workshop
Paris, Genoa

Alessandra Alborghetti
Massimo Alvisi
Marco Amosso
Eric Audoye
Emanuela Baglietto
Roger Baumgarten
François Bertolero
Giorgio G. Bianchi
Gianfranco Biggi
Rosella Biondo
Gail Borden
Carola Brammen
John Breshears
Stefania Canta
Daniela Cappuzzo
Mark Carroll
Dante Cavagna
Antoine Chaaya
Patrick Charles
Christophe Colson
Ivan Corte
Loïc Couton
Toma Damisch
Stefano D'atri
Andreas Degn
Olaf De Nooyer
Vittorio Di Turi
Giorgio Ducci
Birgit Eistert
Johannes Florin
Pierre Furnemont
Alain Gallissian
Alberto Giordano
Giovanna Giusto
Philippe Goubet
Giorgio Grandi
Donald Hart
Margrith Hartmann
Oliver Hempel
Michelle Howard

Shunji Ishida
Charlotte Jackman
Misha Kramer
Giovanna Langasco
Domenico Magnano
Claudio Manfreddo
Ester Manitto
Flavio Marano
Luca Massone
William Matthews
Gian Mauro Maurizio
Jonathan Mc Neal
Nayla Mecattaf
Daniela Miccolis
Sylvie Romet Milanesi
Gianni Modolo
Joost Moolhuijzen
Jean-Bernard Mothes
Eric Novel
Sonia Oldani
Mara Ottonello
Nicola Pacini
Michael Palmore
Hembert Penaranda
Morten Busk Petersen
Ronan Phelan
Daniele Piano
Lia Piano
Renzo Piano
Mario Piazza
Marie Pimmel
Bernard Plattner
Antonio Porcile
Sophie Purnama
Dominique Rat
Emilia Rossato
Paola  Rossato
Stefano Rossi
Caroline Roux
Joachim Ruoff

Angela Sacco
Maria Salerno
Susanna Scarabicchi
Ronnie Self
Franc Somner
Susanne Stacher
Hélène Teboul
Anne H. Temenides
Vittorio Tolu
Renzo V. Truffelli
Harrie Van Der Meiys
Mauritz Van Der Staay
Maurizio Varratta
William Vassal
Maria Veltcheva
Paul Vincent
Erik Volz
Philippe Von Matt
Nicole Westermann
Sarah Wong

Camilla Aasgard
Sebastien Abbado
Laurie Abbot
Peter Ackermann
Kamran Afshar Naderi
Emilia Agazzi
Francesco Albini
Alessandra Alborghetti
Jean Philippe Allain
Michele Allevi
Michel Alluyn
Massimo Alvisi
Marco Amosso
Arianna Andidero
Sally Appleby
Andrea Arancio
Catherine Ardilley
Magda Arduino
Stefano Arecco
Eric Audoye
P. Audran
Veronique Auger
Frank August
Alexandre Autin
Carmela Avagliano
Patrizio Avellino
Rita Avvenente

Carlo Bachschmidt
Jack Backus
Alessandro Badi
Susan Baggs
Emanuela Baglietto
Antonella Balassone
Nicolò Baldassini
Francois Barat
Henry Bardsley
Giulia Barone
Sonia Barone
Laura Bartolomei
Fabrizio Bartolomeo
Mario Bartylla
Cristopher Bartz
Bruna Bassetti
Kathy Bassiere
Mario Bassignani
Sandro Battini
Roger Baumgarten
Paolo Beccio
Eva Belik
Annie Benzeno

Jan Berger
François Bertolero
Alessandro Bianchi
Giorgio G. Bianchi
Patrizia Bianchini
Gianfranco Biggi
Gregoire Bignier
Germana Binelli
Judy Bing
Rosella Biondo
Jean François Blassel
A. Blassone
William Blurock
Paolo Bodega
Marko Bojovic
William Boley
Sara Bonati
Manuela Bonino
Gilles Bontemps
Gail Borden
Antonella Bordoni
Andrea Bosch
Pierre Botschi
Marjolijne Boudry
Sandrine Boulay
Bret Bowin
Carola Brammen
Ross Brennan
John Breshears
Gaelle Breton
Flore Bringand
Maria Brizzolara
Cuno Brullmann
Michael Burckhardt
Christiane Burklein
Mary Byrne
Hans-Peter Bysaeth

Federica Caccavale
Alessandro Calafati
Crystel Calafelle
Benedetto Calcagno
Patrick Callegia
Maurizio Calosso
Michele Calvi
Stefan Camenzind
Nunzio Camerada
Danila Campo
Florence Canal
Andrea Canepa
Stefania Canta
Vittorio Caponetto
Daniela Cappuzzo
Alessandro Carisetto
Monica Carletti
Elena Carmignani
Isabella Carpiceci
Gilbert Carreira
Emanuele Carreri
Mark Carroll
Elena Casali
Marta Castagna

Cristina Catino
Maria Cattaneo
Enrica Causa
Dante Cavagna
Simone Cecchi
Giorgio Celadon
Ottaviano Celadon
Massimo Cella
Alessandro Cereda
Antoine Chaaya
Patricia Chappell
Patrick Charles
Jean Luc Chassais
Pierre Chatelain
Hubert Chatenay
Ariel Chavela
Tina Chee
Laura Cherchi
Raimondo Chessa
Cristopher Chevalier
Catherine Clarisse
Geoffrey Cohen
Franc Collect
Daniel Collin
Christophe Colson
Shelly Comer
Philippe Convercey
Pier Luigi Copat
Michel Corajoud
Colman Corish
Monica Corsilia
Ivan Corte
Giacomo Costa
Leopoldo Costa
Raffaella Costa
Loïc Couton
Rosa Coy
Paolo Crema
Belmondi R. Croce
A. Croxato
Mario Cucinella
Irene Cuppone
Catherine Cussoneau
Lorenzo Custer

Isabelle Da Costa
Toma Damisch
Michel Dananco
Paul Darmer
Lorenzo Dasso
Stefano D'Atri
K. Matthew Daubmann
Mike Davies
Daniela Defilla
S. Degli Innocenti
Andreas Degn
Silvia De Leo
Evelyne Delmoral
Alessandro De Luca
Dalia De Macina
Simona De Mattei
Alessio Demontis

Michel Denance
Olaf De Nooyer
Julien Descombes
Daria De Seta
Michel Desvigne
Laura Diaichelburg
Carmelo Di Bartolo
Ottavio Di Blasi
Helene Diebold
Maddalena Di Sopra
Brian Ditchburn
Vittorio Di Turi
John Doggart
Olivier Doizy
Eugenio Donato
Francois Doria
Catherine D'Ovidio
Michael Dowd
Mike Downs
Klaus Dreissigacker
Delphine Drouin
Serge Drouin
Frank Dubbers
Giorgio Ducci
P. Du Boisson Du Mesnil
Susan Dunne
Jean Luc Dupanloup
Philippe Dupont
Susanne Durr
John Dutton

Mick Eekhout
Stacy Eisenberg
Birgit Eistert
Ahmed El Jerari
Lukas Epprecht
James Evans
Allison Ewing

Roberta Fambri
Roberto Faravelli
Giorgio Fascioli
Maxwell Fawcett
Monica Fea
David Felice
Alfonso Femia
Jacques Fendard
Prado Fernandez Ruben
Agostino Ferrari
Maurizio Filocca
Eileen Fitzgerald
Richard Fitzgerald
Peter Flack
Johannes Florin
Renato Foni
M. Fordam
Gilles Fourel
Gianfranco Franchini
Hughes Frank
Kenneth Fraser
Nina Freedman

Marian Frezza
Enrico Frigerio
Junya Fujita
Pierre Furnemont

Rinaldo Gaggero
Sergio Gaggero
Alain Gallissian
Andrea Gallo
Antonio Gallo
Carla Garbato
Robert Garlipp
Maurizio Garrasi
G. Gasbarri
Angelo Ghiotto
Davide Gibelli
Alain Gillette
Sonia Giordani
Alberto Giordano
Roberto Giordano
Antonella Giovannoni
Giovanna Giusto
Marion Goerdt
Marco Goldschmied
Enrico Gollo
Anahita Golzari
Alessandro Gortan
Philippe Goubet
Françoise Gouinguenet
Robert Grace
Giorgio Grandi
Cecil Granger
Walter Grasmug
Don Gray
Nigel Greenhill
Magali Grenier
Paolo Guerrini
Domenico Guerrisi
Alain Gueze
Barnaby Gunning
Ranjit Gupta

Anton Hahne
Greg Hall
Donald Hart
Thomas Hartman
Margrith Hartmann
Gunther Hastrich
Ulrike Hautsch
Adam Hayes
Christopher Hays
Eva Hegerl
Oliver Hempel
Pascal Hendier
Pierre Henneguier
Marie Henry
Gabriel Hernandez
Caroline Herrin
Cristopher Hight
Kohji Hirano
Harry Hirsch
Andrew Holmes

Eric Holt
Abigail Hopkins
Masahiro Horie
Helene Houizot
Michelle Howard
Bruno Hubert
Jean Huc
Ed Huckabi
Charles Hussey

Filippo Icardi
Frediano Iezzi
Akira Ikegami
Djenina Illoul
Paolo Insogna
Shunji Ishida

Charlotte Jackman
Angela Jackson
Tobias Jaklin
Robert Jan Van Santen
Amanda Johnson
Luis Jose
Frederic Joubert

Shin Kanoo
Jan Kaplicky
Elena Karitakis
Robert Keiser
Christopher Kelly
Paul Kelly
Werner Kestel
Irini Kilaiditi
Tetsuya Kimura
Laurent Koenig
Tomoko Komatsubara
Akira Komiyama
Misha Kramer
Eva Kruse
Bettina Kurtz

Jean Baptiste Lacoudre
Antonio Lagorio
Giovanna Langasco
Frank Lariviere
Stig Larsen
Marc Fischer Laurent
Denis Laville
François Laville
Jean Lelay
Renata Lello
Claudia Leoncini
Laurent Le Voyer
Riccardo Librizzi
Olivier Lidon
Lorraine Lin
Bill Logan
Johanna Lohse
Federica Lombardo
François Lombardo
Steve Lopez
Riccardo Luccardini

Simonetta Lucci
Rolf-Robert Ludwig
Claudine Luneberg
Massimiliano Lusetti

Paola Maggiora
Domenico Magnano
C. Maxwell Mahon
Nicholas Malby
Milena Mallamaci
Natalie Mallat
Claudio Manfreddo
Ester Manitto
Roberta Mantelli
Paolo Mantero
Flavio Marano
Andrea Marasso
Francesco Marconi
Massimo Mariani
A. Marré Brunenghi
Cristina Martinelli
Luca Massone
Daniela Mastragostino
Manuela Mattei
William Matthews
Marie Helene Maurette
Gian Mauro Maurizio
Kathrin Mayer
Ken Mc Bryde
Katherine Mclone
Grainne Mc Mahon
Jonathan Mc Neal
Nayla Mecattaf
Simone Medio
Barbara Mehren
Roberto Melai
Mario Menzio
Evelyne Mercier
Benny Merello
Gabriella Merlo
Peter Metz
Jean C. M'fouara
Daniela Miccolis
Marcella Michelotti
Paolo Migone
Sylvie Romet Milanesi
Emanuela Minetti
Takeshi Miyazaki
Gianni Modolo
Sandro Montaldo
Elisa Monti
Joost Moolhuijzen
Gerard Mormina
Ingrid Morris
Julia Moser
Jean-Bernard Mothes
Farshid Moussavi
Mariette Muller
Philip Murphy
Andrea Musso
Hanne Nagel
Shinichi Nakaya

Hiroshi Naruse
Denise M. Nascimento
Roberto Navarra
Pascale Negre
Andrew Nichols
Hiroko Nishikawa
Susanne Nobis
David Nock
Elisabeth Nodinot
Marco Nouvion
Eric Novel
Koung Nyunt

Alphons Oberhoffer
Anna O'Carrol
Stefan Oehler
Noriaki Okabe
Antonella Oldani
Sonia Oldani
Grace Ong
Patrizia Orcamo
Stefania Orcamo
Roy Orengo
Carlos Osrej
Tim O'Sullivan
Piero Ottaggio
Mara Ottonello
Nedo Ottonello

Antonella Paci
Nicola Pacini
Filippo Pagliani
Michael Palmore
Roger Panduro
Giorgia Paraluppi
Chandra Patel
Pietro Pedrini
Roberto Pelagatti
Luigi Pellini
Danilo Peluffo
Gianluca Peluffo
Hembert Penaranda
Lionel Penisson
Mauro Penna
Patrizia Persia
Morten Busk Petersen
Claire Petetin
Gil Petit
Ronan Phelan
Paul Phillips
Alberto Piancastelli
Carlo Piano
Daniele Piano
Lia Piano
Matteo Piano
Renzo Piano
Mario Piazza
Enrico Piazze
Gennaro Picardi
Alessandro Pierandrei
Fabrizio Pierandrei
Massimo Pietrasanta

Claudia Pigionanti
Marie Pimmel
Alessandro Pisacane
Sandra Planchez
Bernard Plattner
Monica Poggi
Jean A. Polette
Andrea Polleri
Antonio Porcile
Roberta Possanzini
Fabio Postani
Nicolas Prouvé
Costanza Puglisi
Sophie Purnama

Gianfranco Queirolo

Michele Ras
Maria Cristina Rasero
Roberto Rasore
Dominique Rat
Neil Rawson
Judith Raymond
Antonella Recagno
Olaf Rechtenwald
Philippe Reigner
Daniele Reimondo
Luis Renau
Bryan Reynolds
Tom Reynolds
Elena Ricciardi
Kieran Rice
Nemone Rice
Peter Rice
Jean Yves Richard
Giuseppe Rocco
Richard Rogers
Renaud Rolland
Emilia Rossato
Paola Rossato
Stefano Rossi
Caroline Roux
Bernard Rouyer
Tammy Roy
Lucio Ruocco
Joachim Ruoff
Ken Rupard

Antonella Sacchi
Angela Sacco
Gerard Saint Jean
Riccardo Sala
Maria Salerno
Maurizio Santini
Francesca Santolini
Paulo Sanza
Carola Sapper
Paul Satchell
Alessandro Savioli
Susanna Scarabicchi
Maria Grazia Scavo
Stefan Schafer

Helga Schlegel
Giuseppina Schmid
Jean François Schmit
Maren Schuessler
Andrea Schultz
C. Segantini
Daniel Seibold
Ronnie Self
Barbara-Petra Sellwig
Patrik Senne
Anna Serra
Kelly Shannon
Randy Shields
Aki Shimizu
Madoka Shimizu
Cecile Simon
Davide Simonetti
Thibaud Simonin
Alessandro Sinagra
Luca Siracusa
Jan Sircus
Alan Smith
Stephanie Smith
Franc Somner
Richard Soundy
Claudette Spielmann
Susanne Stacher
Adrian Stadlmayer
Alan Stanton
Graham Stirk
Eric Stotts
David Summerfield
Jasmin Surti
Christian Susstrunk

J. Taborda Barrientos
Hiroyuki Takahashi
Norio Takata
Noriko Takiguchi
Hélène Teboul
Anne H. Temenides
Carlo Teoldi
Peter Terbuchte
G. L. Terragna
David Thom
John Thornhill
Cinzia Tiberti
Luigi Tirelli
Elisabeth Tisseur
Vittorio Tolu
Taichi Tomuro
Bruno Tonfoni
Graziella Torre
Laura Torre
Olivier Touraine
Franco Trad
Alessandro Traldi
Renata Trapani
Renzo V. Truffelli
Leland Turner
Mark Turpin
Yoshiko Ueno

Kiyomi Uezono
Peter Ullathorne

Colette Valensi
Maurizio Vallino
Harrie Van Der Meiys
M. Van Der Staay
Michael Vaniscott
Antonia Van Oosten
Robert-Jan Van Santen
Arijan Van Timmeren
Maurizio Varratta
Paolo Varratta
Claudio Vaselli
William Vassal
Francesca Vattuone
Bernard Vaudeville
Martin Veith
Maria Veltcheva
Reiner Verbizh
Laura Vercelli
Maria Carla Verdona
Eric Vestrepen
Silvia Vignale
Antonella Vignoli
Mark Viktov
Alain Vincent
Paul Vincent
Patrick Virly
Marco Visconti
Lorenzo Viti
Bettina Volz
Eric Volz
Philippe Von Matt

Louis Waddell
Jean Marc Weill
Florian Wenz
Nicole Westermann
Nicolas Westphal
Chris Wilkinson
Niel Winder
Martin Wollensak
Jacob Woltjer
Sarah Wong

George Xydis

Masami Yamada
Sugako Yamada
Hiroshi Yamaguchi
Tatsuya Yamaguchi
Emi Yoshimura
John Young

Gianpaolo Zaccaria
E. K. Zammit
Lorenzo Zamperetti
Antonio Zanuso
Martina Zappettini
Walter Zbinden
Maurizio Zepponi

Massimo Zero
Alessandro Zoppini
Ivana Zunino

# Bibliography

## Articles

### 1966

R. Piano, R. Foni, G. Garbuglia, L. Tirelli, M. Filocco. "Una struttura ad elementi standard per la copertura di medie e grandi luci." *La Prefabbricazione*, Jan. 1966.

Z. S. Makowski. "Structural plastics in Europe." *Arts and Architecture*, Aug. 1966, 20–30.

### 1967

M. Scheichenbauer. "Progettare con le materie plastiche." *Casabella* 316, 1967.

"Ricerca sulle strutture in lamiera e in poliestere rinforzato." *Domus* 448, Mar. 1967, 8–22.

### 1968

"Il grande numero." *Domus* 466, Sept. 1968.

"Nuove tecniche e nuove strutture per l'edilizia." *Domus* 468, Nov. 1968, 6.

### 1969

R. Piano. "Progettazione sperimentale per strutture a guscio." *Casabella* 335, 1969.

R. Piano. "Nasce con le materie plastiche un nuovo modo di progettare architetture." *Materie plastiche ed elastometri*, Jan. 1969.

Z. S. Makowski. "Plastic structures of Renzo Piano." *Systems, Building and Design*, Feb. 1969, 37–54.

Z. S. Makowski. "Les structures plastiques de Renzo Piano." *Plastique batiment* 126, Feb. 1969, 10–17.

R. Piano. "Italie recherche de structure." *Techniques et Architecture*, May 1969, 96–100.

R. Piano. "Experiments and projects with industrialised structures in plastic material." *P.D.O.B.* 16–17, Oct. 1969.

"Uno studio-laboratorio." *Domus* 479, Oct. 1969, 10–14.

### 1970

"Un cantiere sperimentale." *Casabella* 349, 1970.

R. Piano. "Verso una pertinenza technologica dei componenti." *Casabella* 352, 1970, 37.

A. Cereda. "Alcune recenti esperienze nel campo della industrializzazione edilizia—tre architetture di Renzo Piano." *Lipe*, Mar. 1970, 1–12.

"L'Italia a Osaka." *Domus* 484, Mar. 1970.

"Renzo Piano." *Architectural Design*, Mar. 1970, 140–45.

"Rigging a Roof." *Architectural Forum*, Mar. 1970, 64–69.

Z. S. Makowski. "Strukturen aus Kunststoff von Renzo Piano." *Werk, Bauen + Wohnen*, Apr. 1970, 112–21.

"Il poliestere rinforzato protagonista del padiglione dell'industria italiana." *Materie plastiche ed elastometri*, May 1970, 470–77.

R. Piano. "Architecture and technology." Trans. T. M. Stevens. *A.A. Quarterly*, July 1970, 32–43.

"Italian Industry Pavilion, Expo '70, Osaka." *Architectural Design*, Aug. 1970, 416.

R. Piano. "Il Padiglione dell'Industria Italiana all'Expo '70 di Osaka." *Acciaio*, Nov. 1970, 1.

### 1971

"R. Piano, Per un'edilizia industrializzata." *Domus* 495, Feb. 1971, 12–15.

"Industrial building." *Architectural Forum*, Apr. 1971.

"Industrialisierung." *Deutsche Bauzeitung*, Apr. 1971, 405–7.

"Le materie plastiche nella produzione edilizia per componenti." *Materie plastiche ed elastometri*, May 1971.

"Grand Piano." *Industrial Design*, Oct. 1971, 40–45.

"Piano e Rogers: Beaubourg." *Domus* 503, Oct. 1971, 1–7.

M. Cornu. "Concours Beaubourg, 'Est-ce un signe de notre temps?'" *Architecture, Mouvement, Continuité*, Nov. 1971, 8–9.

R. Piano. "L'Acciaio nell'edilizia industrializzata." *Acciaio*, Nov. 1971, 1–4.

### 1972

"Le Projet lauréat." *Paris projet* 7, 1972, 48–57.

"Projects de lauréats." *Techniques et Architecture*, Feb. 1972, 48–55.

"Padiglione dell'Industria Italiana all'Expo 70 di Osaka." *Casabella*, Mar. 1972.

"Aktualitat: Esso Tankstellen Wettbewerd in Italien." *Werk, Bauen + Wohnen*, June 1972, 280.

"A Parigi, per i parigini l'evoluzione del progetto Piano + Rogers per il Centre Beaubourg." *Domus* 511, June 1972, 280.

"Paris Centre Beaubourg." *Deutsche Bauzeitung*, Sept. 1972, 974–76.

### 1973

"Centre Culturel du Plateau Beaubourg." *L'Architecture d'Aujourd'hui* 168, July-Aug. 1973, 34–43.

"Centre Plateau Beaubourg." *Domus* 525, Aug. 1973.

"Piano + Rogers." *L'Architecture d'Aujourd'hui* 170, Nov.-Dec. 1973, 46–58.

### 1974

"Le Centre Beaubourg." *Chantiers de France* 68, 1974, 1–6.

"Piano." *Zodiac* 22, 1974, 126–47.

"Edificio per gli uffici B & B a Novedrate." *Domus* 530, Jan. 1974, 31–36.

"Expressive Einheit von Tragkonstruktion und Installationsanlagen." *Werk, Bauen + Wohnen*, Feb. 1974, 71–74.

R. Piano, R. Rogers. "B & B Italia Factory." *Architectural Design*, Apr. 1974, 245–46.

"Beaubourg au transparence." *Architecture intérieure* 141, June-July 1974, 72–77.

"Centre Beaubourg a Paris." *Techniques et Architecture* 300, Sept.-Oct. 1974, 58.

"Factory Tadworth, Surrey." *Architectural Review* 934, Dec. 1974, 338–45.

### 1975

"Etablissement publique du Centre Beaubourg, Paris." *Werk oeuvre*, Feb. 1975, 140–48.

F. Marano. "Una struttura tubolare per un nuovo edificio per uffici a Novedrate." *Acciaio*, Feb. 1975, 1–7.

"A Parigi musica underground." *Domus* 545, Apr. 1975, 9–12.

R. Piano, R. Rogers. "Piano + Rogers." *Architectural Design* 45, May 1975, 75–311.

R. Bordaz. "Le Centre Georges Pompidou." *Construction*, Sept. 1975, 5–30.

P. Rice. "Main Structural Framework of the Beaubourg Centre, Paris." *Acier, Stahl, Steel*, Sept. 1975, 297–309.

P. Rice, L. Grut. "Renzo Piano: la struttura del Centre Beaubourg a Parigi." *Acciaio*, Sept. 1975, 3–15.

### 1976

"L'IRCAM design process." *RIBA Journal*, Feb. 1976, 61–69.

"Novedrate Italia, Edificio per uffici." *Architecture Contemporaine*, Apr. 1976, 35–37.

K. Menomi. "Nel prato una struttura policroma. Edificio per uffici B & B." *Ufficio stile*, June 1976, 76–79.

"Piano + Rogers: Architectural Method." *A+U* 66, June 1976, 63–122.

R. Piano, R. Rogers. "Beaubourg furniture internal system catalogue." *Architectural Design* 46, July 1976, 442–43.

"L'IRCAM: Institut de recherche et coordination acoustique/musique." *Chantiers de France*, Sept. 1976, 2–13.

"Strukturen und Hullen." *Werk oeuvre*, Nov. 1976, 742–48.

### 1977

"Le Centre Beaubourg." Ministère des Affaires Culturelles/Ministère de L'Education National, 1977.

"Centre Georges Pompidou." *AD Profiles* 2, 1977.

Y. Futagawa. "Centre Beaubourg: Piano + Rogers." *GA Global Architecture* 44, 1977, 1–40.

C. Mitsia, M. Zakazian, C. Jacopin. "Eiffel vs. Beaubourg." *Werk-Archithese* 9, 1977, 22–29.

G. Neret. "Le Centre Pompidou." *Connaissance des Arts*, 1977, 3–15.

"Staatliches Kunst und Kulturzentrum Georges Pompidou/Paris." *DLW-Nachrichten* 61, 1977, 34–39.

"Centre National d'Art et de Culture Georges Pompidou, Paris." *Domus* 566–75 (special issue), Jan. 1977, 5–37.

"Piano + Rogers." *RIBA Journal*, Jan. 1977, 11–16.

"Le défi de Beaubourg." *L'Architecture d'Aujourd'hui* 189, Feb. 1977, 40–81.

"Frankreichs Centre National d'Art et de Culture Georges Pompidou Paris." *Bauwelt* 11, Mar. 1977, 316–34.

J. Bub, W. Messing. "Centre National d'Art et de Culture G. Pompidou, ein Arbeitsbericht von zwei Architekturstudenten." *Bauen + Wohnen*, Apr. 1977, 132–39.

M. Fadda. "Dal Beaubourg al progetto collettivo." *Laboratoria* 1, Apr.-June 1977, 69–73.

G. Lentati. "Centro Beaubourg, un'architettura utensile." *Ufficio stile* 10, May 1977, 74–87.

"Piano & Rogers 4 progetti." *Domus* 570, May 1977, 17–24.

"The Pompidolium." *Architectural Review* 963, May 1977, 270–94.

"Piano + Rogers." *Architectural Design* 47, July-Aug. 1977, 530.

R. Piano. "Per un'edilizia evolutiva." *Laboratorio*, Sept.-Nov. 1977, 7–10.

"Intorno al Beaubourg." *Abitare* 158, Oct. 1977, 69–75.

P. Restany, C. Casati. "Parigi: l'oggetto funzional." *Domus* 575, Oct. 1977, 1–11.

R. Piano. "Mobilités de hypothèses alternatives de production." *Werk-Archithese*, Nov.-Dec. 1977, 32.

P. Chemetov. "L'Opera Pompidou." *Techniques et Architecture* 317, Dec. 1977, 62–63.

M. Cornu. "Ce diable Beaubourg." *Techniques et Architecture* 317, Dec. 1977, 64–66.

A. Darlot. "Le centre national d'art et de culture G. Pompidou." *Revue Francaise de l'electricité* 259, Dec. 1977, 48–55.

### 1978

A. Paste. "Il Centro d'Arte e di Cultura G. Pompidou." *L'industria delle costruzioni* 76, Feb. 1978, 3–30.

"Centro Beaubourg Paris." *Informes de la Costrucion* 30, no. 299, Apr. 1978, 13–23.

R. Continenza. "Il centro nazionale d'arte e cultura G. Pompidou a Parigi." *L'Ingegnere* 53, June 1978, 187–98.

"Tipologie evolutive." *Domus* 583, June 1978, 12–13.

G. Biondo, E. Rognoni. "Materie plastiche ed edilizia industrializzata." *Domus* 585, Aug. 1978, 25–28.

"Esperienza di cantiere. Tre domande a R. Piano." *Casabella* 439, Sept. 1978, 42–51.

"IRCAM." *A.A.* 199, Oct. 1978, 52–63.

"Tipologie evolutive, lo spazio costruito deve adattarsi all'uomo." *Domus* 587, Oct. 1978, 30–31.

**1979**

R. Continenza. "Architettura e technologia aspetti dell'opera di R. Piano e R. Rogers." *Costruttori Abruzzesi* 2, 1979, 15–18.

"R. Piano, the Mobile Workshop in Otranto." *ILA & UD Annual Report*, Urbino, 1979, 60–63.

"Da uno spazio uguale due cose diversissime." *Abitare* 171, Jan.-Feb. 1979, 2–21.

"Wohnboxen in Mailand." *M.D.*, June 1979.

"Una recentissima proposta di R. Piano: Laboratorio mobile per lavori di recupero edilizio." *Modulo*, July-Aug. 1979, 855.

L. Wright. "Heimatlandschaft." *Architectural Review* 990, no. 166, Aug. 1979, 120–23.

"Mobiles-Quartier Laboratorium." *Werk, Bauen + Wohnen*, Sept. 1979, 330–32.

R. Continenza. "L'Opera di Piano & Rogers." *L'Ingegnere* 54, Oct. 1979, 469–85.

"Il Laboratorio di quartiere a Otranto." *Domus* 599, Oct. 1979, 2.

"Per il recupero dei Centri storici. Una proposta: Il laboratorio di quartiere." *Abitare* 178, Oct. 1979, 86–93.

"Operazione di recupero." *Casabella* 453, Dec. 1979, 7.

L. Rossi. "Piano + Rice + Ass. Il Laboratorio di quartiere." *Spazio + Società* 8, Dec. 1979, 27–42.

**1980**

"Enveloppes identiques—diversité interne Milano-Cusago I." *AC* 97, no. 25, Jan. 1980, 6–11.

"Free-Plan Four House Group." *Toshi Jutaku*, Feb. 1980, 14–23.

"Contemporary Design in Two Cities." *Building & Remodelling Guide*, July 1980, 108–13.

"Fiat's Magic Carpet Ride." *Design* 379, July 1980, 58.

"Centre Georges Pompidou." *Nikkei Architecture*, Aug. 1980, 83–85.

"Art News." *Geijutsu Shincho*, Sept. 1980.

"La technologia n'est pas toujours industrielle." *A.A.* 212, Dec. 1980, 51–54.

**1981**

"C. G. Pompidou." *A.A.* 213, Feb. 1981, 92–95.

M. T. Mirabile. "Centro Musicale a Parigi." *Industria delle Costruzioni* 114, Apr. 1981, 68–69.

"Sul mestiere dell'Architetto." *Domus* 617, May 1981, 27–29.

G. Lentari. "Quale ufficio?" *Ufficio stile*, June 1981, 60–69.

P. Santini. "Colloquio con R. Piano." *Ottagono* 16, no. 61, June 1981, 20–27.

"Wohnhausgruppe bei Mailand." *Die Kunst*, June 1981.

"Pianoforte." *Building Design* 556, July 1981, 11–14.

R. Pedio. "Renzo Piano Itinerario e un primo bilancio." *L'Architettura*, Nov. 1981,

614–62.

R. Piano. "Renzo Piano Genova." *Casabella* 474–75, Nov.-Dec. 1981, 95–96.

Ranieri, Valli. "Progetto e partecipazione." *Edilizia Popolare* 163, Nov.-Dec. 1981, 66–68.

**1982**

"Il Centro Congressi del World Trade Center Italiano." *Ufficio stile* 15, no. 67, 1982, 24–30.

"Piano in Houston." *Skyline*, Jan. 1982, 4.

"Italia." *Nikkei Architecture*, Feb. 1982, 52–56.

"Renzo Piano monografia." *A.A.* 219 (monographic issue), Feb. 1982.

"Fiat vettura sperimentale e sottosistemi." *Abitare* 202, Mar. 1982, 8–9.

"Tecnoarchitettura vettura sperimentale e sottosistemi." *Ottagono*, Mar. 1982.

"People's office ufficio fabbrica." *Ufficio stile*, Apr. 1982, 49–52.

M. Dini. "La città storica." *Area* 5, June-July 1982, 47.

S. Fox. "A Clapboard Treasure House." *Cite*, Aug. 1982, 5–7.

R. Piano. "Still in Tune." *Building Design* 606, Aug. 1982, 10–11.

"Piano Demonstration in Texas." *Progressive Architecture*, Sept. 1982.

"Abitacolo e abitazione." *Casabella* 484, Oct. 1982, 14–23.

"Renzo Piano." *The Architectural Review* 1028, Oct. 1982, 57–61.

L. Sacchetti. "Si chiude la scena comincia il congresso." *Costruire per Abitare* 3, Oct. 1982, 117–20.

M. T. Carbone. "Renzo Piano: Il molo degli specchi, il cantiere di quartiere." *Costruire per Abitare* 5, Dec.-Jan. 1982–83, 76–78.

M. T. Carbone. "Sei progetti e un fuoco di paglia." *Costruire per Abitare* 5, Dec.-Jan. 1982–83, 76–78.

**1983**

Renzo Piano. "Artisan du futur." *Techniques et Architecture* 350, 1983, 121–38.

"La macchina espositiva." *Abitare* 212, Mar. 1983, 90–91.

G. Ferracuti. "Il Laboratorio di Quartiere." *Recuperare*, Mar.-Apr. 1983, 120–23.

P. A. Croset. "Parigi 1989." *Casabella* 47, no. 490, Apr. 1983, 18–19.

"Design of the Future." *Wave*, Apr. 1983, 51–54.

A. L. Rossi. "La macchina climatizzata." *Domus* 638, Apr. 1983, 10–15.

"Tra il dire e il fare." *Costruire* 9, May 1983, 71.

B. Costantino. "Taller de Barrio: Coloquio con Renzo Piano y Gianfranco Dioguardi." *Modulo* 11, June 1983, 20–33.

"Des Technologies nouvelles pour l'habitat ancien." *Techniques et Architecture* 348, June-July 1983, 51–61.

C. Béret. "L'espace-flexible." *Art press* 2,

June-Aug. 1983, 22–23.

"Piano Machine." *The Architectural Review* 169, no. 1038, Aug. 1983, 26–31.

"Un boulevard flottant." *Urbanisme* 197, Sept. 1983, 44–45.

M. Brandli. "L'allestimento di Renzo Piano per la mostra di Calder." *Casabella* 47, no. 494, Sept. 1983, 34–36.

O. Fillion. "Schlumberger a Montrouge." *Architecture Intérieure* 196, Sept. 1983, 118–23.

M. Pawley. "Piano's Progress." *Building Design* 23, Sept. 1983, 32–34.

O. Pivetta. "Postindustriale sarà lei." *Costruire* 12, Sept. 1983, 100–105.

J. P. Robert. "Un Chantier experimental a Montrouge." *Le Moniteur* 40, Sept. 1983, 60–67.

L. Rossi. "La cultura del fare." *Spazio e Società* 6, no. 23, Sept. 1983, 50–62.

"S. Boidi: Io, il mestiere i miei strumenti." *Costruire* 14, Nov. 1983, 82, 83, 112.

"Calder a Torino." *Domus* 644, Nov. 1983, 56–59.

M. Margantini. "Instabil Sandy Calder." *Modo* 64, Nov. 1983, 53–57.

"Piano Rehab." *The Architectural Review* 174, no. 1041, Nov. 1983, 68–73.

R. Pedio. "Retrospettiva di Calder a Torino." *L'Architettura* 29, Dec. 1983, 888–94.

R. Rovers. "Recent Werk van Renzo Piano." *Bouw* 25, Dec. 1983, 9–12.

**1984**

O. Boisère. "Paris x Paris." *Domus* 646, Jan. 1984, 22–27.

"The Menil Collection." *Arts + Architecture*, Jan. 1984, 32–35.

G. Plaffy. "R. Piano: Sub-Systems Automobile." *Omni*, Jan. 1984, 112–15.

A. Pélissier. "Renzo Piano, participer, inventer de nouvelles méthodes de travail et de nouvelles maisons." *Histoire de participer* 93, Feb. 1984, 64–69.

"Una tensostruttura per l'insegna della mostra di Calder a Torino." *Acciaio* 25, Feb. 1984, 53–57.

M. Fazio. "A Torino Calder." *Spazio e Società*, Mar. 1984, 66–69.

"Lingotto Piano/Schein." *Building Design*, May 1984, 26–28.

P. Rumpf. "Fiat-Lingotto: Change oder Danaergeschenk fur Turin?" *Bauwelt* 17, May 1984, 733.

M. Zardini. "Venti idee per il Lingotto." *Casabella* 502, May 1984, 30–31.

Y. Pontoizeau. "Renovation du site industriel Schlumberger, Montrouge." *L'Architecture d'Aujourd'hui* 233, June 1984, 14–23.

"UUL, Unità Urbanistiche Locali." *Costruire* 20, June 1984, 36–38.

"Exposition itinerante de technologie informatique." *Techniques et Architecture* 354, June-July 1984, 144–45.

R. Marchelli. "Un involucro di policarbonato per una mostra itinerante." *Materie Plastiche ed Elastometri*, July-Aug. 1984,

424–27.

"Beaubourg analogo." *Rassegna*, Sept. 1984, 94–97.

A. Castellano. "Venti Progetti per il futuro del Lingotto." *La mia casa* 170, Sept. 1984, 48–51.

"IBM Exhibit Pavilion, Paris Exposition." *A+U* 168, Sept. 1984, 67–72.

A. Mladenovic. "Renzo Piano." *Nas Dom*, Sept. 1984, 26–29.

"Una mostra itinerante per far conoscere il computer." *Abitare* 227, Sept. 1984, 4–6.

C. Di Bartolo. "Creatività e Progetto." *Modo*, Oct. 1984, 36–40.

Y. Pontoizeau. "Projects & Realisations." *L'Architecture d'Aujourd'hui* 235, Oct. 1984, 59–65.

"Technologia: teconologie leggere." *Modulo*, Oct. 1984, 1003–9.

"Un'arca veneziana per i suoni di 'Prometeo.'" *AD/Mondadori*, Nov. 1984, 48–50.

"Arcadian Machine." *The Architectural Review* 1053, Nov. 1984, 70–75.

"Boeri e Crosety, Dinosaur with a brain." *Blueprint*, Nov. 1984, 12–13.

"L'Expo IBM." *GA Document*, Nov. 1984.

R. Pedio. "Exhibit IBM, padiglione itinerante di tecnologia informatica." *L'Architettura*, Nov. 1984, 818–24.

"Riflessioni sul 'Prometeo.'" *Casabella* 507, Nov. 1984, 38–39.

A. Castellano. "Renzo Piano e l'Arca del Prometeo." *La mia casa* 173, Dec. 1984, 48–53.

"Piano + Nono." *The Architectural Review* 1054, Dec. 1984, 53–57.

**1985**

R. Buchanan. "The Traps of Technology." *Forum* 29, 1985, 138–44.

"Renzo Piano and His Methods." *SD* 85-01 High-Tech 244, Jan. 1985, 47–67.

"Prometeo." *Interni* 348, Mar. 1985, 73.

G. Sansalone. "Questo gruppo spara su tutto." *Costruire* 27, Mar. 1985, 49.

G. Simonelli. "La grande nave lignea." *Modulo*, Mar. 1985, 164–70.

A. Castellano. "L'architettura sperimentale di Renzo Piano." *La mia casa* 176, Apr. 1985, 32–53.

M. Milan. "Il Prometeo." *Acciaio*, Apr. 1985, 166–70.

J.M.H. "Restructuration d'un site industriel à Montrouge." *Technique et Architecture* 359, Apr.-May 1985, 42–53.

A. Burigana. "Renzo Piano." *Architectural Digest* 47, May 1985, 32–38.

E. Caminati. "L'arte di costruire." *Costruire* 29, May 1985, 162–68.

"France: Le printemps des musées." *Le Moniteur*, May 1985.

J. Glancey. "Piano Pieces." *The Architectural Review* 1059, May 1985, 58–63.

R. Piano, S. Ishida. "Music Space for the Opera 'Prometeo' by L. Nono." *A+U* 118, June 1985, 67–74.

O. Fillion. "Natura, la revanche." *Archi-*

*Crée* 207, Aug.-Sept. 1985, 64–69.
"Il Prometeo." *Daidalos* 17, Sept. 1985, 84–87.
"Cité Descartes." *Techniques et Architecture* 362, Oct. 1985, 135–37.
"Italia 1984." *Industria delle Costruzioni* 168, Oct. 1985, 64–73.
A. Pelissier. "Entretien avec Renzo Piano." *Techniques et Architecture* 362, Oct. 1985, 101–11.
J. P. Robert. "La Schlumberger a Montrouge di Renzo Piano." *Casabella* 517, Oct. 1985, 26–29.
E. Hubeli. "Kunstliches und Naturliches." *Werk, Bauen + Wohnen*, Nov. 1985, 23–28.
"IBM." *Architects Magazine*, Nov. 1985, 249–50.
"Des chantiers permanents." *L'Architecture d'Aujourd'hui* 242, Dec. 1985, 12–15.
N. Okabe. "Urban Conversion of the Schlumberger Factories." *Global Architecture* 14, Dec. 1985.

**1986**
"Immeuble de bureaux." *Architecture contemporaine*, 1986, 182–85.
G. Negro. "Un architetto per Lione." *Costruire* 37, Feb. 1986, 86–89.
"Eine mobile Oper und ein 'Quartierlabor.'" *Werk, Bauen + Wohnen*, Apr. 1986, 4–9.
"Reazione spaziale di Renzo Piano negli uffici Lowara a Vicenza." *Architettura*, Apr. 1986, 246–53.
"Un open space transparente." *Habitat Ufficio*, June-July 1986, 48–55.
"Houston, Texas, De Menil Museum." *Abitare* 247, Sept. 1986, 382–84.
D. Mangin. "Piano de A à W." *L'Architecture d'Aujourd'hui* 246, Sept. 1986, 1–37.
M. Prusicki. "Renzo Piano, Progetto Lingotto a Torino." *Domus* 675, Sept. 1986, 29–37.
"Aspettando Colombo." *Costruire* 44, Oct. 1986, 42–49.
F. Zagari. "Progetto Bambù." *Abitare* 248, Oct. 1986, 28–31.
"A. Robecchi, La religiosa attesa dell'atto." *Costruire* 45, Nov. 1986, 126–30.
"Vicenza, Una mostra di Renzo Piano." *Abitare* 249, Nov. 1986, 111.
O. Boissière. "Il Museo de Menil a Houston." *L'Arca* 2, Dec. 1986, 28–35.
D. Smetana. "Piano and Palladio, virtuoso duet." *Progressive Architecture*, Dec. 1986, 25, 33.
M. Vogliazzo. "Conversando con Renzo Piano." *Gran Bazaar*, Dec. 1986, 22–25.
"Renzo Piano: Menil Collection a Houston." *Ilaud*, 1986–87, 76–77.

**1987**
B. Galletta. "Concorso per la Sede del Credito Industriale Sardo, a Cagliari." *Industria delle Costruzioni* 183, Jan. 1987, 27–33.
"Piano Lessons." *AJ* 21, Jan. 1987, 20–21.

"Piano Solo." *Building Design* 23, Jan. 1987, 14–15.
"Piano's Sketches for the Final Composition." *Design Week* 23, Jan. 1987.
"Le Synchrotron de Grenoble." *Le Moniteur*, Jan. 1987, 58–59.
A. Castellano. "Il Forum industriale." *L'Arca* 3, Jan.-Feb. 1987, 29–37.
"Facciata continua strutturale." *Domus* 681, Mar. 1987.
E. M. Farrelly. "Piano Practice." *The Architectural Review* 1081, Mar. 1987, 32–59.
R. Piano. "La modernità secondo Piano." *L'Arca* 5, Apr. 1987, 59–65.
B. Nerozzi. "L'Architettura ritrovata." *Gran Bazaar* 55, Apr.-May 1987, 47–54.
P. Papademetriou. "The Responsive Box." *Progressive Architecture*, May 1987, 87–97.
"Simplicity of Form, Ingenuity In the Use of Daylight." *Architecture*, May 1987, 84–91.
"Trenward System aus glasfaserverstaktem Beton." *Detail* 27, May 1987, 1–4.
R. Ingersoll. "Pianissimo, the very quiet Menil Collection." *Texas Architecture* 3, May-June 1987, 40–47.
R. Banham. "In the Neighborhood of Art." *Art in America*, June 1987, 124–29.
A. Benedetti. "Ristrutturazione e riuso di un'area industriale a Montrouge, Parigi." *Industria delle Costruzioni* 188, June 1987, 6–23.
H. F. Debailleux. "Piano à Houston." *Beaux-Arts Magazine* 47, June 1987, 68–73.
M. Filler. "A Quiet Place for Art." *House & Garden*, June 1987, 74–75.
R. Piano. "Uno stadio per Bari," *Domus* 684, June 1987, 7.
"Renzo Piano, lo Stadio di Bari e il sincrotone di Grenoble." *Casabella* 536, June 1987, 1–37.
M. Keniger. "The Art of Assembly." *Australia Architecture* 5, July 1987, 63–67.
Ranzani, Guazzoli. "Renzo Piano, Museo Menil, Houston." *Domus* 685, July-Aug. 1987, 32–43.
L. Caprile. "Il Museo con la cassaforte sul tetto una nuova 'contestazione' di Renzo Piano." *Arte* 177, Sept. 1987, 25.
E. M. Farrelly. "The Quiet Game." *The Architectural Review* 1087, Sept. 1987, 70–80.
"A Homely Gallery." *The Architect*, Sept. 1987, 38–41.
G. K. Koenig. "Piano: la Basilica palladiana non si tocca." *Ottagono* 86, Sept. 1987, 48–53.
"The de Menil Collection." *Transaction*, Oct. 1987, 44–51.
"Piano, retour près de Beaubourg." *L'Architecture d'Aujourd'hui* 253, Oct. 1987, 48–50.
J. F. Pousse. "Renzo Piano: la métamorphose de la technologie (Menil, Bari, Schlumberger, Lingotto, Lovara)." *Techniques et Architecture* 374, Oct.-Nov. 1987, 146–65.

R. Banham, S. Ishida. "Renzo Piano." *A+U* 206, Nov. 1987, 39–122.
A. Castellano. "Poesia e geometria per Bari." *L'Arca*, Nov. 1987, 80–85.
S. Heck. "Piano's entente cordiale." *RIBA Journal*, Nov. 1987, 28–35.
S. Ishida. "The Menil Art Museum." *SD*, Nov. 1987, 48–50.
V. Magnago Lampugnani, E. Ranzani. "Renzo Piano: sovversione, silenzio e normalità." *Domus* 688, Nov. 1987, 17–24.
"Konstruktionen für das Licht." *Werk, Bauen + Wohnen*, Dec. 1987, 30–39.
"Sammlung Menil in Houston." *Baumeister*, Dec. 1987, 36–41.

**1988**
"Atélier Municipaux, Paris 19ème." *Usine*, 1988, 82–85.
V. Borel, E. Daydé. "L'IRCAM au Faite." *Septe à Paris* 6, Jan. 1988, 35.
R. de la Nouve, I. Cazes. "Donjon Final. La tour de l'Ircam sera le campanile du beau Bourg." *Sept à Paris* 6, Jan. 1988, 34–35.
C. Ellis. "Umbau eines Industriecomplex und Landschaftsgestaltung in Montrouge, Paris." *Bauwelt*, Jan. 1988, 29–31.
F. Irace. "Destinazione museo." *Abitare* 261, Jan. 1988, 192–97.
G. de Bure. "Renzo Piano: l'homme aux semelles de vent." *Decoration International* 102, Feb. 1988, 110–23.
"Wood Framing (IBM)." *Progressive Architecture*, Feb. 1988, 92.
M. Giordano. "La catarsi genovese del '92." *L'Arca* 14, Mar. 1988.
D. Marabelli. "Leggera e integrata." *Modulo* 140, Apr. 1988, 478–83.
"L'invention constructive, les avancées technologiques." *Architecture et Informatique* 27, May-June 1988, 20–23.
"Menil Collection Museum in Houston, Texas." *Detail* 3, May-June 1988, 285–90.
"Menil—Sammlung in Houston." *DBZ*, June 1988, 795–98.
"Genua." *Werk, Bauen + Wohnen*, Sept. 1988, 48–55.
"Il Lingotto." *Rassegna* 10, no. 35, Sept. 1988, 110–13.

**1989**
"Concorso Kansai International Airport." *The Japan Architect* 2, 1989, 191–97.
"Piano Plays Nature's Theme." *World Architecture* 2, 1989, 72–77.
"Salir a la luz ampliacion del IRCAM." *A & V* 17, 1989, 75–77.
R. Ingersoll. "Pianissimo—La discreta coleccion Menil." *Arquitectura Viva* 4, Jan. 1989, 15–19.
"Osaka." *Building Design* 918, Jan. 1989, 1.
G. Picardi. "Flying High." *Building Design* 920, Jan. 1989, 26–28.
"Museo a Houston (Texas)." *Abacus* 5, no. 17, Jan.-Mar. 1989, 28–39.
R. Radicioni. "Quale Piano e per chi?" *Spazio & Società* 12, no. 45 Jan.-Mar. 1989,

104–6.
A. Pelissier. "Kansai: la course contre le temps." *Techniques et Architecture* 382, Feb. 1989, 65–68.
"Football Stadium." *GA Document* 23, Feb.-Mar. 1989, 44–46.
"Il concorso per il nuovo aeroporto di Osaka." *Casabella* 53, no. 555, Mar. 1989, 22–23.
P. Davey. "Piano's Lingotto." *The Architectural Review* 1105, Mar. 1989, 4–9.
F. Mellano. "Vuoti a rendere." *Modulo* 149, Mar. 1989, 272–81.
"Kansai International Airport." *Architectural Design*, Mar.-Apr. 1989, 52–60.
"Arvedi space." *Acciaio* 30, no. 4, Apr. 1989, 168–73.
"Il Building Workshop di Renzo Piano compie 25 anni." *L'Arca* 26, Apr. 1989, 118.
M. Desvigne. "Ensemble touristique dans la baie di Sistiana." *L'Architecture d'Aujourd'hui* 262, Apr. 1989, 52–54.
M. Desvigne. "Musée d'art moderne à Newport." *L'Architecture d'Aujourd'hui* 262, Apr. 1989, 50–51.
D. Ghirardo. "Piano Quays—aeroporto di Osaka." *The Architectural Review* 185, no. 1106, Apr. 1989, 84–88.
"Italy's Brunel." *Blueprint* 56, Apr. 1989, 52–54.
S. Redecke. "La cultura del fare." *Bauwelt* 3, Apr. 1989, 614–17.
"L'artificio assoluto." *Gran Bazaar* 67, Apr.-May 1989, 29–34.
V. M. Lampugnani. "Il concorso per l'areoporto internazionale di Kansai," *Domus* 705, May 1989, 34–39.
"Renzo Piano: una mostra e la presentazione del progetto Lingotto." *Abitare* 274, May 1989, 149.
E. M. Moreno. "What Makes a Museum Environment Successful?" *Architecture* 78, June 1989, 70.
F. Montobbio. "Prospettive ed evoluzione verso un nuovo disegno della città." *Urbanistica* 95, June 1989, 110–13.
"Turin-Gênes." *CREE*, June-July 1989.
"Bari Bowl." *Construction Today*, July 1989, 26.
"A Gate for Malta." *Building Design* 22, Sept. 1989, 20–21.
"Home for a Hero." *Building Design* 22, Sept. 1989, 22–25.
M. Dini. "Oltre lo 'styling,'" *Architetti Liguria* 9, no. 7, Sept.-Oct. 1989, 30.
C. Davies. "Piano quartet, *Architectural Review* 186, no. 112, Oct. 1989, 60–75.
"Extension de l'Ircam, Paris." *Techniques et Architecture* 386, Oct.-Nov. 1989, 114–23.
C. Mulard. "Le musée d'art de Newport Harbor, par Renzo Piano." *CREE* 232 Oct.-Nov. 1989, 27.
"Raison de forme: Centre Commercial de Bercy." *Techniques et Architecture* 386, Oct.-Nov. 1989, 114–23.
"Una mostra al Lingotto." *Rassegna* 9, no.

40/4, Dec. 1989, 90–93.

E. Ranzani. "Renzo Piano: Allestimento al Lingotto." *Domus* 711, Dec. 1989, 14–16.

"Fusion Horizontale." *Techniques et Architecture* 387, Dec.-Jan. 1989–90, 144–45.

**1990**

*A & V* 23 (monographic issue), Edit. Avisa, Madrid, 1990.

"Centre George Pompidou." *Connaisance des Arts,* 1990, 1–76.

"Cruise Princess." *G.B. Progetti* (monographic issue), Milan, 1990.

V. M. Lampugnani. "Renzo Piano Building Workshop." *A & V* 23, 1990, 1–88.

R. Piano. "Abitazioni a tipologia evolutiva a Corciano." *Edizioni Over,* 1990, 21–22.

O. di Blasi. "Renzo Piano: Libreria, Teso, Fontana Arte." *Domus* 712, Jan. 1990, 76–79.

F. Bertamini. "Il regalo di Colombo." *Costruire* 81, Feb. 1990, 27–30.

F. Lenne. "Une usine modulaire en foret." *Le Moniteur* 4499, Feb. 1990, 64–67.

E. Ranzani. "Ampliamento dell'Ircam a Parigi." *Domus* 713, Feb. 1990, 38–47.

"Stade de Bari, Italie." *L'Architecture d'Aujourd'hui* 267, Feb. 1990, 120–21.

C. Mattongo. "I sassi di Renzo." *Costruire* 83, Apr. 1990, 68–70.

J. Melvin. "Special Report: Shopping Centres." *Building Design,* Apr. 1990, 11–19.

"Bari." Stadt *Bauwelt* 24, May 1990, 1220–21.

G. Lorenzelli. "All'ultimo stadio." *Costruire* 84, May 1990, 46.

E. Ranzani. "Renzo Piano, Stadio di Calcio e atletica leggera, Bari." *Domus* 716, May 1990, 33–39.

"Schmuckstücke und Skandale." *Deutsche Bauzeitung,* May 1990, 163–64.

V. Magnago Lampugnani. "La terminal de la isla." *Arquitectura Viva* 12, May-June 1990, 14.

M. Barda. "Bari: estadio San Nicola." *Arquitectura Urbanismo* 6, no. 30, June 1990, 34–35.

A. Demerle. "Le stade de Bari." *Le Moniteur Architecture* 12, June 1990, 32–39

"Grand Stand." *New Civil Engineering* 7, June 1990, 10–11.

R. Laera, C. Riccardi. "Bari: Il nuovo stadio, un fiore nel deserto." *Il Nuovo Cantiere,* abstract, June 1990, 10–11.

J. M. Montaner. "Innovacion en la arquitectura de museos." *Architectural Digest* 31, June 1990, 118–22.

"Libreria Teso." *Techniques et Architecture* 390, June-July 1990, 162.

R. Ingersoll. "La trastienda del Mundial." *Arquitectura Viva* 13, July-Aug. 1990, 52–53.

"Parigi: Un dirigibile in legno e acciaio." *Il Nuovo Cantiere* 24, no. 7–8, July-Aug. 1990, 14–16.

M. Beretta. "203.000 Kilometri di coda."

*Oice* 4–5, July-Oct. 1990, 71–72.

"Extension of the IRCAM Studios in Paris." *Detail* 4, Aug.-Sept. 1990, 395–98.

B. Marzullo, A. Castellano. "La nave delfino." *L'Arca* 41, Sept. 1990, 72–81.

"Ort und Stadium." *Werk, Bauen + Wohnen,* Sept. 1990, 22–29.

L. P. Puglisi. "I sassi di Matera: recupero di Palazzo Venusio e del suo intorno." *Industria Costruzioni* 24, no. 227, Sept. 1990, 48–52.

"Soft Shore." *The Architectural Review* 1123, Sept. 1990, 71–73.

G. F. Brambilla. "Renzo Piano: ampliamento dell'IRCAM." *Costruire in Laterizio* 3, no. 17, Sept.-Oct. 1990, 358–61.

"The San Nicola Stadium." *The Arup Journal* 25, no. 3, Autumn 1990, 3–8.

"Industrial Revolution." *Building Design* 19, Oct. 1990, 30.

"Raumschiff Mit Zentraler Bühne: Futballstadion in Bari." *Architektur Aktuell* 139, Oct. 1990, 82–85.

B. Marzullo. "Centri Storici: a Genova per noi." *Il Nuovo Cantiere* 24, no. 11, Nov. 1990, 38–40.

"L'automobile, produzione e design a Milano 1879–1949." *Rassegna* 12, no. 44, Dec. 1990, 98–101.

"Parte il Metrogenova." *Vetro Spazio* 19, Dec. 1990, 10–16.

"Transatlantici." *Rassegna* 12, no. 44, Dec. 1990.

"Le Grand Souffle: Stade de Carbonara, Bari, Italie." *Techniques et Architecture* 393, Dec.-Jan. 1990–91, 44–49.

**1991**

J. Ferrier. "Usine optronique Thomson–Guyancourt 1990" *Usines*, vol. 2, Editions du Moniteur, 1991, 64–73.

"Fontana Arte: 'Teso.'" *Abitare* 292, Jan. 1991, 145.

"Ponti per il Porto di Ushibuka." *Space Design*, Jan. 1991, 88–91.

"Antologia 3." *Casabella* 55, no. 575–76, Jan.-Feb. 1991, 89.

S. Ishida, N. Okabe. "Renzo Piano Building Workshop." *GA Document* 28, Mar. 1991, 60–95.

"The Menil Collection Museum." *Space Design*, Mar. 1991, 74–76.

V. Travi. "Trieste: la baia delle meraviglie." *Il Nuovo Cantiere,* Mar. 1991, 55–56.

"Verselbstandigter Turm." *Baumeister,* Mar. 1991, 20–21.

"Un nuovo porto antico per Genova." *Presenza Tecnica* 9, no. 2, Mar.-Apr. 1991, 10–23.

"Kansai International Airport." *GA Document* 29, Apr. 1991, 70.

"Lyon, Citè International de la Tête d'Or." *Techniques et Architecture* 395, Apr.-May 1991, 52–57.

F. J. A., "Eastern Promise." *The Architectural Review* 1131, May 1991, 83–90.

B. Marzullo. "Aree dismesse: due progetti importanti. L'area Caleotto." *Cantiere* 25,

no. 5, May 1991, 48–49.

J. P. Menard. "Détail: Renzo Piano Façades en briques et composite." *Le Moniteur Architecture* 21, May 1991, 51–61.

E. Ranzani. "La trasformazione delle città: Genova." *Domus* 727, May 1991, 44–71.

"Raumschiff." *DB,* May 1991, 64–67.

"Columbus exhibition." *GB Progetti* 7 (monographic issue), May-June 1991.

"Kansai International Airport Passenger Terminal Building Design Development Process." *Space Design*, June 1991.

R. Morganti. "Centro Commerciale a Bercy II, Parigi." *L'Industria delle Costruzioni* 25, no. 236, June 1991, 22–30.

"Piano a Bercy." *L'Architecture d'Aujourd'hui* 269, June 1991, 162–66.

"Expo 92: un grande progetto di recupero." *Allestire* 8, no. 73, June-July 1991, 50–54.

"French Connection." *The Architectural Review* 189, no. 1133, July 1991, 59–63.

J. F. P. "Côte Jardin." *Techniques et Architecture* 189, no. 1133, July 1991, 38–47.

"Complesso residenziale a Parigi." *Domus* 729, July-Aug. 1991, 27–39.

"La facciata strutturale in alluminio." *Ufficio stile* 24, no. 7, Sept. 1991, 138–49.

M. Dumont. "Renzo Piano, l'aéroport du Kansai à Osaka." *L'Architecture d'Aujourd'hui* 276, Sept. 1991, 45–50.

L.M. "La sede dell'ISML sperimenta una facciata continua di nuova concezione." *AxA* 1, no. 2, Sept. 1991, 50–57.

"Il ruolo dell'acciaio inox nel metrò di Genova." *Inossidabile* 105, Sept. 1991, 8.

J. Cervera. "A flor de piel." *Arquitectura Viva* 20, Sept.-Oct. 1991, 42–47.

"Centre Cultural Kanak à Nouméa." *L'Architecture d'Aujourd'hui* 277, Oct. 1991, 9–13.

C. Mattogno. "Piano torna al Beaubourg." *Costruire* 101, Oct. 1991, 107.

F. Peyouzere. "Le Centre National d'Art et de Culture George Pompidou (1977)," *Architecture Intérieure* 246, Dec.-Jan. 1991–92, 87.

**1992**

C. Garbato. "Das Experiment im Werk Renzo Pianos." *Detail* 6, 1992, 557–60.

"Renzo Piano Building Workshop 1964–1991: In search of a balance." *Process Architecture* 100, 1992.

"Fiat factory gets Renzo Piano retread." *Architectural Record,* Jan. 1992, 18.

Leucos. "Il vetro in architettura." *Abitare* 303, Jan. 1992, 42–43.

"Longements Rue de Meaux, Paris XIXe." *Le Moniteur* 27, Jan. 1992, 84–85.

"Piano." *Le Moniteur* 27, Jan. 1992, 18.

"Piano's magic carpet." *The Architectural Review* 1139, Jan. 1992.

"Progetto per l'esposizione internazionale Genova 1992." *Phalaris* 18, Jan.-Feb. 1992, 44–47.

"Renzo Piano, attraverso Parigi" *Arredo*

*Urbano* 47–48, Jan.-Apr. 1992, 116–21.

P. Buchanan. "Pacific Piano." *The Architectural Review* 1141, Mar. 1992, 61–63.

A. Castellano. "Renzo Piano, Aereoporto Kansai." *Abitare* 305, Mar. 1992, 229–34.

T. Fisher. "Flights of Fantasy." *Progressive Architecture,* Mar. 1992.

L. Gelhaus. "Il Grande Bigo." *Rassegna* 41, no. 1, Mar. 1992, 114–17.

"Kansai International Airport." *De Architect* 46, Mar. 1992, 60–65.

P. Righetti. "La nuova sede del Credito Industriale Sardo." *Modulo* 179, Mar. 1992, 170–80.

"Una città ed il mare." *L'Arca* 59, Apr. 1992.

T. Fisher. "The Place of Sports." *Progressive Architecture,* Apr. 1992, 94–95.

M. Barda. "Um Aeroporto sobre o mar." *AU architetura urbanismo* 41, Apr.-May 1992, 54–63.

F. Bertamini, G. Salsalone. "La scoperta di Genova." *Costruire* 108, May 1992, 26–38.

E.H. "Trompe l'oeil." *Werk, Bauen + Wohnen,* May 1992, 54–57.

M. Toffolon. "Sotto le ali di una tenda." *Modulo* 181, May 1992, 488–91.

M. Champenois. "Piano, rénovation du port de Gênes." *L'Architecture d'aujourd'hui* 281, June 1992, 78–85.

F. Irace. "Piano per Genova-La città sul mare." *Abitare* 308, June 1992, 133–36.

"Genèse d'un Paysage." *Teräsrakenne* 402, June-July 1992, 88–93.

"Gènes d'un Paysage." *Techniques et Architecture* 402, June-July 1992, 88–93.

R. Ingersoll, S. Ishida. "Renzo Piano Building Workshop: Shopping Center Bercy; Bari Soccer Stadium; Subway Station, Genoa." *A+U* 262, July 1992, 70–114.

C. F. Kusch. "Internationale Columbus Ausstellung, Genoa." *DBZ,* July 1992, 1033–35.

C. Minoletti. "Genova Domani." *Quaderni* 12, July 1992, 19–24.

"Una corte per abitare." *Abitare* 308, July-Aug. 1992, 192.

Z. Freiman. "Perspectives Genoa's historic port reclaim." *Progressive Architecture,* Aug. 1992, 78–85.

R. Maillinger. "Colombo '92 in Genua." *Baumeister,* Aug. 1992, 40–45.

C. Garbato. "Il porto Vecchio." *Sport & Città* 12, July 1992, 10–16.

A. Valenti. "Berlino. Renzo Piano a Potsdamer Platz: 'L'Eclettico e il disciplinato dell'Architettura,'" *Arredo Urbano* 50–51, Sept. 1992, 30–33.

N. Baldassini. "Genova, Le celebrazioni Colombiane." *Flare* 7, Oct. 1992, 4–13.

F. De Pasquali. "Per la Cateristica e l'acciaio, uno sviluppo che viaggia in parallelo" *Acciaio* 4, Oct. 1992, 23–27

J. C. Garcias. "Deux Etoiles Italiennes." *L'Architecture d'Aujourd'hui* 283, Oct. 1992, 92–97.

G. Paci. "Il delfino Bianco" *Casa Vogue*

245 (supplement), Oct. 1992, 58–61

P. Righetti. "Gli ex Magazzini del Cotone." *Modulo* 185, Oct. 1992, 1024–33.

"Colombo '92—Esposizione di Genova, Sala Congressi-Auditorium Aquarium" *Habitat Ufficio* 58, Oct.-Nov. 1992, 62–63.

Y. Futagawa. "Renzo Piano, Unesco Laboratory Columbus International Expo '92, Thomson CSF Factory." *GA* 35, Nov. 1992, 40–59.

S. Ishida. "Unesco Workshop," "Columbus International Exposition." "Thomson CSF Factory." *GA* 35, Nov. 1992.

"Dal bullone al territorio." *L'Architettura* 446, Dec. 1992, 884–86.

"Esposizione Internazionale 1992 nel porto antico." *L'Architettura* 446, Dec. 1992, 862–63.

P. Rumpf. "Progetti per l'area della Potsdamerplatz, Berlino." *Domus* 744, Dec. 1992, 44–55.

"Un sistema, illuminotecnico funzionale." *Rassegna* 52, no. 4, Dec. 92, 94–97.

**1993**

D. Cruickshank. "Cross Roads Berlin." *The Architectural Review* 1151, Jan. 1993, 20–28.

D. Cruickshank. "Genoa Drama." *The Architectural Review* 1151, Jan. 1993, 36–41.

R. Dorigati. "Un parco culturale per la città il Lingotto." *L'Arca* 78, Jan. 1993, 48–53.

L. Pogliani. "Piano per tre." *Costruire* 117, Jan. 1993, 48.

"Renzo Piano Aereoporto di Kansai, Osaka." *Domus*, Jan. 1993, 52–59.

R. Stefanato. "Trasporto Ferroviario, speranze tra i binari." *Olce Temi*, Jan. 1993, 33–37.

"Crown Princess." *Interni* 427, Jan.-Feb. 1993, 120–21.

C. Sattler. "Potsdamer Platz—Leipziger Platz, Berlin 1991." *AD* 1, Jan.-Feb. 1993, 18–23.

"Sistemazione degli spazi esterni dell'industria Thomson a Guyancourt." *Casabella* 597–98, Jan.-Feb. 1993, 110–11.

G. Ullmann. "Zwischen Seelandschaft und Piazza." *Werk, Bauen + Wohnen*, Jan.-Feb. 1993, 41–48.

D. Albrecht. "Renzo Piano Exhibit in NY." *Architecture*, Feb. 1993, 22–23.

P. Arcidi. "Renzo Piano Exhibit opens in NY." *Progressive Architecture*, Feb. 1993, 19.

"Elektronikfabrik in Gyancourt." "Das Experiment im Werk, Renzo Piano." *Detail* 6, Feb. 1993, 593–97.

"Er(b)folge am Potsdamer Platz." *Baumeister*, Feb. 1993.

"Un Modello su cui muoverci." *L'Arca* 68, Feb. 1993, 98.

"Lingotto: una completa gamma illuminotecnica ad alto contenuto tecnologico." *Rassegna* 53, Mar. 1993, 90–93

"Mecanico e Organico." *Arquitectura Viva* 29, Mar.-Apr. 1993, 52–59.

"Renzo Piano Spazio Scenico per Moby-Dick: 'Ulisse e la Balena Bianca,'" *Domus* 29, Mar.-Apr. 1993.

E. Morteo. "Renzo Piano." *Domus* 748, Apr. 1993, 87–89.

R. Piano. "Un nuevo rodaje para el Lingotto." *Diseno/Diseño Interior* 24, Apr. 1993, 26–27.

E. Regazzoni. "Unesco & Workshop." *Abitare* 317, Apr. 1993, 156–69.

N. Baldassini. "La luce nell'architettura Hi-Tech." *Flare* 8, May 1993, 26–28.

S. Brandolini. "Il terminal passeggeri del Kansai International Airport nella baia di Osaka." *Casabella* 601, May 1993.

"Le Centre Culturel Jean-Marie Tjibaou." *MWA VEE* 1, May 1993, 48–53.

"Genova Acquario Oceanico. Protezione delle superfici esterne in cemento." *Arkos* 20, May 1993, 30.

D. O. Mandrelli. "Lungo il fiume, tra gli alberi." *L'Arca* 71, May 1993.

A. L. Nobre. "Renzo Piano, presença na America." *Architetura Urbanismo* 47, May 1993, 28.

O. Touraine. "Aeroport International du Kansaui." *Le Moniteur* 41, May 1993, 44–49.

J. Sainz. "Hipergeometriàs, el ordenador en el studio de Renzo Piano." *Arquitectura Viva* 30, May-June 1993, 96–97.

"Lingotto Fiere: montanti eccezionali per diaframmi luminosi" *Proporzione* 1, June 1993, 32–40

M. Tardis. "La grande Vague." *Techniques et Architecture* 408, June-July 1993, 114–21.

"Ushibuka Fishing Port Connecting Bridge." *JA* 10, Summer 1993, 212–17.

R. P. Red. "Solitärs in der periurbanen Würste." *Werk, Bauen + Wohnen*, July-Aug. 1993, 20–25.

"Haltestelle Brin in Genua." *Detail* 4, Aug.-Sept. 1993, 414–17.

"Osaka: 'Aereoporto,'" *GB Progetti* 19, Sept. 1993, 4.

F. Premoli. "Amsterdam: 'Musei,'" *GB Progetti* 19, Sept. 1993, 16.

"Kansai International Airport, Passenger Terminal Building." *JA* 11, Autumn 1993, 54–69.

"Ushibuka—Giappone: Ponti." *GB Progetti* 21, Nov. 1993, 10.

J. M. Alvarez Enjuto. "Arquitectura en la confluencia de los limites." *Lapiz* 98, Dec. 1993, 45–49.

G. Messina. "Progetti di Renzo Piano in mostra itinerante." *Industria delle Costruzioni* 266, Dec. 1993, 64–65.

"Nuovo Teatro Margherita." *Casabella* 607, Dec. 1993, 38.

M. Rognoni. "Un Edificio Residenziale a Parigi: Rue de Meaux." *Maiora* 18, Dec. 1993, 4–11.

**1994**

"Daimler-Benz." *A&V* 50, 1994, 36–45.

G. Grasso. "Padre Pio per un luogo d'incontro." *Chiesa oggi* 10, 1994, 70–71.

"Kansai Airport." *Lifescape* 54, 1994, 9–17.

R. Dorigati. "Un Parco Culturale per la Città, il Lingotto." *L'Arca* 78, Jan. 1994, 48–53.

"Kansai Airport." *Kenchiku Bunka* 567, Jan. 1994, 161–76.

"Presentato a Bari, il progetto per l'ex Teatro Margherita." *Industria delle Costruzioni* 267, Jan. 1994, 74

"Berlino—Riqualificazione area della Potsdsamer Platz." *GB Progetti* 23, Mar. 1994, 11.

"Kansai Airport." *Kenchiku Bunka* 570, Apr. 1994, 21–74.

R. Keiser. "Flugzeugträger." *Werk, Bauen + Wohnen*, Apr. 1994, 49–53.

A. Bugatti. "Un lingotto di tecnologia." *Costruire* 132, May 1994, 125–28.

"Kansai Airport." *Kenchiku Bunka* 572, June 1994, 25–44.

M. Kloos. "Het juiste gebaar." *Archis*, June 1994, 5–7.

"L'Auditorium al Lingotto di Torino." *Casabella* 614, July-Aug. 1994, 52–59.

V. D. Danner. "Woge, Der Kansai-Airport in der Burcht von Osaka." *AIT*, no. 5779 E, July-Aug. 1994, 26–35.

"Kansai Airport." *GA Japan* 9, July-Aug. 1994, 24–80.

"Museo Beyeler a Riehen, Basilea." *Domus: Museums Dossier* 2, July-Aug. 1994, 30–33.

"Kansai Airport." *Kenchiku Bunka* 574, Aug. 1994, 89–118.

D. Cruickshank. "Piano Forte." *Perspectives* 5, Sept. 1994, 34–37.

"The Hills are Alive." *Building Design* 1190, Sept. 1994, 16–19.

"Kansai Airport." *Kenchiku Bunka* 575, Sept. 1994, 91–98.

"Kansai Airport Artificial Landscape." *Progressive Architecture*, Sept. 1994, 22.

L. Verdi. "Un nuovo Lingotto per Torino." *Modulo* 204, Sept. 1994, 284–91.

R. Miyake. "Special report Renzo Piano Building Workshop, Creating Harmony from Technology and Nature." *Approach* 3, Autumn 1994, 1–23.

"Kansai International Airport Passenger Terminal Building." *JA* 15, Autumn 1994

"Auditorium Lingotto." *GB Progetti* 29, Oct. 1994.

A. Castellano. "Kansai International Airport." *L'Arca* 86, Oct. 1994, 2–27.

M. C. Clemente. "Leggero come l'aria." *Costruire* 137, Oct. 1994, 46–49.

L. Gazzaniga. "Renzo Piano Building Workshop, Aeroporto Internazionale di Kansai, Osaka, Giappone." *Domus* 764, Oct. 1994, 7–23.

"Le Quai en bonne voie." *Actua Cité* 2, Oct. 1994.

"Die Wachenschau—Neue Töne." *Bauwelt* 39, Oct. 1994, 60–61.

N. Baker. "Tears in the reunited city." *Building Design* 1198, Nov. 1994, 22.

P. Buchanan. "Kansai." *Architectural Review* 1173, Nov. 1994, 30–81.

V. Cappelli. "Il nuovo Auditorium di Roma, una sfida Urbanistica." *Amadeus* 11, no. 60, Nov. 1994, 43–45.

R. Keiser. "Vorwärtsstrategien." *Werk, Bauen + Wohnen*, Nov. 1994, 6–17.

C. F. Kusch. "Hafenanlage von Genua." *DBZ*, no. 1D8471E, Nov. 1994, 67–70.

A. Rocca. "Noumea Paris." *Lotus International* 83, Nov. 1994, 42–55.

A. Rocca. "Renzo Piano." *Lotus International* 83, Nov. 1994.

P. Buchanan. "Dunas de metal." *Arquitectura Viva* 36, Nov.-Dec. 1994, 46–47.

M. P. Belki. "Le piazze perdute." *Costruire* 139, Dec. 1994, 114–15.

V. M. Lampugnani. "Eine Stuck Gosstadt als Experiment." *DAM Hatje*, Dec. 1994

G. Messina. "Renzo Piano: un Auditorium per Roma." *Industria delle Costruzioni* 278, Dec. 1994, 40–42.

G. de Whithy. "Luci della Cité." *Costruire* 139, Dec. 1994, 38–40.

P. Buchanan. "Padre Pio Pilgrimage Church: Italy." *Scroope* 6, 1994–95, 28–29.

"Stadium in Bari." *Detail* 6, Dec.-Jan. 1994–95.

**1995**

"Auditorium Roma. Piano's monument for musical culture." *World Architecture* 39, 1995, 86.

A. Castellano. "Come casse armoniche." *L'Arca* 91, 1995, 4–9

"Kansai—Vertigos finimilenarios: imagenes del flujou." *AV monografias* 51–52, 1995, 14–26.

P. Buchanan. "Plane Geometry." *Architecture*, Jan. 1995, 84–103.

P. Dilley, A. Guthrie. "Kansai International Airport Terminal Building." *The Arup Journal* 30, Jan 1995, 14–23.

J. Melvin. "Best Fiat Forward." *Building Design* 1203, Jan. 1995, 12–13.

C. Garbato. "Metropolis auf der Inael." *Architecture aktuel* 175–76, Jan.-Feb. 1995, 48–61.

"Postdamer Platz." *L'Architecture d'Aujourd'hui* 297, Feb. 1995, 66–73.

C. A. Bottigelli, M. G. Alessi. "Il futuro in cantiere." *Costruire* 142, Mar. 1995, 44–46.

P. Giordano. "Postdamer Platz." *Domus Dossier* 3, Mar. 1995, 68–89, 74–75, 82–83.

K. Kuche. "Plywaiace Iotnisko." *Architektura & Biznes* 4, no. 33, Mar. 1995, 20–21.

N. Okabe. "Appunti di volo per Kansai Airport." *Vetro Spazio* 36, Mar. 1995, 18–26.

D. Dillon. "Cy Twombly Gallery." *Architecture*, Apr. 1995, 24.

J.F.P. "Cité D'Avenir. Cité International de Lyon." *Techniques et Architecture* 419, Apr.-May 1995, 72–77.

V.G.E. "De la Terre et du Feu." *Impact* 53, May-June 1995, 7–9.

L. Spagnoli. "Ircam parigi. Il terziario fra current architecture neotradizionalismo hi-tech." *Costruire in laterizio* 45, May-

June 1995, 162–67.
M.G.Z. "Roma va Piano." *Cree* 265, May-June 1995, 22.
A. Castellano. "Fede e tecnologia." *Ecclesia* 1, June 1995, 48–57.
C. Garbato. "Il Lingotto di Piano." *Finestra* 6, June 1995, 176–85.
P. Rumpf. "La città dei concorsi: Berlino del dopo muro." *Rassegna* 61, June 1995, 45–55.
M. Toffolon. "Un Auditorium tutto in legno." *Modulo* 212, June 1995, 494–95.
"Crown Princess il bianco delfino d'acciaio." *Idea* 7, July 1995, 26–31.
L. L. Pirano, M. Gatto. "Al cantiere della cité internazionale de Lyon." *GB Progetti* 38, July-Aug. 95, 34–35
P. Buchanan. "Natural workshop." *Architectural Review* 1183, Sept. 1995, 76–80.
P. Buchanan. "Organiczna maszyna (Kansai Airport)." *Architektura murator* 9, Sept. 1995, 34–41.
"Lione: la città internazionale." *Abitare* 343, Sept. 1995, 85–86.
"Saitama arena competition." *GB Progetti* 39, Sept. 1995, 8–13.
G. Sgali. "La conchiglia d'argento (Lyon)." *Area* 23, Sept. 1995, 26–33.
"Cy Twombly Annex at the Menil Collection." *A+U* 302, Nov. 1995, 6–17.
N. Okabe. "Ushibuka Bridge." *At architecture magazine* 107, Nov. 1995, 44–49.
M. Bédarida. "Lione: la politica degli spazi." *Casabella* 629, Dec. 1995, 8–23.
V. V. de Raulino. "Compass." *Architektur aktuell* 186, Dec. 1995, 40–45.

## 1996

B. Camerana. "L'Aeroporto internazionale di Kansai Osaka, Giappone, 1988–1994." *Eden rivista dell'architettura nel paesaggio* 3, 1996, 15–26.
B. Camerana. "Il centro culturale Kanak Jean-Marie Tjibaou, Nouméa, Nuova Caledonia." *Eden rivista dell'architettura nel paesaggio* 3, 1996, 33–38.
B. Camerana. "La trasformazione della fabbrica Fiat, Lingotto, Torino, Italia, 1991–" *Eden rivista dell'architettura nel paesaggio* 3, 1996, 27–32.
G. Gabbi. "Genova, nuova capitale del Mediterraneo: fronte del porto." *Airone* 181, 1996, 45–49.
I. Lupi. "Germania, da Berlino verso Est." *Abitare* 352, 1996, 104–5.
"Ray uczestnictwa." *Architektura murator* 6, no. 21, 1996, 32–37.
"Tate frames architecture." *Any* 13, 1996 45–51.
"Vesima." *Lifescape* 57, 1996, 1–12.
"Vision of Universe." *Art & Deco Art Graphics*, 1996, 24–27.
"The Key to the City (Lyon)." *Architectural Review* 1187, Jan. 1996.
R. Laera. "San Nicola: Bari-Soltanto per Bari." *Costruire* 152, Jan. 1996, 30–31.
"Renzo Piano." *Domus* 778, Jan. 1996, 61.
L. L. Sorensen. "Auditorium Roma."

*Arkitekten Magasin* 2, Jan. 1996, 8–11.
A. Dominoni. "Berlino-Cantiere laboratorio." *Grap Casa* 123, Jan.-Feb. 1996, 96–101.
"Kanak." *Casabella* 360–61, Jan.-Feb. 1996, 84.
"The Menil Collection." *Casabella* 360–61, Jan.-Feb. 1996, 126–27.
"La Cité internationale de Lyon." *Archis*, Mar. 1996, 38–45.
"Cité internationale in Lyon." *Bauwelt* 87, Mar. 1996, 424.
I. Maisch. "Renzo Piano." *Hauser*, Mar. 1996, 51–62.
C. Garbato. "La configurazione dello spazio." *Mercedes* 1, May-Apr. 1996, 20–27.
W. F. Stern. "The Twombly and the Making of Place." *Culture Zones* 34, Spring 1996, 16–19.
D. Chetrit. "Lyon. Une eurocité." *Parcours* 100, Apr. 1996, 66–69.
"Centre for Business and Art in Turin." *Detail* 3, Apr.-May 1996, 331–37.
C. Schittich. "Alt und New Ein interview mit Renzo Piano." *Detail* 3, Apr.-May 1996, 280–90.
"1896–1996: The first 100 years, *The Architectural Review* 1191, May 1996, 91, 100.
K. Frampton. "Kenneth Frampton: universalismo e regionalismo." *Domus* 782, May 1996, 4–8.
K. Kliche. "Cité international Rodanem." *A & B* 5, May 1996, 10–11.
C. F. Kusch. "Eine Architektur der ortsbezogenen technology, *DBZ* 5, May 1996, 83–90.
R. Piano. "Il mestiere più antico del mondo." *Micromega* 2, May-June 1996, 107–9.
"The Craft of the Diversity (RP general)." *Building Design* 1269, June 1996, 16–19.
P. Restany. "Susumu Shingu poeta e filosofo dello spazio." *Domus* 783, June 1996, 84–88.
P. Paoletti. "L'uomo del vulcano." *Affari & Mercati* 2, June-July 1996, 16–18.
C. Garbato. "Un luminoso rigore." *Ottagono* 119, June-Aug. 1996, 50–53.
L. Pagani, A. Perversi. "Luce, spazio e visione." *Ottagono* 119, June-Aug. 1996, 43.
J. Rodermond. "Manifest of non place (Amsterdam)." *De Architect Dossier*, July 1996, 16.
"Urbane Zukunftsvision (Lyon)." *DBZ* 7, July 1996, 26–27.
M. G. Alessi. "La fiducia di ricominaciare da capo Berino: instancabile marciapiede." *Controspazio Architettura urbanistica* 4, July-Aug. 1996, 96.
C. A. Boyer. "Cité Internationale, Lyon." *Domus* 784, July-Aug. 1996, 16–25.
"La Ferrari e Maranello, Maranello e la Ferrari." *Abitare* 353, July-Aug. 1996.
"Stuttgart 21." *Bauwelt* 31–32, Aug. 1996, 1752–53.
"L'Ircam en trois actes et quatre batiments." *Architecture intérieure cree* 272, Aug.-Sept. 1996, 74–77.

"Lyon. Bâtiment pour installations." *Architecture intérieure cree* 272, Aug.-Sept. 1996, 66–69.
"Nouméa centre Jean-Marie Tjibaou." *Architecture intérieure cree* 272, Aug.-Sept. 1996, 50–55.
D. Elco. "Technologie Museum NINT/Impuls Science and Technology center." *Jaarslag 1995*, Oct. 1996, 1–25.
"Al Lingotto." *Abitare* 355, Oct. 1996, 96.
G. Muratore. "Ferrovia e città." *L'Arca* 108, Oct. 1996, 6–9.
C. Wolf. "Renzo Piano: Kolumbus der neuen architektur." *Ideales Heim* 10, Oct. 1996, 57–63.
C. Wolf. "Renzo Piano: Kolumbus der neuen architektur." *Atrium Haus und Wohnen International* 6, Nov.-Dec. 1996, 84–91.
I. Meier. "B & B Innovative technik und zeitmässes design." *Atrium Haus und Wohnen International* 6, Nov.-Dec. 1996, 126–29.

## Books

*International Conference on Space Structures.* Exhibition catalog. London, 1966.
E. Poleggi, G. Timossi. *Porto di Genova, Storia e Attualità.* Genoa, 1977.
*IRCAM.* Paris 1977.
*Costruire e ricostruire.* Udine, 1978.
A. Fils. *Das Centre Pompidou in Paris.* Munich, 1980.
R. Piano, M. Arduino, M. Fazio. *Antico è bello.* Rome/Bari, 1980.
G. Donin. *Renzo Piano, Piece by Piece.* Rome: Casa del Libro Editrice, 1982.
*La modernité, un projet inachevé.* Exhibition catalog. Paris, 1982.
M. Dini, R. Piano. *Progetti e Architetture 1964–1983.* Milan: Electa, 1983; French edition, Paris: Electa Moniteur, 1983; English edition, New York: Rizzoli, 1984.
*Storia di una mostra.* Milan: Fabbri Editori, 1983.
L. Nono. *Verso Prometeo.* Venice: La Biennale/Ricordi editori, 1984.
Associazione Industriali Provincia di Genova. *Genova Ieri, Oggi, Domani.* Genoa: Rizzoli Editore, 1985.
R. Piano. *Chantier, ouvert au public.* Paris: Arthaud editeur, 1985.
*1992, Genova città di Colombo: immagini e progetti.* Genoa: Columbus 1992 editore, 1986.
R. Piano. *Dialoghi di cantiere.* Bari: Laterza Editrice, 1986.
L. Miotto. *Renzo Piano.* Exhibition catalog. Paris: Editions du Centre Georges Pompidou, 1987.
R. Piano, R. Rogers. *Du Plateau Beaubourg au Centre Georges Pompidou.* Paris: Editions du Centre Georges Pompidou, 1987.
*A+U Monograph.* Tokyo, 1989.
Eco, Zeri, Piano, Graziani. *Le Isole del*

*tesoro.* Milan: Electa, 1989.
*Renzo Piano.* Exhibition catalog. Tokyo: Edit. Delphi Research, 1989.
R. Piano. *Buildings and Projects, 1971–1989.* New York: Rizzoli, 1990.
R. Piano. *Il Nuovo Stadio di Bari.* Milan: Ediz. L'Archivolto, 1990.
*Colombo '92: la città, il porto, l'esposizione.* Quaderni di Mostrare (Exporre), 1992.
*Renzo Piano Building Workshop Exhibit/Design.* Libra Immagine, 1992.
P. Buchanan. *Renzo Piano Building Workshop Complete Works.* vol 1. London: Phaidon Press, 1993; Italian edition, Turin: Allemandi, 1994; French edition, Paris: Flammarion, 1994; German edition, Stuttgart: Hatje Cantz, 1994.
*The Making of Kansai International Airport Terminal, Osaka, Japan; Renzo Piano Building Workshop.* Tokyo: Kodansha, 1994.
*Renzo Piano, progetti e architetture 1987–1994*, vol. 3, Milan: Electa, 1994.
P. Buchanan. *Renzo Piano Building Workshop Complete Works*, vol. 2. London: Phaidon Press, 1995; Italian edition, Turin: Allemandi, 1996; German edition, Stuttgart: Hatje Cantz, 1996.

## Photography Credits

Thanks to the Renzo Piano
Building Workshop for providing
the graphic material for this
book, and to the following
photographers:
P. Adenis, G. Basilico, G. Berengo
Gardin, G. G. Bianchi, R. Bryant
(Arcaid), M. Carrol, CineFiat,
Commune of Amsterdam,
M. Denancé, H. Edgerton,
R. Einzing, Fiat Auto, M. Folco,
Fregoso & Basalto, D. Gilbert
(Arcaid), S. Goldberg, R. Halbe,
D. Hart, Y. Hata, P. Hester,
Hickey & Robertson, K. Hiwatashi,
Horn, K. Hosokawa, S. Ishida,
T. Kitajima, Maeda, G. Maschetti,
E. Minetti, G. Muciaccia, A. Muhs,
Y. Newspaper, P. A. Panz,
Publifoto, Réunion des Musées
Nationaux, F. Reuter, M. Riboud,
C. Richters, C. Rives, Rotta,
P. Ruault, R. Schäffer,
Shinkenchiku-Sha, Sky Front,
Ben Smusz, Studio Gui,
F. Taccone, W. Vassal,
D. Von Schaewen.